THE **BIG** BOOK OF **PASTA**

HILAIRE WALDEN

THE **BIG** BOOK OF
PASTA

365

**QUICK AND
VERSATILE RECIPES**

dbp

DUNCAN BAIRD PUBLISHERS

LONDON

The Big Book of Pasta
Hilaire Walden

First published in the United Kingdom and Ireland in 2007 by
Duncan Baird Publishers Ltd
Sixth Floor
Castle House
75–76 Wells Street
London W1T 3QH

Conceived, created and designed by Duncan Baird Publishers

MANAGING EDITOR: Grace Cheetham
EDITOR: Gillian Haslam
MANAGING DESIGNER: Manisha Patel
DESIGNER: Sailesh Patel
STUDIO PHOTOGRAPHY: William Lingwood
FOOD STYLIST: Marie-Ange La-Pierre
PROP STYLIST: Helen Trent

British Library Cataloguing-in-Publication Data:
A CIP record for this book is available from the British Library

ISBN: 978-1-84483-430-3

10 9 8 7 6 5 4 3 2

Typeset in Gill Sans Condensed
Colour reproduction by Scanhouse, Malaysia
Printed in China by Imago

PUBLISHER'S NOTE: While every care has been taken in compiling
the recipes in this book, Duncan Baird Publishers, or any other
persons who have been involved in working on this publication,
cannot accept responsibility for any errors or omissions,
inadvertent or not, that may be found in the recipes
or text, nor for any problems that may arise as
a result of preparing one of these recipes.

UNLESS OTHERWISE STATED:
• Use medium eggs
• Use fresh herbs
• Do not mix metric and imperial measurements
• 1 tsp = 5ml
  1 tbsp = 15ml
  1 cup = 250ml

Contents

INTRODUCTION 7

FIRST COURSES & SNACKS
CHAPTER 1 21

FISH & SHELLFISH
CHAPTER 2 61

MEAT & POULTRY
CHAPTER 3 105

VEGETABLE & VEGETARIAN DISHES
CHAPTER 4 153

INDEX 214

Introduction

Although internationally popular and wonderfully versatile,
pasta remains quintessentially Italian and it is arguably most
enjoyable when it is accompanied by other Mediterranean ingredients.

Pasta is a healthy food, and its nutrition can be enhanced by
the ingredients used with it in the traditional restrained Italian
style, rather than large amounts of fattening cream, butter and
cheese. Tossed with judicious amounts of freshly cooked vegetables,
herbs and perhaps a little cheese, pasta makes a nutritious dish.

Pasta can be dressed up or down. Despite its inherent simplicity,
it can still be the ideal dish for a special occasion, provided the
ingredients are first class and fresh. What's more, the many
dishes can be prepared and cooked in a matter of minutes.

The range of pasta that is available continues to increase, but it
is important to buy good-quality brands, which are usually Italian.
Simply look for the words 'durum wheat', and 'pure egg' if it is egg
pasta, on the packaging. If other ingredients are present, even water,
put the packet back on the shelf. Good fresh pasta can also be found
in quality Italian delicatessens. With such a wide choice of commercially
produced pasta, few people make their own. It does take a little while
to get the knack of making it, especially if the stretching is done
by hand, but once the skill has been acquired, the superiority
of the results makes the effort of learning well worthwhile.

PASTA QUANTITIES

The amount of pasta you cook per person depends on appetite, the role the pasta dish is to play in the meal, and the character of the sauce: less pasta would be needed if a rich creamy sauce were to accompany it rather than a light vegetable one.

As a general guide, allow 70g (2½oz) dried pasta for a first course portion, 85–115g (3–4oz) for a main course serving. Slightly more fresh pasta is usually needed.

DRIED PASTA

Semolina flour, made from durum wheat, is traditionally used in dried pasta. The flour is much tougher than other wheat flours and it is this quality which gives dried pasta its durability, preventing it from breaking easily when dried. It is a very strong flour and the dough needs industrial machinery to work it properly, and atmosphere- and temperature-controlled conditions for the drying that is required for long storage. Dried flour-and-water pasta made from durum wheat includes spaghetti, as well as many other shapes.

Dried egg pasta also includes some soft flour with the durum wheat flour. It has a silkier, smoother texture when cooked, a richer flavour, and is more expensive.

It is sometimes considered that fresh egg pasta is always better than dried, but this is not the case. Good-quality dried pasta (i.e. pasta made from durum wheat by a reputable, and usually Italian, company) is far better than poor-quality bought fresh egg pasta (some don't even contain much egg). However, the growing popularity of pasta in general, and fresh pasta in particular, has meant an increase in sales of low-quality fresh pasta. The best fresh egg pasta can usually be found in Italian delicatessens that make their own.

QUICK GUIDE TO PASTA SHAPES

There are hundreds of pasta shapes. Names can be confusing as sometimes one name can refer to different shapes, while different names can be used in various parts of Italy. The name ending provides a clue: -ini and -ette imply small, while -oni implies large. See page 12 for more information on shapes and sizes of home-made pasta.

LONG ROUND PASTA includes spaghetti; spaghettini (thin spaghetti); vermicelli (fine spaghetti); capelli d'angelo, 'angel hair' (threadlike pasta); tonnarelli (home-made square spaghetti); bucatini or perciatelli (chunky spaghetti with hollow centres); bigoli (the only traditional pasta made with wholemeal flour).
LONG FLAT RIBBONS include tagliatelle; taglierini, taglioni and bavette (thinner tagliatelle); fettuccine (narrower tagliatelle); frappe (delicate ribbons with wavy edges); trenette (a cross between tagliatelle and linguine); linguine (resembling flattened spaghetti); paglia e fieno, 'straw and hay' (nests of green and plain fettuccine); tagliolini (home-made version of linguine); pappardelle (wide ribbons); lasagnette (wide with fluted edges).
TUBULAR PASTA includes macaroni; ziti (similar to macaroni); penne (short tubes cut on the diagonal, penne lisce is smooth and penne rigate is ridged); pennette (shorter, thinner penne); rigatoni (ridged, hollow chunky tubes); marille (double rigatoni); sedani (short, ridged tubes with straight ends); elicoidali (narrower rigatoni with spiral ridges and straight ends), denti d'elefante, 'elephants' teeth', (fairly long, ridged tubes with straight ridges and flat ends); garganelli (home-made ridged scroll-shapes); cavatappi (corkscrew shapes); chifferi (small curved tubes).
SHAPED PASTA includes fusilli (spirals); orecchiette (ear-shapes); rotelle (wheels); farfalle (butterfly-shapes); conchiglie (shells); smooth or ribbed conchigliette/conchiglioni (small/large conchiglie); riccioli (short with wide ridges); radiatori (shaped like old-fashioned radiators); gnocchi (dumplings); cavatieddi (small, mussel-shaped); lumache (shells formed out of hollow pasta), eliche (short, thin spirals); trofie (rolls of pasta with pointed ends, sometimes open along one side); strozzapreti (twists), gemelli and caserecce (similar to strozzapreti); ballerine (bell-shaped, with frilly edges); campanelle (similar to ballerine).
FILLED PASTA (RIPIENA) includes cannelloni (tubes); cappelletti (small squares folded into hat shapes); ravioli (squares); ravioloni (large ravioli); agnolotti or raviolini (half-moons); tortelli (squares, larger than raviolini — the smaller version, tortellini, are rounder in shape, although tortelloni can also be large, square shapes).
SOUP PASTA are small shapes (pastina) that are used in soups, with names often ending in -ini, -etti or -ette. For example, tubettini, anellini, quadretti, conchigliette, stelline and ditali.

HOME-MADE PASTA

The best pasta is undoubtedly home-made pasta, particularly home-made egg pasta. In fact, very few people make anything but egg pasta. You need only two ingredients, flour and eggs. Both influence the flavour. A wide range of different flours can be used — see below. Good-quality, free-range and preferably organic eggs will give the best flavour; the richer the colour of the yolk, the better the colour of the pasta. Any size can be used; simply adjust the amount of flour accordingly. See page 10 for the different flavour variations you can experiment with.

Flours

The type of flour used governs the texture of the pasta:

DURUM WHEAT: This is not used for home-made pastas. Fresh egg pasta is usually undried so it is not necessary to use durum wheat, although some people like to use plain semolina in the dough to give it some durability.

GOOD-QUALITY UNBLEACHED PLAIN FLOUR: This makes a dough that is malleable and easy to roll, and pasta that is quite soft and not particularly resilient (springy and slightly elastic).

STRONG BREAD FLOUR: This produces a firmer dough that requires more effort to roll, but the pasta will have a more conventional, firmer, more chewy texture with a decent amount of resilience.

GROUND SEMOLINA/SEMOLINA FLOUR: These add to the texture, colour and firmness of pasta, making it chewy and quite coarse, but not very resilient. Dough that contains only semolina and no other flour is much harder to roll, tears more easily and is the hardest to stretch thinly. However, it is easier to cut and is less likely to stick. Dough made with semolina requires more flour per egg than other flours, and it can be tricky getting the proportions right. A good compromise, therefore, is to use one quarter to one half semolina to bread flour.

TIPO/DOPIO 00: This is a very soft, highly refined Italian flour. The dough is more grainy than other pasta doughs at first but it becomes smoother and more silky after kneading for a few minutes. The dough is the easiest to work with and produces pasta that is lighter, softer and not particularly firm, but it has greater resilience. It also takes slightly less time to cook than pasta made with other flours.

The consistency of the dough also influences the texture of the pasta. A stiff dough will produce firmer pasta, whereas a soft dough makes pasta that is soft and silky. However, a soft dough is also more difficult to handle, tends to stick when cut and takes longer to dry. It is easier to add more flour to a dough that is too soft.

PASTA-MAKING EQUIPMENT

If you wish to make your own pasta, there are just a few essential pieces of kitchen equipment that you will require:

- Spacious, firm working area, at least 60cm (24in) deep, 90cm (36in) wide.
- Smooth warm surface — traditionally, pasta is made on a large smooth wooden board. In modern kitchens, laminated worktops are good alternatives. Marble, slate or granite are too cold.
- Long rolling pin — a 60cm (24in) long rolling pin, up to 5cm (2in) in diameter, is ideal for rolling a 3-egg quantity of pasta.
- Tea towels — several clean tea towels are needed for absorbing moisture from the pasta dough when it is left to dry.
- Clingfilm — for covering the ball of dough lightly when it is left to rest.
- Pasta machine — this makes stretching the pasta dough much easier in terms of effort and skill. Made of stainless steel, the machine has rollers for pressing out the dough as thinly as possible. The distance between the rollers can be adjusted, so the dough can be rolled progressively thinner and thinner until the required thickness is achieved. Cutters for producing various widths of noodles are available for attaching to the machine. A hand-operated pasta machine is usually considered to give better results than one operated by a motor.
- Large, sharp knife for cutting noodles and shapes.
- Pastry wheel for cutting stuffed pasta shapes, and for giving wavy edges to wide noodles such as pappardelle and lasagnette.
- Biscuit cutters for cutting out some stuffed pasta shapes.

FRESH PASTA DOUGH

PREPARATION TIME: it's hard to be precise as so much depends on whether you work by hand or use a machine, your skill and experience and the shape required. With a little experience, doing everything by hand and cutting simple noodles would take about 35–40 minutes, plus drying, making about 350g (12oz) pasta.

200G (7oz/1¾ CUPS) FLOUR (SEE PREVIOUS PAGE)
2 LARGE FREE-RANGE EGGS, PREFERABLY ORGANIC, AT ROOM TEMPERATURE

Flavour variations

Try adding the following ingredients for different flavours. A little extra flour will probably be needed for most variations during the kneading, cutting and rolling stages.

HERB: stir 3 tbsp finely chopped mixed herbs such as basil, rosemary, parsley or oregano into the eggs.

BLACK PEPPER: stir 1½ tbsp coarsely ground black peppercorns into the eggs.

LEMON: add 2 tbsp lemon juice and the finely grated zest of 2 lemons to the eggs; about 25g (1oz/2 tbsp) or more extra flour will probably be needed.

SPINACH: cook 150g (5oz) spinach in a covered pan, shaking the pan occasionally, until wilted and tender. Drain well, chop finely and squeeze out surplus moisture. Spread on paper towels to dry. Add to the eggs. As much as an extra 100g (3½oz/packed ½ cup) flour will be needed.

SAFFRON: crush a pinch of saffron threads, soak for 30 minutes in 1 tbsp boiling water, then add to the eggs. About 25g (1oz/2 tbsp) extra flour will probably be needed.

CHILLI: stir 1–2 tsp crushed chilli flakes into the eggs.

BLACK OLIVE: beat 2 tbsp black olive paste into the eggs.

SQUID: add a 6g sachet of squid ink to the eggs.

SUN-DRIED TOMATO PASTE: beat 2 tbsp sun-dried tomato paste into the eggs.

PESTO OR RED PESTO: beat 2 tbsp pesto into the eggs.

For a 3-egg quantity, use 300g (10oz/2¼ cups) flour and 3 large eggs. This produces about 500g (1lb 2oz) of pasta.

You can either mix the dough by hand (see below) or use a food processor or food mixer (see facing page for instructions).

Hand mixing

This is generally considered better than using a food processor because it is easier to judge the moistness of the dough and thus add the right amount of flour. Flours vary in the amount of liquid they absorb depending on their storage conditions and the humidity and temperature of the kitchen. Eggs can also vary slightly in size. It is far easier to add more flour to a soft dough than it is to add more egg to a dry dough.

1   Tip the flour into a bowl and make a well in the centre. Add the eggs. Using a fork, break up the eggs slightly while bringing in some of the flour from the sides. Continue working with your hands, mixing in as much flour as needed to make a rough, semi-soft dough. You may not need all the flour, but if the dough is too sticky, sprinkle on a little more. If you add too much flour, correct it by adding a little more egg or good-quality olive oil.

2   Form the dough into a ball and transfer to a work surface lightly dusted with flour. Knead the dough for about 10 minutes, pushing a portion of the dough away from you with the heel of your hand, then fold the dough back on itself, so that it faces towards you.

3   Continue with this action, turning the dough through a few degrees occasionally so all the dough is worked, until it is elastic, smooth and soft. If the dough is to be passed through a machine, it does not have to be kneaded for quite as long as hand-rolled dough. Avoid using too much flour during the kneading otherwise the dough will become too dry and will be tough. Just enough flour to stop the dough sticking is all that is needed.

Using a food processor

Put all the ingredients in and work until they come together into a ball that leaves the sides of the bowl clean. Transfer the dough to a floured work surface and knead by hand for about 2 minutes.

Using a food mixer

With the dough hook attached, put the flour and eggs into the bowl and mix on medium speed until they come together to form a tight dough. Transfer the dough to a floured work surface and work by hand for about 1 minute.

Resting the dough

Place the kneaded dough under a bowl or wrap in clingfilm and leave to relax at room temperature for 30 minutes. If the kitchen is hot, refrigerate the dough, but allow it to warm up again to room temperature before rolling.

Rolling by hand

Hand-rolling produces pasta that has a more interesting texture, is more porous and absorbs a sauce better than machine-rolled pasta. It does require a certain amount of energy, practice and time until you get used to doing it.

1   Divide the unwrapped dough into four balls. Re-cover three balls. Working on a lightly floured surface, knead the unwrapped ball for a minute or so, then, with the flat of your hand, flatten it slightly into a disc before rolling out from the centre, and stopping at the edge.

2   Using a fair amount of pressure and always rolling away from you, stretch the dough rather than flatten it. Without using any pressure, roll the pin back to the centre and repeat four times. Give the dough a slight turn and repeat. Continue in this way until the dough is about 6mm (¼in) thick all over. Dust the surface and the pin frequently with flour.

3   Next, roll the top (far) edge of the dough, about one third of the way down, on to the rolling pin. Grip it with one hand, curling your fingers around the dough and pin. Grab the bottom edge of the dough with your other hand and, pulling gently in both directions, stretch the dough slightly. Be careful: too much pressure and you'll tear the dough, too little pressure and it won't stretch. Unroll the pin, give the dough a quarter turn and repeat, working your way around the dough, until it is about 2–3mm (½–⅛in) thick.

4   Place the rolling pin on the dough. Gently stretch and roll the dough tightly on to the pin from the top towards you, with both your hands cupped over the centre of the pin (keep a firm hold of the edge of the dough nearest you). Stop when you have rolled up about one quarter of the dough on to the pin.

5   Place the balls of your hands on the dough on the pin, right on top. Begin rolling the pin towards you, while at the same time sliding the palms of your hands away from each other towards the ends of the pin, dragging them against the surface of the dough. Roll up some more of the dough, quickly roll backwards and forwards while repeating the same stretching action with the palms of your hands until the sheet is completely rolled up. Aim for a total of about 12–14 stretching actions.

6   Unroll the pasta, turn it slightly, and dust lightly with flour if sticky. Working as quickly as possible, repeat the rolling and stretching action until the pasta is wafer-thin, less than 2mm (⅟₁₆in) thick, depending on the type of pasta you are making. Should a hole appear, simply patch it with a piece of dough from the edge. If you take more than 8–10 minutes to achieve this, the pasta will dry out and lose its elasticity, making it impossible to roll further.

7   If you are making stuffed pastas, omit steps 4, 5 and 6. Roll up the pasta sheet on to the rolling pin, then roll it out again on to a large clean dry towel spread on a table, letting about one third of the sheet hang over the edge of the table. Leave for 10 minutes before turning it so another third hangs down. Repeat with the last third. When the surface begins to look leathery and the dough is still pliable, it is ready for cutting. If the kitchen is very hot, the drying time will probably need to be reduced; if the dough dries out too much, it will become brittle and crack.

8   Roll the dough on to the rolling pin and unroll it again on the work surface. Cut into the required sizes using a large sharp knife or a pastry wheel. Push the noodles slightly apart so the air can circulate. Alternatively, the dough can be folded over and over into a flat roll, about 6cm (2½in) wide, then cut across the roll to make the width of noodles you require. With floured fingertips, tweeze the noodles apart. This is a quicker method, but you will have to unravel the folded strips and they might have fold marks in them.

Using a pasta machine

Divide the dough into four balls. Re-cover three of them so they do not dry out. Using the base of your palm, flatten the fourth ball slightly, then pass it through a lightly floured pasta machine on the thickest setting. Fold the two ends of the sheet in towards the middle and repeat four more times. Move the notch or handle of the machine down one setting and repeat.

Continue passing the sheet through the machine in this way until you have gone through all the settings, or all but the last one (this is often considered too thin), until the pasta is about 1–1.15mm thick (or the required thickness for the noodles you are making — see below for traditional thicknesses). Repeat with the remaining balls of dough. See page 13 for storage instructions.

Cut sheets about 20–23cm (8–9in) long. Pass them through the appropriate cutters on the machine or cut noodles by hand. Leave for 5 minutes to firm up before cooking.

Pasta size

These are the traditional widths for the different types of flat pasta:
Tagliatelle (rolled to 1mm thick): 8mm (⅓in)
Tagliarini (rolled to 1mm thick): 2mm (½in)
Tagliolini (rolled to 1mm thick): 2mm (½in)
Tonnarelli (rolled to 1.5mm thick): 1.5mm (¼in)
Fettuccine/trenette (rolled to 1mm thick): 5mm (⅓in)
Pappardelle (rolled slightly thicker, about 1.5mm): 2cm (¾in)
Lasagnette (rolled slightly thicker, about 1.5mm): 2.5–3cm (1–1¼in)
Lasagne (rolled slightly thicker, about 1.5mm): 12.5–15cm x 7.5–10cm (5–6 x 3–4in), or whatever your preference

Making pasta shapes

When making shapes, be sure to keep the dough you are not working on covered, and work as quickly as possible, otherwise the dough will become too dry. Listed below are the easiest shapes to create with home-made pasta — see page 8 for details of the many dried pasta shapes now available in supermarkets and Italian delicatessens.

BRANDELLI: this is the simplest of all pasta shapes: simply tear pieces of the rolled-out pasta sheet into pieces.

FARFALLE: using a fluted pasta or pastry wheel, cut the pasta sheets into rectangles measuring 4 x 2.5cm (1¼ x 1in). Pinch the long sides of each rectangle between your index finger and thumb, squeezing hard enough to make a bow-tie shape. If the pasta fails to hold its shape, moisten your fingers with water and squeeze again. Lay the bow ties out on tea towels, sprinkle with a little flour and leave to dry for about 15 minutes before cooking.

GARGANELLI: cut the pasta sheets into 5cm (2in) squares. Lay an old-fashioned butter pat (paddle), ridged side uppermost, on the work surface. Lay a pasta sheet across the pat so that a pointed end of the sheet is in the centre of the top side of the pat. Put a lightly floured clean pencil or round chopstick diagonally across the corner of the sheet that is nearest you, and, pressing down on the uncovered sides of the pencil, roll it away from you across the pat, enclosing the pasta, which should be marked with the pat ridges. Stand the pencil on its end, give a light tap on the surface so the roll slips off. Spread the garganelli on a tea towel to dry for 10–15 minutes.

GNOCCHI: roll a small amount of pasta into a small sausage, about 2.5cm (1in) long. Press the piece on to a ridged butter pat, and press and push firmly to form a hollow sausage.

MALTAGLIATI: as the name means badly cut, these can be made from pieces of leftover dough, as well as being specially cut. They can be random shapes, or cut into neater triangles. Traditionally, maltagliati are used in soups, but they can also be used in other dishes.

ORECCHIETTE: roll lengths of pasta into sausages about 30cm (12in) in length and 1cm (½in) in diameter. Cut into 1cm (½in) lengths and roll each length into an even ball. Press on each ball in turn, at the same time pushing it away from you slightly so that the pasta curls into an ear or shell shape.

QUADRUCCI: these are similar to maltagliati, but cut into squares.

Stuffed pastas

The sizes given here are the most usual ones, but they can vary according to preference. Any dough that is leftover can be cut into shapes such as brandelli and maltagliati (see page 12). Surplus filling can be used as sandwich or omelette filling, for filling mushroom caps, or formed into balls or sausage shapes and fried, depending on type.

AGNOLOTTI (ALSO KNOWN AS RAVIOLINI): using a 5cm (2in) fluted or plain pastry cutter, cut out circles of pasta dough. Place or pipe about ½ tsp of filling on one half of each circle. Dampen the edges of the circles using a pastry brush and fold the uncovered halves of the circles over the filling. Press the edges together to seal.

CAPPELLETTI/CAPPELLACCI: these are made in the same way as tortellini except that the dough is cut into squares. When formed, they should resemble bishops' mitres.

RAVIOLI (CALLED TORTELLONI IN ROMAGNA): if necessary, using a floured large sharp knife, cut the rolled sheet into 45–50cm (18–20in) lengths. Fold in half lengthways to mark a central long fold. Keep the sheets you are not working on covered. Using a teaspoon or piping bag fitted with a large plain nozzle, place or pipe small mounds of filling about 4–5cm (1½–2in) apart along either side of the fold of one of the lengths, spacing them evenly. With a pastry brush, carefully brush a little water around each mound. Lay a second sheet of dough over the first one. Press gently with your fingertips, between the mounds, pushing out all trapped air. Sprinkle lightly with flour. Cut along each long side of the strip with a pastry or pasta wheel, then in between the mounds, to make squares. Repeat with the remaining sheets and filling. The ravioli can now be cooked, or dried further by being laid on a tea towel, spaced apart, until dried.

RAVIOLONI: the same as ravioli, but larger.

TORTELLINI: using a fluted or plain pastry cutter, cut out 5cm (2in) circles of pasta dough. Place or pipe about ½ tsp of filling on one half of each circle. Dampen the edges of the circles with water using a pastry brush and fold the uncovered halves of the circles over the filling. Press the edges together to seal. Bend the two corners towards each other, wrapping them around the end of your index finger. Pinch the tips together to seal.

TORTELLINI (FROM BOLOGNA): these are made like cappelletti with the dough being cut into 7.5cm (3in) squares.

Once the pasta has been cut and shaped as required, make sure the strands or shapes do not touch because they will stick to each other. Leave for 5 minutes to dry slightly and become firmer, if you are going to cook them straight away.

STORING FRESH PASTA

If you are not using the pasta straightaway or if you have made a large quantity, sprinkle noodles lightly with flour or semolina and then form into loose 'nests' for longer storage. Alternatively, spread on clean tea towels laid on baskets or trays, or drape the pasta over a clothes airer or a clean broom handle suspended between two chairs. Leave to dry for 24 hours and wrap carefully.

The pasta should then keep for 3–4 days stored in a rigid container in a cool place. Lacking durum wheat, home-made pasta can become brittle and crack if it is kept for longer. Lasagne sheets and shapes should be left to dry, spread out.

PASTA DOUGH: This freezes well for up to 1 month, rolled into a ball and covered.

FILLED PASTAS: These can be kept for up to 3 days in the fridge. Leave them spread out to dry. Then store on sheets of greaseproof paper in an airtight container in the fridge. Filled pastas with moist fillings do not freeze successfully, but meat-filled pastas freeze well. Spread out the shapes on a tray and open-freeze for 2–3 hours, then carefully transfer them to a rigid freezer-proof container. Freeze for up to 3 months. Cook from frozen, allowing them an extra 5 minutes cooking.

PASTA DISHES: Uncooked pasta dishes for baking, such as lasagne or cannelloni, can be covered and refrigerated for up to a day. Return the dish to room temperature 1–2 hours before cooking, or bake for an additional 5–10 minutes (uncovered) in the oven, depending on the size of the dish. Pasta dishes can also be frozen. Cover and chill before freezing for up to 2 months. Thaw overnight in the fridge before baking as instructed in the recipe.

SAUCES

Italians are very adept at matching a pasta shape to a sauce and only use certain combinations, but there are no rules set in stone. However, some combinations are more successful than others. The shape and thickness of pasta are significant. They are an integral part of its texture, which affects the way it combines with a sauce. As a general guideline match the thickness of the pasta to the weight of the sauce.

- Long, thin pasta, such as linguine, spaghettini and spaghetti, is thought to be best with simple sauces based on olive oil, and with sauces containing finely chopped ingredients. Spaghetti is sturdy enough to also go with a wide variety of sauces.
- Long, thick pasta, such as bucatini, and flat ribbons like tagliatelle go well with cream sauces, and with sauces containing small amounts of vegetables, fish and meat.
- Pappardelle and other wide pastas, pasta tubes such as penne, and pasta shapes like orecchiette are usually partnered with robust vegetable or meat sauces, or used in baked dishes.
- Tubular pasta, twists, shells and similar shapes go well with chunkier meat and vegetable sauces.
- Fresh pasta is traditionally considered to suit delicate cream sauces better than dried pasta.

The 'ideal' amount of sauce to an Italian is enough to coat the pasta lightly without leaving a covering or pool on the plate when the pasta is eaten. Again, this is a matter of taste, and if you prefer more sauce, use it.

EQUIPMENT FOR COOKING PASTA

These are the basics you will need:

- Large, deep saucepan: the most useful and safest pans if you cook pasta frequently are those with an inner perforated draining basket that can simply be lifted from the pan when the pasta is cooked.
- Wide, deep frying pan: for cooking lasagne.
- Long-handled fork: for stirring pasta during cooking to keep the strands separate, and for tossing the pasta with the sauce.
- Wooden pasta rake: resembles a flat wooden spoon with prongs attached to one side, at right angles to it. It is effective because pasta does not slip off when it is lifted.
- Tongs: these are very effective for lifting strands of spaghetti and other tubular pastas.
- Long-handled slotted spoon or straining/skimming spoon: for lifting shapes and stuffed pastas from the water.
- Parmesan grater: a special, very sharp grater that is specifically designed for grating hard cheeses such as Parmesan or pecorino.
- Parmesan knife: a short-bladed knife for cutting Parmesan and pecorino and for creating shavings.

COOKING PASTA

To be at its best, pasta should be served as soon as it is cooked (unless being used for a salad), so it is important to time the cooking of the sauce to be ready at the same time. This might occasionally mean taking the sauce off the heat when it is cooked, then reheating it just before the pasta is done. Because of the time taken for the pasta water to boil, it often makes sense to put it on before preparing the sauce. This is especially true for fresh pastas.

Whilst it is important to have enough water, there is no need, and indeed is wasteful, to have vast amounts. Provided the pasta is covered by about 7.5cm (3in) of water, it will cook perfectly well if it is stirred immediately after being added to the water and 2–3 times during cooking, and the water is kept at a gentle rolling boil.

Bring a covered pan of water to the boil, add salt if you like (this is purely a matter of taste and not essential), then add all the pasta at once (oil is unnecessary), without breaking it; coil spaghetti into the water as it softens. Stir, cover the pan and return the water quickly to the boil. Remove the lid and boil the pasta until shortly before you think it will be done, and start testing. The pasta should be just firm to the bite; it will continue to cook in its own heat after draining.

Fresh pasta can be cooked in as little as 1 minute or as much as 5 minutes, depending on the type of flour and the length of drying. The normal range is 2–4 minutes. Commercial dried pastas should be cooked according to the instructions on the pack, but begin testing a couple of minutes before the stated time. Stuffed pastas take about 4–7 minutes.

Drain pasta as soon as it is ready, either by tipping it into a large, preferably warmed, colander in the sink, or by lifting out the saucepan's integral straining basket. Give the colander or basket two or three sharp shakes, but do not drain the pasta too thoroughly. Long pasta should remain slippery and slightly dripping with water. Shapes and short tubes should be drained slightly more thoroughly to dislodge any trapped water, but they should still be slippery. Fresh egg pasta needs the least thorough draining, and should remain very slippery because it will tend to absorb more of the sauce than dried pasta.

It is a good idea to get into the habit of reserving a little of the cooking water (some recipes specify this), to moisten the dressed pasta if it is too dry. This water is better than hot tap water because the starch it contains will add body as well as moisture to the sauce.

Combining pasta and sauce

Pasta should be tossed with its sauce as soon as it is cooked, or with a little olive oil or cooking water to prevent it sticking together. If it does happen to stick, tip it into a colander and pour boiling water through it. For tossing, the pasta can returned to the hot pan in which it was cooked, the sauce ingredients added and everything tossed together; or the pasta can be added to the pan of sauce; or it can be tipped into a hot, roomy serving bowl, the sauce added and the two tossed together. Some recipes specify gently heating the pasta and sauce together, and care must be taken not to use too high a temperature or heat for too long. To toss pasta and sauce, use two large, long-handled spoons or forks, or a spoon and a fork and lift the pasta, reaching right down into the bottom of the bowl, and toss gently. If, after tossing, the sauce seems too thick, add a little of the reserved cooking water.

Cooking stuffed pastas

Stuffed pastas, such as ravioli, are more fragile than ordinary types so require more gentle handling and cooking to prevent them being damaged and the filling escaping. Don't boil them too hard, and, for preference, use a large slotted spoon or a draining/skimming spoon to remove them from the pan when cooked.

Pasta for baked dishes

Because of the cooking in the oven, pasta for a baked dish should be boiled for slightly less time than normal: usually 1–2 minutes, depending on the length of time in the oven.

Lasagne sheets and cannelloni tubes should be cooked in batches, in a shallow, wide pan rather than a deep, narrower one. As they are difficult to stir to separate, and don't move about as much as other pastas, it is worth adding 1–2 tbsp olive oil to the water. Cook according to the instructions on the packet, then drain well and rinse under running cold water to remove surplus starch and prevent sticking. Drain again, and then spread on a tea towel to dry. Cannelloni tubes should be handled more gently than lasagne sheets.

The texture of no-pre-cook types will benefit from similar cooking until they are just pliable, which will probably be about 1 minute. If a recipe specifies pre-cooking and you do not give it, it is a good idea to use a little more sauce than the recipe specifies, or make the sauce thinner.

Cooking in a microwave

Short pasta shapes and soup pasta, and quantities under 225g (8oz) are the only types that are worth cooking in a microwave, although the results won't be quite as good as conventionally cooked pasta. It doesn't really make sense to cook larger amounts because the large volume of water required means that they would have to be cooked in batches, so time is not saved.

Microwave ovens can be useful, though, for thawing frozen dishes, and for reheating pre-cooked pasta dishes such as lasagne and cannelloni, especially individual portions. Microwaves can also be used for thawing and reheating pasta sauces.

To cook less than 225g (8oz) pasta shapes in a microwave, put the pasta in a suitable large bowl, pour over boiling water to cover by 2.5cm (1in), stir and put the bowl in the microwave. Cook on 100% (HIGH) power for 3–4 minutes for fresh pasta, 8–10 minutes for dried. Leave to stand for 5 minutes before draining.

SERVING PASTA

Pasta bowls or deep soup plates make the best serving dishes. Because pasta loses its heat so quickly, be sure to warm the dishes well. Pasta salads are best served warm or cold, not chilled.

001
ragù

PREPARATION TIME 10 minutes COOKING TIME 1¾–2¼ hours SERVES 4

I ONION, FINELY CHOPPED
I SMALL CARROT, FINELY CHOPPED
I SMALL CELERY STICK, FINELY CHOPPED
OLIVE OIL
2 GARLIC CLOVES, FINELY CHOPPED
350G (12OZ) LEAN MINCED BEEF
225ML (8FL OZ/1 CUP) MILK

175ML (6FL OZ/¾ CUP) MEDIUM-BODIED DRY
   WHITE WINE
500G (1LB 2OZ) RIPE WELL-FLAVOURED TOMATOES,
   CHOPPED
I TBSP SUN-DRIED TOMATO PASTE
I BOUQUET GARNI
SALT AND FRESHLY GROUND BLACK PEPPER

1   Fry the onion, carrot and celery in a little olive oil in a heavy pan until soft and lightly browned. Add the garlic and fry for a further 1–2 minutes. Stir in the beef to break it up, and cook, stirring, until it loses its pink colour.

2   Once the meat has changed colour, pour in the milk in three stages; let the liquid simmer and evaporate between each addition. Repeat with the wine. Do not allow the sauce to boil otherwise the meat will become tough.

3   Stir in the tomatoes, tomato paste, bouquet garni, seasoning and 225ml (8fl oz/scant 1 cup) water. Continue to simmer, uncovered, very gently for 1½–2 hours, stirring occasionally, until it has thickened. Discard the bouquet garni.

4   Use immediately, or leave to cool, cover and refrigerate for 2–3 days. Alternatively, freeze for up to 1 month. Thaw in the fridge overnight before using; the sauce will probably thicken so it might be necessary to stir in a little additional liquid.

002
quick ragù

PREPARATION TIME 10 minutes COOKING TIME 50 minutes SERVES 4

I LARGE ONION, FINELY CHOPPED
I CARROT, FINELY CHOPPED
I CELERY STICK, FINELY CHOPPED
OLIVE OIL
2 GARLIC CLOVES, FINELY CHOPPED
450G (1LB) MINCED BEEF
300ML (10FL OZ/SCANT 1¼ CUPS) RED WINE

300ML (10FL OZ/SCANT 1¼ CUPS) BEEF STOCK
400G CAN CHOPPED TOMATOES
I TBSP SUN-DRIED TOMATO PASTE
2 TSP DRIED OREGANO
SALT AND FRESHLY GROUND BLACK PEPPER
2 TBSP (1½ TBSP) CHOPPED FLAT-LEAF PARSLEY

1   Fry the onion, carrot and celery in a little oil until soft and flecked with brown. Add the garlic, fry for 1 minute then stir in the beef and cook, stirring, until lightly browned. Stir in the wine, stock, tomatoes, tomato paste and oregano.

2   Heat until just simmering, half cover and then simmer gently, stirring occasionally, for about 40 minutes until the beef is very tender and the sauce reduced. If the sauce becomes too dry, add a little water, or remove the lid if the sauce has not reduced enough. Season and stir in the parsley.

003
béchamel sauce

PREPARATION TIME 5 minutes, plus 30 minutes infusing COOKING TIME 10 minutes SERVES 4

570ML (1 PINT/SCANT 2½ CUPS) MILK
1 BAY LEAF
1 ONION SLICE
1 CLOVE

2 PARSLEY SPRIGS
50G (2OZ/SCANT ¼ CUP) UNSALTED BUTTER
4 TBSP (3 TBSP) PLAIN FLOUR
SALT AND FRESHLY GROUND BLACK PEPPER

1   Gently heat the milk with the bay leaf, onion, clove and parsley until bubbles appear around the edge. Cover, remove from the heat and leave for 30 minutes.
2   Melt the butter in a heavy pan until sizzling but not browned, then stir in the flour and cook for 1–2 minutes. Off the heat, slowly strain in the milk, whisking or stirring. Return to the heat and bring to the boil, stirring or whisking. Lower the heat and simmer for 5 minutes, stirring occasionally. Season.
3   If not using the sauce straight away, cover the surface closely with clingfilm, leave to cool, then store in the fridge for up to 3 days. When reheating the sauce, it may be necessary to stir in a little more milk to restore the correct consistency.

Note:
    The thickness of a béchamel sauce (and therefore the proportions of butter, flour and milk) can vary from recipe to recipe. The flavourings — the bay leaf, onion, clove and parsley — remain the same.

004
simple white sauce

PREPARATION TIME 5 minutes COOKING TIME 10 minutes SERVES 4

570ML (1 PINT/SCANT 2½ CUPS) MILK
35G (1¼OZ/3 TBSP) PLAIN FLOUR
40G (1½OZ/2½ TBSP) UNSALTED BUTTER

1 BAY LEAF
SALT AND FRESHLY GROUND BLACK PEPPER

1   Put all the ingredients into a small saucepan and bring to the boil over a moderate heat, whisking constantly, and simmer until the sauce thickens, still whisking.
2   Reduce the heat and let the sauce simmer very gently for 2–3 minutes, stirring occasionally. Discard the bay leaf. Season.

Variation:
    Cheese sauce: stir 50g (2oz) grated Parmesan cheese into the sauce after discarding the bay leaf. Do not boil once the cheese has been added.

005
fresh tomato sauce

PREPARATION TIME 5 minutes COOKING TIME 25–30 minutes SERVES 4

I SMALL ONION, FINELY CHOPPED
VIRGIN OLIVE OIL
2 GARLIC CLOVES, LEFT WHOLE
I BAY LEAF
3 THYME SPRIGS

3 PARSLEY SPRIGS
ABOUT IKG (2¼LB) WELL-FLAVOURED TOMATOES,
 QUITE FINELY CHOPPED
SALT AND FRESHLY GROUND BLACK PEPPER
SUGAR OR SUN-DRIED TOMATO PASTE (OPTIONAL)

1 Fry the onion in a little oil in a large frying pan for 2 minutes. Stir in the garlic and herbs
   and cook over a medium heat for 8–10 minutes until the onion is soft but not coloured.
2 Add the tomatoes, raise the heat and cook until the sauce is no longer watery. Season, and add
   a pinch or two of sugar, or a little sun-dried tomato paste, if necessary, to enhance the flavour.
   Discard the garlic and herbs.
3 The sauce should have some texture; if you prefer a smooth sauce, purée it and pass through
   a non-metallic sieve. Use immediately, or leave to cool, cover and refrigerate for 2–3 days.
   Alternatively, freeze for up to I month; thaw in the fridge overnight before using.

Variation:
   Grilled tomato sauce: grill 1kg (2¼lb) tomatoes on the lowest rung under the grill, turning as required,
   until evenly blistered and lightly charred. Remove any blackened skin, then purée coarsely so there is
   still some texture. Fry two chopped shallots in a little oil until soft, then stir in the purée and simmer
   until thickened. Season and add a pinch of sugar, if necessary, to bring out the flavour. Store as above.

006
pesto

PREPARATION TIME 5 minutes COOKING TIME 5 minutes SERVES 4

50G (2oz) BASIL LEAVES
2 GARLIC CLOVES, CRUSHED
2 TBSP PINE NUTS
115ML (4FL OZ/SCANT ½ CUP) EXTRA-VIRGIN OLIVE OIL

50G (2oz) PARMESAN CHEESE, FRESHLY GRATED
SALT AND FRESHLY GROUND BLACK PEPPER
SQUEEZE OF LEMON JUICE (OPTIONAL)

1 Put the basil, garlic, pine nuts and a little of the oil into a blender and pulse to a fairly smooth paste.
   Mix in the remaining oil.
2 Transfer to a bowl and stir in the Parmesan. Season, and add a squeeze of lemon juice, if liked.
   Pesto will keep in a covered container in the fridge for up to I week.

007
red pesto

PREPARATION TIME 5 minutes COOKING TIME 5 minutes SERVES 4

50G (2oz) SUN-DRIED TOMATOES IN OIL, DRAINED

2 GARLIC CLOVES, CRUSHED

40G (1½oz) BASIL LEAVES

3 TBSP PINE NUTS, LIGHTLY TOASTED

6 TBSP MIXED EXTRA-VIRGIN OLIVE OIL AND OIL
  FROM THE TOMATOES

4 TBSP FRESHLY GRATED PARMESAN CHEESE

SALT AND FRESHLY GROUND BLACK PEPPER

½–2 TSP BALSAMIC VINEGAR

1   Put the tomatoes, garlic, basil, pine nuts and a little of the oils into a blender and pulse to a fairly
    smooth paste. Mix in the remaining oils.
2   Transfer to a bowl and stir in the Parmesan. Season, taking care with the salt but adding plenty
    of black pepper. Add balsamic vinegar, to taste. Red pesto will keep in a covered container
    in the fridge for up to 1 week.

008
winter tomato sauce

PREPARATION TIME 20 minutes COOKING TIME 30–35 minutes SERVES 4

1 ONION, CHOPPED

1 CARROT, CHOPPED

1 CELERY STICK, CHOPPED

OLIVE OIL OR OIL FROM THE SUN-DRIED TOMATOES

2 GARLIC CLOVES, CHOPPED

2 X 400G CAN CHOPPED TOMATOES

2 TBSP SUN-DRIED TOMATO PASTE

150ML (5FL OZ/SCANT ⅔ CUP) RED
  OR MEDIUM-BODIED DRY WHITE WINE

150ML (5FL OZ/SCANT ⅔ CUP) VEGETABLE STOCK

50G (2oz) SUN-DRIED TOMATOES IN OIL,
  DRAINED AND SLICED

SALT AND FRESHLY GROUND BLACK PEPPER

1   Fry the onion, carrot and celery in a little oil until softened and beginning to colour. Add the garlic,
    cook for 1 minute, then stir in the canned tomatoes, tomato paste, wine and stock. Simmer, uncovered,
    for about 30 minutes until thickened, stirring occasionally.
2   Purée the sauce, then add the sun-dried tomatoes and seasoning.

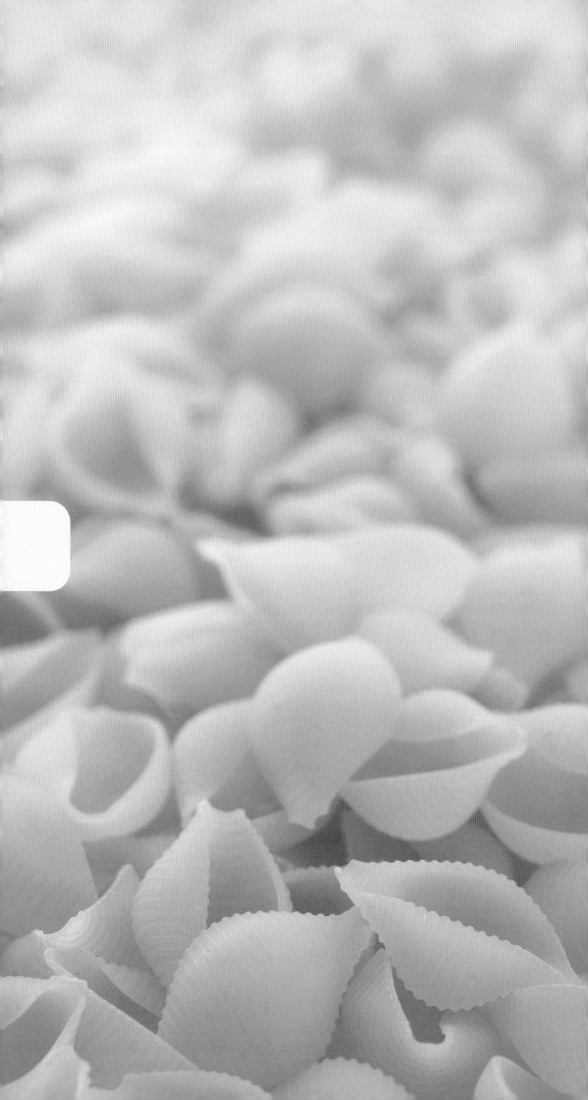

first courses
& snacks

First-course pasta dishes are lighter than those served for main courses, containing less pasta and with fewer ingredients. If you would like to serve one of the recipes in this chapter as a main course, simply serve larger portions to fewer people. First-course pasta dishes are generally quick and easy to prepare, and often made from simple store cupboard or fridge ingredients. An exception to the 'quick' rule is gnocchi, the dumplings made from mashed potato, spinach and ricotta, or semolina, but these can be made in advance. Some simple classics appear in this chapter, such as Spaghetti alla Carbonara and Herb Fettuccine all'Alfredo, plus some variations on traditional recipes, like Trenette with Red Pesto and Ricotta and Spaghetti with Summer Puttanesca Sauce. This chapter also features soup recipes containing pasta.

009

vegetable, borlotti & pasta soup

PREPARATION TIME 10 minutes COOKING TIME 50 minutes SERVES 6

I ONION, CHOPPED

I SMALL LEEK, THINLY SLICED

2 CELERY STICKS, CHOPPED

3 GARLIC CLOVES, CHOPPED

3–4 THYME SPRIGS

OLIVE OIL

1.2 LITRES (2 PINTS/4½ CUPS) VEGETABLE STOCK

400G CAN BORLOTTI BEANS, DRAINED AND RINSED

I COURGETTE, DICED

5 TOMATOES, CHOPPED

150G (5oz) FRENCH BEANS, HALVED

150G (5oz) BABY BROAD BEANS

50G (2oz) FRESH MALTAGLIATI,
   OR SMALL PASTA SHAPES FOR SOUP

LEAVES FROM A SMALL BUNCH OF
   FLAT-LEAF PARSLEY, CHOPPED

SALT AND FRESHLY GROUND BLACK PEPPER

PESTO (SEE PAGE 18) AND SHAVED PECORINO,
   TO SERVE

1   Fry the onion, leek, celery, garlic and thyme in oil in a large saucepan until soft but not coloured.
    Add the stock, cover and simmer for 30 minutes.
2   Add the borlotti beans, courgette, tomatoes, French and broad beans, simmer for a further 10 minutes,
    then add the pasta and parsley, stir and cook for about 5 minutes until the pasta is tender.
3   Season, discard the thyme and serve with pesto swirled in and scattered with pecorino shavings.

010

chunky vegetable & pasta soup

PREPARATION TIME 5 minutes COOKING TIME 25 minutes SERVES 6–8

2.3 LITRES (4 PINTS/8⅓ CUPS) VEGETABLE STOCK

2–3 GARLIC CLOVES, CHOPPED

450G (1LB) POTATOES, DICED

2 LEEKS, THINLY SLICED

3 CARROTS, DICED

350G (12oz) COURGETTES, DICED

175G (6oz) FRENCH BEANS, HALVED

400G CAN CANNELLINI BEANS, DRAINED AND RINSED

400G CAN CHOPPED PLUM TOMATOES

115G (4oz) FARFALLINE OR
   OTHER SMALL PASTA FOR SOUP

115G (4oz) CHESTNUT MUSHROOMS, SLICED

OLIVE OIL, FOR FRYING

PESTO (SEE PAGE 18) AND FRESHLY GRATED
   PECORINO, TO SERVE

1   Bring the stock and garlic to the boil in a large saucepan. Add the potatoes, leeks and carrots.
    Cover and simmer gently for 20 minutes until the vegetables are very tender.
2   Add the courgettes, French beans, cannellini beans and tomatoes. Bring to the boil, stir in the
    pasta and simmer for about 10 minutes until the pasta is al dente.
3   Meanwhile, fry the mushrooms in a little oil until softened. Add to the soup for the final 5 minutes
    of its cooking. Serve in warmed large soup plates accompanied by pesto and pecorino.

chicken soup with tortellini

PREPARATION TIME 5 minutes COOKING TIME 10 minutes SERVES 4

I LITRE (1¾ PINTS/4 CUPS) GOOD CHICKEN STOCK
I QUANTITY SPICED CHICKEN TORTELLINI
  (SEE PAGE 120), OR BOUGHT FRESH
  CHICKEN TORTELLINI OR RAVIOLI

2 WELL-FLAVOURED PLUM TOMATOES,
  SEEDED AND FINELY CHOPPED
FINELY CHOPPED FLAT-LEAF PARSLEY AND
  FRESHLY GRATED PARMESAN, TO SERVE

1   Bring the stock to the boil in a saucepan, add the tortellini and cook for 4–5 minutes.
2   Lower the heat so the stock is just simmering, add the tomatoes and warm through
    for a couple of minutes. Serve sprinkled with Parmesan and parsley.

012
golden squash & conchigliette soup

PREPARATION TIME 15 minutes COOKING TIME 30 minutes SERVES 4

I ONION, FINELY CHOPPED

VIRGIN OLIVE OIL

2 GARLIC CLOVES, FINELY CHOPPED

500G (1LB 2OZ) BUTTERNUT OR ONION SQUASH,
    CUT INTO 1CM (½IN) PIECES

I LARGE BAY LEAF, TORN ACROSS

1.4 LITRES (2½ PINTS/5½ CUPS) VEGETABLE STOCK

115ML (4FL OZ/½ CUP) MEDIUM-BODIED DRY WHITE
    VERMOUTH

115G (4OZ) CONCHIGLIETTE, OR OTHER SMALL
    PASTA SHAPES FOR SOUP

FRESHLY GRATED PARMESAN, TO SERVE

1   Fry the onion in a little oil until soft. Stir in the garlic, squash and bay leaf and cook gently for
     2 minutes. Pour in the stock and wine and simmer for 10–15 minutes until the squash is tender.
2   Remove 1–2 cups of the soup, purée the liquid and then return to the pan. Bring to the boil, add the
     conchigliette, stir, and cook for 6–8 minutes until the pasta is just tender. Serve with grated Parmesan.

Note:

This soup is particularly good served with Parmesan croûtons: cut 3 thick slices of bread, remove
the crusts and spread with garlic butter made by pounding a small knob of unsalted butter with
a crushed garlic clove. Sprinkle over 2 tbsp freshly grated Parmesan. Place on an oiled baking sheet
and cut into cubes, spacing them well apart. Bake in a preheated oven at 200°C/400°F/gas 6
for 8–10 minutes until golden.

013
crab & prawn soup

PREPARATION TIME 10 minutes COOKING TIME 30 minutes SERVES 4

1 ONION, FINELY CHOPPED

1 SMALL FENNEL BULB, FINELY CHOPPED,
　FEATHERY TOPS RESERVED

OLIVE OIL

2 GARLIC CLOVES, FINELY CHOPPED

2 THYME SPRIGS

PINCH OF CHILLI FLAKES

1 LITRE (1¾ PINTS/4 CUPS) SHELLFISH
　OR FISH STOCK

350ML (12FL OZ/SCANT 1½ CUPS) PASSATA

65G (2¼OZ) FUNGHETTI OR
　OTHER SMALL PASTA SHAPES

175G (6OZ) CRAB MEAT

115G (4OZ) PEELED COOKED PRAWNS

1 LARGE BOTTLED GRILLED RED PEPPER IN OIL,
　DRAINED AND CHOPPED

SALT AND FRESHLY GROUND BLACK PEPPER

PINCH OF SUGAR (OPTIONAL)

LEAVES FROM A SMALL BUNCH OF
　FLAT-LEAF PARSLEY, CHOPPED

1　Fry the onion and fennel in a little oil until soft and translucent, adding the garlic, thyme and chilli
　flakes towards the end of cooking. Pour in the stock and passata, bring to the boil and then simmer
　for about 15 minutes.

2　Return the soup to the boil, stir in the pasta and cook according to the packet instructions.
　Lower the heat, add the crab, prawns and red pepper and heat through gently. Do not boil.
　Season, adding a pinch of sugar, if necessary. Sprinkle over the reserved fennel tops and parsley.

014
chicken & pasta soup

PREPARATION TIME 10 minutes COOKING TIME 25 minutes SERVES 4

4–6 CHICKEN THIGHS, PREFERABLY UNBONED
1 ROSEMARY SPRIG
2 BAY LEAVES
5 GARLIC CLOVES
200ML (7FL OZ/ ¾ CUP) MEDIUM-BODIED DRY
   WHITE WINE
700ML (1¼ PINTS/2⅔ CUPS) CHICKEN STOCK
1 ONION, FINELY CHOPPED

1 CARROT, DICED
OLIVE OIL
50G (2OZ) SMALL FARFALLINE,
   OR OTHER SMALL PASTA SHAPE FOR SOUP
1 SMALL COS LETTUCE, SHREDDED
2 TBSP CHOPPED FLAT-LEAF PARSLEY
SALT AND FRESHLY GROUND BLACK PEPPER
FRESHLY GRATED PARMESAN, TO SERVE

1 Put the chicken, rosemary, bay, 4 garlic cloves, wine and stock into a saucepan. Slowly bring just to the boil, then simmer gently for 10–15 minutes, depending on size and whether the chicken has bone, until the chicken is just cooked through. Transfer the chicken to a plate using a slotted spoon. Reserve the stock.
2 Chop the reserved garlic clove. Fry the onion, carrot and chopped garlic in a little oil in a saucepan until softened. Strain in the stock, bring to the boil and then add the pasta. Stir and cook for about 5 minutes until the pasta is tender.
3 Meanwhile, chop the chicken quite finely. Add to the soup with the lettuce and parsley, when the pasta is cooked. Heat gently until the lettuce has wilted. Season. Serve sprinkled with Parmesan.

015
courgette, broad bean & tagliatelle soup

PREPARATION TIME 5 minutes COOKING TIME 25 minutes SERVES 4

1 ONION, FINELY CHOPPED
2 GARLIC CLOVES, CRUSHED
4 TBSP OLIVE OIL
225G (8OZ) BROAD BEANS
350G (12OZ) SMALL-MEDIUM COURGETTES, GRATED
1.4 LITRES (2½ PINTS/6 CUPS) VEGETABLE STOCK,
   BOILING

150G (5OZ) TAGLIATELLE,
   BROKEN INTO SHORT LENGTHS
2 TBSP FINELY CHOPPED
   FLAT-LEAF PARSLEY
SALT AND FRESHLY GROUND BLACK PEPPER
FRESHLY GRATED PARMESAN, TO SERVE

1 Fry the onion and the garlic in the oil in a saucepan until soft and very lightly coloured. Stir in the beans and courgettes for 1–2 minutes, then add the stock. Bring to the boil, stir and then simmer, uncovered, for 10–15 minutes.
2 Remove half the vegetables, purée them and return to the soup.
3 Meanwhile, cook and drain the pasta according to the packet instructions. Add to the soup with the parsley, season and reheat. Serve sprinkled with freshly grated Parmesan.

spring minestrone

PREPARATION TIME 10 minutes COOKING TIME 15 minutes SERVES 4–6

175G (6oz) SMALL CARROTS, QUITE FINELY CHOPPED

85G (3oz) MINIATURE FENNEL BULBS (ABOUT 4),
    QUITE FINELY CHOPPED, OR I SMALL FENNEL BULB

OLIVE OIL

3 BABY LEEKS, THINLY SLICED

175G (6oz) SMALL COURGETTES,
    QUITE FINELY CHOPPED

1.3 LITRES (2¼ PINTS/5¼ CUPS) GOOD-QUALITY
    VEGETABLE STOCK

85G (3oz) VERMICELLI OR
    SMALL PASTA SHAPES FOR SOUP

200G (7oz/1¼ CUPS) SHELLED PEAS,
    OR FROZEN PETITS POIS

200G (7oz/1¼ CUPS) SHELLED BROAD BEANS,
    OR FROZEN BABY BROAD BEANS

3 WELL-FLAVOURED TOMATOES,
    SEEDED AND SLICED

100G (3½oz) BABY SPINACH LEAVES

SALT AND FRESHLY GROUND BLACK PEPPER

PESTO (SEE PAGE 18), TO SERVE

1   Fry the carrots and fennel in a little oil until beginning to soften. Add the leeks and
     courgettes, fry for 2–3 minutes and then add the stock. Bring to the boil, add the
     pasta and cook until just tender, adding the peas, beans and tomatoes 4–5 minutes
     before the end of the cooking.

2   Stir in the spinach. Season as soon as it has wilted, and serve with pesto.

anelli siciliani, chickpea & sage soup

PREPARATION TIME 10 minutes COOKING TIME 25 minutes SERVES 4

1 CELERY STICK, CHOPPED,

1 LEEK, CHOPPED

1 CARROT, FINELY CHOPPED

VIRGIN OLIVE OIL

3 GARLIC CLOVES, FINELY CHOPPED

8 SMALL SAGE LEAVES, FINELY CHOPPED

400G CAN CHICKPEAS, DRAINED AND RINSED

400G CAN CHOPPED PLUM TOMATOES

ABOUT 825ML (1½ PINTS/3⅓ CUPS) VEGETABLE STOCK

100G (3½OZ) ANELLI SICILIANI,
    OR OTHER SMALL PASTA SHAPES FOR SOUP

SALT AND FRESHLY GROUND BLACK PEPPER

FRESHLY GRATED PARMESAN, TO SERVE

1   Fry the celery, leek and carrot in a little oil in a saucepan until lightly browned. Add the garlic
    and sage, fry for 1 minute, then add the chickpeas, tomatoes and stock. Simmer for 15–20 minutes.
    Pour most of the soup into a food processor and reduce to a thick, nubbly purée. Return to the pan.
2   Meanwhile, cook and drain the pasta. Add to the soup and heat through, adjusting the thickness,
    if necessary, by boiling so that excess water evaporates, or adding more stock if too thick. Season.
    Serve with freshly grated Parmesan.

linguine with herbs, lemon & garlic crumbs

PREPARATION TIME 10 minutes COOKING TIME 10 minutes SERVES 4

300G (10oz) LINGUINE*
EXTRA-VIRGIN OLIVE OIL
1 PLUMP GARLIC CLOVE, CRUSHED
50G (2oz) FRESH BREADCRUMBS
1 SHALLOT, FINELY CHOPPED

LEAVES FROM A BUNCH OF MIXED HERBS SUCH
   AS PARSLEY, OREGANO, BASIL AND FENNEL,
   PLUS A FEW CHIVES, ALL FINELY CHOPPED
JUICE OF 1 LEMON
1 TSP LEMON ZEST
SALT AND FRESHLY GROUND BLACK PEPPER

1   Cook and drain the pasta according to the packet instructions.
2   Meanwhile, heat about 3 tbsp oil in a frying pan, add the garlic and breadcrumbs and cook over
    a low heat, stirring frequently, until golden. Stir in the shallot towards the end.
3   At the same time, gently warm 2 tbsp oil with the herbs, lemon juice, zest and seasoning in a pan.
4   Toss the pasta with the herb mixture, scatter over the breadcrumbs and serve.

*   Spaghetti or bucatini can also be used.

tagliarini with artichokes & gremolata

PREPARATION TIME 10 minutes, plus 30 minutes standing COOKING TIME 10 minutes SERVES 4

8 ROAST ARTICHOKES IN OIL, RINSED AND QUARTERED
2 TBSP SMALL CAPERS
6 SPRING ONIONS, FINELY CHOPPED
2–3 TBSP LEMON JUICE, TO TASTE
EXTRA-VIRGIN OLIVE OIL
SALT AND FRESHLY GROUND BLACK PEPPER

GRATED ZEST OF 1 LEMON
3 GARLIC CLOVES, FINELY SLICED
HANDFUL OF FLAT-LEAF PARSLEY, CHOPPED
250G (9oz) TAGLIARINI
FRESHLY GRATED PARMESAN, TO SERVE

1   Put the artichokes, capers, spring onions and lemon juice into a small bowl and pour over enough oil
    to cover. Season using plenty of black pepper. Leave for 30 minutes.
2   To make the gremolata, combine the lemon zest, garlic and parsley in a small bowl.
3   Cook and drain the tagliarini according to the packet instructions. Toss with the artichoke mixture and
    serve with the lemon and garlic gremolata scattered over, accompanied by freshly grated Parmesan.

020

spaghetti with lemon, basil & parmesan

PREPARATION TIME 5 minutes COOKING TIME 10 minutes SERVES 4–6

85ML (3FL OZ/SCANT ⅓ CUP) VIRGIN OLIVE OIL
2 GARLIC CLOVES, FINELY CHOPPED
JUICE AND GRATED ZEST OF I LEMON
400G (14oz) SPAGHETTI

50G (2oz) PARMESAN, FRESHLY GRATED
HANDFUL OF BASIL LEAVES, SHREDDED
SALT AND FRESHLY GROUND BLACK PEPPER

1   Warm the oil, garlic and lemon juice in a small saucepan over a very low heat.
2   Meanwhile, cook and drain the spaghetti according to the packet instructions. Toss with the warmed oil, the Parmesan, basil and seasoning. Serve with the lemon zest sprinkled over.

021

pasta, basil & goats' cheese frittata

PREPARATION TIME 10 minutes COOKING TIME 15–20 minutes SERVES 3–4

115G (4oz) COOKED ANGELS' HAIR PASTA
   (50G/2oz UNCOOKED WEIGHT)
4 EGGS, LIGHTLY BEATEN
2 GARLIC CLOVES, FINELY CHOPPED
2 TBSP CHOPPED FLAT-LEAF PARSLEY
SALT AND FRESHLY GROUND BLACK PEPPER
OLIVE OIL

85G (3oz) GOATS' CHEESE, FINELY CHOPPED
   OR CRUMBLED
2 WELL-FLAVOURED TOMATOES, CHOPPED
2 TSP BALSAMIC VINEGAR
I TBSP SHREDDED BASIL LEAVES
1½ TBSP FRESHLY GRATED PARMESAN

1   Stir the pasta into the eggs with the garlic, parsley and seasoning.
2   Heat a thin film of oil in an ovenproof frying pan, pour in the egg mixture and spread it out evenly. Cook over a low-medium heat until most of the mixture is set, but the top is still creamy.
3   Scatter over the goats' cheese and put under a preheated grill until the cheese is bubbling.
4   Meanwhile, combine the tomatoes with the balsamic vinegar and basil.
5   Sprinkle the Parmesan over the frittata and serve in wedges, accompanied by the tomatoes.

022

spaghetti with garlic, anchovies & parsley

PREPARATION TIME 5 minutes COOKING TIME 10 minutes SERVES 6

425G (15oz) SPAGHETTI
3 GARLIC CLOVES, FINELY CHOPPED
VIRGIN OLIVE OIL
50G (2oz) CAN ANCHOVIES IN OIL, DRAINED
2 TSP DRIED OREGANO

LEAVES FROM A SMALL BUNCH OF FLAT-LEAF
   PARSLEY, COARSELY CHOPPED
SALT AND FRESHLY GROUND BLACK PEPPER
FRESHLY GRATED PECORINO OR PARMESAN, TO SERVE

1   Cook and drain the spaghetti according to the packet instructions.
2   Meanwhile, fry the garlic in a little oil with the anchovies, oregano and parsley, stirring frequently, until the anchovies have dissolved and the garlic is soft and lightly coloured. Season, using plenty of black pepper.
3   Toss with the spaghetti and serve with pecorino or Parmesan.

023
cavatappi with rocket, tomatoes & olives

PREPARATION TIME 10 minutes COOKING TIME 10 minutes SERVES 4

250G (9oz) CAVATAPPI
3 PLUMP GARLIC CLOVES, FINELY SLICED
4 TBSP EXTRA-VIRGIN OLIVE OIL
550G (1¼LB) RIPE WELL-FLAVOURED TOMATOES,
  SEEDED AND CHOPPED

50G (2oz) ROCKET
12 OIL-CURED BLACK OLIVES, PITTED
1 TBSP PINE NUTS, LIGHTLY TOASTED
SALT AND FRESHLY GROUND BLACK PEPPER
FRESHLY GRATED PECORINO OR PARMESAN, TO SERVE

1 Cook and drain the cavatappi according to the packet instructions.
2 Meanwhile, fry the garlic in the oil in a small pan until just beginning to colour. Scoop the garlic from the pan and reserve. Add the tomatoes to the oil and warm over a low heat; do not let them soften.
3 Toss the pasta with the oil and tomatoes, garlic, rocket, olives, pine nuts and seasoning. Serve with pecorino or Parmesan.

024
herb fettuccine all'alfredo

PREPARATION TIME 5 minutes COOKING TIME 10 minutes SERVES 6

45G (1½oz/2½ TBSP) UNSALTED BUTTER
225ML (8FL OZ/1 CUP) DOUBLE CREAM
SMALL PINCH OF FRESHLY GRATED NUTMEG
  (OPTIONAL)

SALT AND FRESHLY GROUND BLACK PEPPER
450G (1LB) FRESH HERB FETTUCCINE (SEE PAGE 10)*
50G (2oz) PARMESAN, FRESHLY GRATED, PLUS EXTRA
  TO SERVE (OPTIONAL)

1 Put a pan of water for the pasta on to boil.
2 Meanwhile, boil the butter with the cream in a large frying pan until reduced by almost a half, stirring frequently. Add the nutmeg, if using, salt and plenty of black pepper.
3 Cook and drain the pasta. Toss with the cream sauce and the cheese. Serve with extra Parmesan, if liked.

* Plain fettuccine can also be used.

025
linguine with anchovies, chilli & olives

PREPARATION TIME 5 minutes COOKING TIME 10 minutes SERVES 6

400G (14oz) LINGUINE
2 WIDE STRIPS OF PARED LEMON RIND
4 TBSP EXTRA-VIRGIN OLIVE OIL
50G (2oz) CAN ANCHOVIES, DRAINED AND CHOPPED
2 GARLIC CLOVES, FINELY CHOPPED
PINCH OF DRIED CHILLI FLAKES

115G (4oz) MIXED PITTED GREEN AND BLACK OLIVES,
  FINELY CHOPPED
2 TBSP CHOPPED FRESH FLAT-LEAF PARSLEY
FRESHLY GROUND BLACK PEPPER
FRESHLY GRATED PARMESAN, TO SERVE

1 Cook and drain the pasta according to the packet instructions, reserving ½ cup of the cooking water.
2 Meanwhile, heat the lemon rind in the oil in a large frying pan over a low heat for about 2 minutes, until sizzling. Stir in the anchovies until they dissolve, then add the garlic, chilli flakes and olives and cook over a fairly high heat for 2–3 minutes. Discard the lemon rind. Add the parsley and season with black pepper. Toss with the pasta and add enough cooking water to moisten. Serve with Parmesan.

026

spaghetti with mixed herb sauce

PREPARATION TIME 10 minutes COOKING TIME 10 minutes SERVES 4–6

85ML (3FL OZ/SCANT ⅓ CUP) EXTRA-VIRGIN OLIVE OIL

1 GARLIC CLOVE, FINELY CHOPPED

2 TBSP CHOPPED FLAT-LEAF PARSLEY

LEAVES FROM A SMALL BUNCH OF SAGE, CHIVES,
    PARSLEY AND THYME, FINELY CHOPPED

SALT AND FRESHLY GROUND BLACK PEPPER

2 TSP LEMON JUICE

375G (13oz) SPAGHETTI

1   Gently heat the oil, garlic and herbs in a saucepan for 1–2 minutes, stirring. Season and then add the lemon juice.

2   Meanwhile, cook and drain the spaghetti according to the packet instructions, reserving ½ cup of the cooking water. Toss with the herb mixture, adding enough reserved water, if necessary, to moisten.

027

linguine with gorgonzola & watercress

PREPARATION TIME 5 minutes COOKING TIME 10 minutes SERVES 4

200G (7oz) LINGUINE

1 BUNCH OF WATERCRESS, THICK STALKS REMOVED

3 TBSP VIRGIN OLIVE OIL

2 TSP LEMON JUICE, TO TASTE

SALT AND FRESHLY GROUND BLACK PEPPER

65G (2¼oz) GORGONZOLA, CRUMBLED

1   Cook and drain the pasta according to the packet instructions.

2   Meanwhile, put the watercress, oil and lemon juice into a blender. Pulse until the watercress is finely chopped. Season and adjust the lemon juice, if necessary. Toss with the pasta and Gorgonzola.

028

fusilli with artichokes, tomatoes & olives

PREPARATION TIME 5 minutes COOKING TIME 10 minutes SERVES 4–6

300G (10oz) FUSILLI*

1 RED ONION, FINELY CHOPPED

6 PIECES SUN-BLUSH TOMATOES IN OIL, DRAINED
    (OIL RESERVED) AND SLICED

10 ROAST ARTICHOKES IN OIL, DRAINED

50G (2oz) PITTED BLACK OLIVES

100G (3½oz) ROCKET

50G (2oz) PECORINO, FRESHLY GRATED

1   Cook and drain the fusilli according to the packet instructions.

2   Meanwhile, fry the onion in 1 tbsp of the reserved tomato oil until softened and turning golden.

3   Coarsely chop the artichokes with the olives and add to the pan with the tomatoes. Heat through. Add the rocket and toss with the pasta and half the cheese. Serve with the remaining cheese scattered over.

*   Eliche can also be used.

029
fidelini with walnut sauce

PREPARATION TIME 5 minutes COOKING TIME 10 minutes SERVES 4

325G (11oz) FIDELINI
85G (3oz) WALNUT HALVES, LIGHTLY TOASTED
1 GARLIC CLOVE, CRUSHED
1 TBSP VIRGIN OLIVE OIL

150G (5oz) RICOTTA
SALT AND FRESHLY GROUND BLACK PEPPER
FINELY CHOPPED FLAT-LEAF PARSLEY AND FRESHLY
    GRATED PECORINO, TO SERVE

1   Cook and drain the pasta according to the packet instructions, reserving ½ cup of the cooking water.
2   Meanwhile, put the walnuts and garlic into a small blender and pulse to chop finely. Add the oil and
    mix briefly to a coarse paste. Transfer to a bowl and work in the ricotta and seasoning. Toss with
    the pasta, adding enough of the reserved cooking water to moisten, if necessary. Serve scattered
    with the parsley and pecorino.

030
tagliatelle with ricotta pesto

PREPARATION TIME 5 minutes COOKING TIME 20 minutes SERVES 4

2 GARLIC CLOVES
250G (9oz) RICOTTA
2 TBSP VIRGIN OLIVE OIL
LEAVES FROM A LARGE BUNCH OF BASIL,
  A FEW RESERVED FOR GARNISH

SALT AND FRESHLY GROUND BLACK PEPPER
225G (8oz) TAGLIATELLE
FRESHLY GRATED PARMESAN, TO SERVE

1   Simmer the garlic cloves in a little water for 10 minutes. Drain well and put into a blender with the
    ricotta, oil and basil. Mix until smooth. Season.
2   Cook and drain the tagliatelle according to the packet instructions, reserving ½ cup of the cooking water.
    Toss immediately with the ricotta pesto, adding some of the reserved cooking water, if necessary,
    to moisten. Serve garnished with basil leaves and accompanied by Parmesan.

031
spaghetti with sun-dried tomato tapenade

PREPARATION TIME 5 minutes COOKING TIME 10 minutes SERVES 4–6

400G (14oz) SPAGHETTI
3 GARLIC CLOVES, CRUSHED
PINCH OF CHILLI FLAKES
4 TBSP VIRGIN OLIVE OIL
70G (2½oz) PITTED OIL-CURED BLACK OLIVES

65G (2¼oz) SUN-DRIED TOMATOES IN OIL
45G (1½oz) CAPERS
LEAVES FROM A SMALL BUNCH OF FLAT-LEAF
  PARSLEY, CHOPPED

1   Cook and drain the pasta according to the packet instructions.
2   Meanwhile, put the garlic, chilli flakes and oil into a blender and add three-quarters of the olives,
    sun-dried tomatoes and capers. Mix together to a smooth sauce. Thinly slice the remaining sun-dried
    tomatoes and quarter the remaining olives.
3   Toss the spaghetti with the sauce, parsley and remaining sun-dried tomatoes, olives and capers.

warm pasta salad with spinach, tomatoes & olives

PREPARATION TIME 10 minutes COOKING TIME 10 minutes SERVES 4

225G (8oz) LINGUINE*	SALT AND FRESHLY GROUND BLACK PEPPER
3 TBSP VIRGIN OLIVE OIL	50G (2oz) BABY LEAF SPINACH
2 TSP WHITE WINE VINEGAR	50G (2oz) PITTED KALAMATA OLIVES, HALVED
I TSP BALSAMIC VINEGAR	115G (4oz) CHERRY TOMATOES, HALVED
2 TSP OREGANO	115G (4oz) FETA, CRUMBLED
I SMALL GARLIC CLOVE, CRUSHED	½ SMALL RED ONION, FINELY CHOPPED

1   Cook and drain the pasta according to the packet instructions.
2   Meanwhile, whisk the oil with the vinegars, oregano, garlic and seasoning until emulsified.
3   Toss the pasta with the oregano dressing and the remaining ingredients. Serve warm.

*   Cavatappi, cavatelli, eliche, fusilli or orecchiette can also be used.

033

fusilli, rocket & tomato frittata

PREPARATION TIME 5 minutes COOKING TIME 25 minutes SERVES 4–6

100G (3½oz) FUSILLI
150G (5oz) WELL-FLAVOURED CHERRY TOMATOES,
  HALVED
125G (4½oz) ROCKET
7 EGGS

50G (2oz) SOFT GOATS' CHEESE, CHOPPED
I TBSP THYME
SALT AND FRESHLY GROUND BLACK PEPPER
VIRGIN OLIVE OIL
115G (4oz) TALEGGIO, FINELY CHOPPED

1   Cook and drain the pasta according to the packet instructions. While it is still warm, stir in the tomatoes and rocket.
2   Meanwhile, beat the eggs into the goats' cheese. Add the thyme, pasta mixture and seasoning.
3   Heat a little oil in a large ovenproof frying pan, pour in the egg mixture and cook gently until the frittata is almost set; it should remain creamy on top. Scatter over the Taleggio and place under a preheated grill until melted. Serve cut into wedges.

034

trenette with tuscan herb sauce

PREPARATION TIME 10 minutes COOKING TIME 10 minutes SERVES 4–6

450G (ILB) FRESH TRENETTE (SEE PAGE 10)
2 GARLIC CLOVES, FINELY CHOPPED
4 TBSP VIRGIN OLIVE OIL
6 ANCHOVY FILLETS, DRAINED
2 TBSP PASSATA
PINCH OF CHILLI FLAKES

LEAVES FROM A SMALL BUNCH OF FLAT-LEAF
  PARSLEY, FINELY CHOPPED
I TBSP THYME
I TBSP CHOPPED MARJORAM
1½ TSP FINELY CHOPPED ROSEMARY
SALT AND FRESHLY GROUND BLACK PEPPER
FRESHLY GRATED PARMESAN, TO SERVE

1   Cook and drain the pasta.
2   Meanwhile, gently fry the garlic in the oil for 2 minutes, then stir in the anchovies until dissolved. Stir in the passata. After I minute add the chilli flakes and herbs. Heat gently for a couple of minutes. Season.
3   Toss with the trenette and serve with Parmesan.

035

trenette with wilted tomatoes

PREPARATION TIME 5 minutes COOKING TIME 10 minutes SERVES 4

300G (10oz) TRENETTE
400G (14oz) WELL-FLAVOURED CHERRY PLUM
  TOMATOES OR WELL-FLAVOURED ORDINARY
  CHERRY TOMATOES, HALVED OR QUARTERED
VIRGIN OLIVE OIL
ABOUT 2 TBSP BALSAMIC VINEGAR, TO TASTE

PINCH OF CASTER SUGAR, TO TASTE (OPTIONAL)
SALT AND FRESHLY GROUND BLACK PEPPER
LEAVES FROM A SMALL HANDFUL OF BASIL,
  SHREDDED
SHAVINGS OF PECORINO OR PARMESAN, TO SERVE

1   Cook and drain the trenette according to the packet instructions.
2   Meanwhile, cook the tomatoes briskly in a large frying pan in a little oil for 1–2 minutes, until just beginning to soften. Remove from the heat and immediately stir in balsamic vinegar to taste. Add a pinch of sugar, to taste, if liked. Season and toss with the pasta. Serve with the basil and pecorino or Parmesan shavings scattered over.

036
fusilli with spinach,
sun-dried tomatoes & olives

PREPARATION TIME 5 minutes COOKING TIME 10 minutes SERVES 4

225G (8oz) FUSILLI*
GOOD HANDFUL OF BABY SPINACH LEAVES
12 SUN-DRIED TOMATOES IN OIL, DRAINED (OIL
    RESERVED) AND SLICED
2–3 GARLIC CLOVES, FINELY CHOPPED
12 PITTED KALAMATA OLIVES, SLICED

1–2 TSP BALSAMIC VINEGAR
PINCH OF CHILLI FLAKES (OPTIONAL)
5 TBSP MIXED EXTRA-VIRGIN OLIVE OIL AND OIL
    FROM THE SUN-DRIED TOMATOES
SALT AND FRESHLY GROUND BLACK PEPPER

1   Cook and drain the pasta according to the packet instructions.
2   Toss with the spinach, and then with the remaining ingredients. Season and serve warm.

*   Eliche or farfalle can also be used.

037
tagliatelle with lemon & parsley sauce

PREPARATION TIME 5 minutes COOKING TIME 5 minutes SERVES 4–6

115G (4oz/SCANT ½ CUP) RICOTTA
3 TBSP LEMON JUICE
2 TBSP GRATED LEMON ZEST
2 TBSP CHOPPED FLAT-LEAF PARSLEY

SALT AND FRESHLY GROUND BLACK PEPPER
400G (14oz) FRESH TAGLIATELLE (SEE PAGE 10)
4 TBSP FRESHLY GRATED PARMESAN

1   Mash the ricotta with the lemon juice and zest until smooth. Mix in the parsley and seasoning.
2   Cook and drain the pasta. Toss with the ricotta mixture, and serve sprinkled with the Parmesan.

038
spaghetti with sun-dried tomatoes,
garlic & chilli

PREPARATION TIME 5 minutes COOKING TIME 10 minutes SERVES 6

400G (14oz) SPAGHETTI*
12–14 SUN-DRIED TOMATOES IN OIL,
    DRAINED AND SLICED
3 GARLIC CLOVES, FINELY CHOPPED

1 TBSP CHOPPED FLAT-LEAF PARSLEY
PINCH OF DRIED CHILLI FLAKES
50ML (2FL OZ/¼ CUP) EXTRA-VIRGIN OLIVE OIL

1   Cook and drain the spaghetti according to the packet instructions.
2   Meanwhile, combine the sauce ingredients and warm gently in a small saucepan.
3   Toss the spaghetti with the sauce, and serve.

*   Bucatini or fusilli can also be used.

039
pancetta-stuffed tomatoes

PREPARATION TIME 15 minutes COOKING TIME 35 minutes SERVES 4

4 RIPE BEEF OR OTHER LARGE TOMATOES

50G (2oz) MACARONI

85G (3oz) PANCETTA, CHOPPED

VIRGIN OLIVE OIL

1 SMALL ONION, FINELY CHOPPED

1 GARLIC CLOVE, FINELY CHOPPED

115G (4oz) MOZZARELLA, FINELY CHOPPED

8 PITTED KALAMATA OLIVES, CHOPPED

2 TBSP CHOPPED FLAT-LEAF PARSLEY

2 TBSP CHOPPED CHIVES

SALT AND FRESHLY GROUND BLACK PEPPER

MAYONNAISE OR AÏOLI, TO SERVE (OPTIONAL)

1   Pre-heat the oven to 190°C/375°F/gas 5.
2   Slice the tops from the tomatoes and reserve. Scoop the seeds and central flesh from the tomatoes into a sieve, leaving the walls intact. Press the flesh and seeds through the sieve into a bowl and reserve the juice. Leave the tomato shells upside down on kitchen paper to drain.
3   Cook the macaroni for 1 minute less than usual. Drain.
4   Meanwhile, fry the pancetta in a little oil until lightly golden and the fat runs. Remove from the pan. Fry the onion and garlic in the pancetta fat until softened but not coloured. Add the reserved tomato flesh and juice and boil until thickened. Toss with the pasta, pancetta, mozzarella, olives, herbs and seasoning.
5   Stand the tomato shells upright in a shallow baking dish and fill with the pasta mixture. Replace the lids and bake in the preheated oven for 20–25 minutes until the tomatoes are soft and beginning to colour. Serve with mayonnaise or aïoli, if liked.

040
tagliatelle with sicilian tomato pesto

PREPARATION TIME 5 minutes COOKING TIME 10 minutes SERVES 4–6

50G (2oz) BASIL LEAVES

2 GARLIC CLOVES, CHOPPED

100G (3½oz) BLANCHED ALMONDS

350G (12oz) WELL-FLAVOURED TOMATOES,
  SEEDED AND CHOPPED

40G (1½oz) PECORINO, FRESHLY GRATED,
  PLUS EXTRA TO SERVE

115–150ML (4–5FL OZ) VIRGIN OLIVE OIL

SALT AND FRESHLY GROUND BLACK PEPPER

ABOUT 1 TBSP SUN-DRIED TOMATO PASTE (OPTIONAL)

350G (12oz) TAGLIATELLE

1   Put the basil, garlic and almonds into a blender and mix to a nubbly paste. Add the tomatoes and cheese and, with the motor running, pour in the oil in a slow, steady stream. Season, and add sun-dried tomato paste if necessary, to boost the tomato flavour.
2   Cook and drain the pasta according to the packet instructions. Toss with half the pesto. Serve with the remaining pesto, if liked.

Note:

It is not practical to make a smaller quantity of the pesto, but any remaining can be kept in a jar, covered by a layer of oil, in the fridge for up to 1 week.

041
fusilli with sun-blush tomatoes, anchovies & olives

PREPARATION TIME 10 minutes COOKING TIME 10 minutes SERVES 4

2 SHALLOTS, FINELY CHOPPED

2 GARLIC CLOVES, FINELY CHOPPED

OLIVE OIL

8 ANCHOVY FILLETS, DRAINED

100G (3½oz) SUN-BLUSH TOMATOES,
  DRAINED AND COARSELY CHOPPED

8 PITTED BLACK OLIVES, FINELY CHOPPED

350G (12oz) FUSILLI

1 TBSP SMALL CAPERS

LEAVES FROM A SMALL BUNCH OF
  FLAT-LEAF PARSLEY, CHOPPED

FRESHLY GROUND BLACK PEPPER

1   Fry the shallots and garlic in a little oil for 1–2 minutes. Stir in the anchovies, sun-blush tomatoes and olives. Heat gently.
2   Meanwhile, cook and drain the pasta according to the packet instructions.
3   Toss the fusilli with the tomato mixture, capers and parsley. Season with plenty of black pepper; salt probably won't be necessary.

spaghetti with anchovies, lemon, chillies & thyme pangritata

PREPARATION TIME 5 minutes COOKING TIME 15 minutes SERVES 4

2 THICK SLICES OF CRUSTLESS BREAD,
  MADE INTO CRUMBS
2½ TSP THYME LEAVES
2 PLUMP GARLIC CLOVES,
  FINELY CHOPPED
VIRGIN OLIVE OIL

350G (12oz) SPAGHETTI
PINCH OF CHILLI FLAKES
12 ANCHOVY FILLETS
ZEST AND JUICE OF 1 SMALL LEMON,
  PLUS EXTRA TO TASTE, IF NECESSARY
SALT AND FRESHLY GROUND BLACK PEPPER

1   To make the pangritata, fry the breadcrumbs, thyme and 1 garlic clove in 115ml (4fl oz) oil, stirring
    frequently, until very crisp and golden. Season and scoop onto kitchen paper to drain.
2   Cook and drain the spaghetti according to the packet instructions.
3   Meanwhile, fry the remaining garlic and the chilli in a little oil for 30 seconds. Stir in the anchovies until
    they dissolve. Remove from the heat and add the lemon juice and zest, and season. Taste and add more
    lemon juice, if necessary. Toss with the spaghetti and serve with the crumbs sprinkled over.

cavatelli with fresh tomatoes, herbs & mozzarella

PREPARATION TIME 10 minutes COOKING TIME 10 minutes SERVES 4–6

225G (8oz) BUFFALO MOZZARELLA,
  CUT INTO 5MM (¼IN) CUBES
675G (1½LB) WELL-FLAVOURED PLUM TOMATOES,
  DICED
1 TBSP SHREDDED BASIL
2 TSP OREGANO

2 TSP THYME
5 TBSP EXTRA-VIRGIN OLIVE OIL
2 TSP LEMON JUICE
SALT AND FRESHLY GROUND BLACK PEPPER
400G (14oz) CAVATELLI*

1   Combine the cheese, tomatoes, herbs, oil, lemon juice and seasoning in a large bowl.
2   Cook and drain the pasta according to the packet instructions. Toss immediately with the tomato mixture.
    If the cheese does not begin to melt, cover for 2 minutes. Serve straight away.

*   Cavatappi or eliche can also be used.

044
herb carbonara

PREPARATION TIME 5 minutes COOKING TIME 10 minutes SERVES 4–6

350G (12oz) LINGUINE*
3 TBSP BASIL, SHREDDED
2 TBSP FINELY CHOPPED FLAT-LEAF PARSLEY
85G (3oz) PARMESAN, FRESHLY GRATED

50G (2oz/scant ¼ cup) UNSALTED BUTTER, MELTED
SALT AND FRESHLY GROUND BLACK PEPPER
4 EGG YOLKS

1   Cook and drain the linguine according to the packet instructions.
2   Meanwhile, stir the herbs, Parmesan, butter and seasoning into the egg yolks. Toss with the linguine
    to make a creamy sauce, and serve.

*   Tagliarini or spaghetti can also be used.

045
spaghetti with summer puttanesca sauce

PREPARATION TIME 10 minutes COOKING TIME 10 minutes SERVES 4

300G (10oz) SPAGHETTI
1 GARLIC CLOVE, FINELY CHOPPED
EXTRA-VIRGIN OLIVE OIL
3 ANCHOVY FILLETS, CHOPPED
350G (12oz) WELL-FLAVOURED TOMATOES,
   SEEDED AND CHOPPED

1 TBSP CAPERS
10 PITTED BLACK OLIVES, SLICED
1 TBSP CHOPPED FLAT-LEAF PARSLEY
FRESHLY GROUND BLACK PEPPER

1   Cook the pasta according to the packet instructions.
2   Meanwhile, cook the garlic in a little oil until it just begins to change colour. Stir in the anchovies until
    they dissolve, then add the tomatoes, capers and olives. Stir around for a few minutes to warm the
    tomatoes. Remove from the heat and add the parsley and black pepper. Toss with the pasta.

046
spaghetti alla carbonara

PREPARATION TIME 5 minutes COOKING TIME 10 minutes SERVES 4

250G (9oz) SPAGHETTI
85G (3oz) PANCETTA, CUT ACROSS INTO STRIPS
SMALL KNOB OF UNSALTED BUTTER
4 TBSP MEDIUM-BODIED DRY WHITE WINE
2 EGGS

1½ TBSP CHOPPED FLAT-LEAF PARSLEY
25G (1oz) PECORINO, FRESHLY GRATED
25G (1oz) PARMESAN, FRESHLY GRATED
SALT AND FRESHLY GROUND BLACK PEPPER

1   Cook and drain the pasta according to the packet instructions.
2   Meanwhile, fry the pancetta in the butter until crisp but not coloured. Add the wine and boil until
    reduced by half.
3   While the pancetta is cooking, in a bowl that is large enough to hold the cooked pasta, beat the eggs
    with the parsley, half of each of the cheeses, a pinch of salt and plenty of black pepper.
4   Drain the pasta and immediately add it to the bowl of eggs. Quickly toss together, adding the pancetta
    as well, until the eggs are creamy. Toss lightly with the remaining cheese and serve.

pasta, prawns & pesto

PREPARATION TIME 5 minutes COOKING TIME 10 minutes SERVES 4–6

350G (12oz) FUSILLI*
4 TBSP VIRGIN OLIVE OIL
4 TBSP PESTO (SEE PAGE 18)
225G (8oz) PEELED COOKED PRAWNS

5 PLUM TOMATOES, CHOPPED
SALT AND FRESHLY GROUND BLACK PEPPER
SHREDDED BASIL LEAVES, TO SERVE

1 Cook and drain the pasta according to the packet instructions.
2 Meanwhile, stir the oil into the pesto.
3 Toss the pesto mixture, prawns and tomatoes with the pasta, season and serve sprinkled with basil leaves.

* Cavatappi, conchiglie or eliche can also be used.

048

spaghetti with simple red pepper sauce

PREPARATION TIME 10 minutes COOKING TIME 10 minutes SERVES 6

2 LARGE, FLESHY RED PEPPERS, GRILLED, PEELED
    AND CHOPPED (SEE PAGE 67)
2 GARLIC CLOVES, CHOPPED
PINCH OF CHILLI FLAKES (OPTIONAL)
5 TBSP PINE NUTS, LIGHTLY TOASTED

5 TBSP EXTRA-VIRGIN OLIVE OIL
½ TSP BALSAMIC VINEGAR, TO TASTE
SALT AND FRESHLY GROUND BLACK PEPPER
400G (14oz) SPAGHETTI
FRESHLY GRATED PARMESAN, TO SERVE

1 Put the peppers, garlic, chilli (if using), pine nuts and oil into a food processor. Pulse until just smooth.
    Add the balsamic vinegar and seasoning, to taste.
2 Cook and drain the pasta according to the packet instructions, reserving ½ cup of the cooking water.
    Toss with the red pepper sauce, adding a little of the reserved cooking water, if necessary.
    Serve with the freshly grated Parmesan.

049

spaghetti with capers,
olives & anchovies

PREPARATION TIME 5 minutes COOKING TIME 10 minutes SERVES 6

400G (14oz) SPAGHETTI
1 GARLIC CLOVE, FINELY CHOPPED
2 TBSP DRIED BREADCRUMBS
115ML (4FL oz/½ CUP) EXTRA-VIRGIN OLIVE OIL
6 ANCHOVY FILLETS, CHOPPED

2 TBSP CAPERS
10 PITTED BLACK OLIVES, SLICED
1 TBSP CHOPPED FLAT-LEAF PARSLEY
FRESHLY GROUND BLACK PEPPER

1 Cook and drain the pasta according to the packet instructions, reserving ½ cup of the cooking water.
2 Meanwhile, cook the garlic and breadcrumbs in the oil until the garlic just begins to change colour, but
    do not let the breadcrumbs brown. Stir in the anchovies until they dissolve, then add the capers and
    olives. Stir around for a minute or so, remove from the heat and add the parsley and black pepper.
    Toss with the pasta and add enough cooking water to moisten.

050
fidelini-stuffed peppers

PREPARATION TIME 10 minutes COOKING TIME 20–25 minutes SERVES 4

40g (1½oz) FIDELINI
2 LARGE RED PEPPERS
2 TBSP MILK
2 TBSP SOFT CHEESE WITH
  GARLIC AND HERBS

2 MEDIUM EGGS, BEATEN
2 TBSP CHOPPED FLAT-LEAF PARSLEY
1 WELL-FLAVOURED TOMATO, SEEDED AND CHOPPED
6 TBSP FRESHLY GRATED PARMESAN

1   Preheat the oven to 180°C/350°F/gas 4.
2   Cook and drain the fidelini according to the packet instructions, but for 1½ minutes less than usual. Snip the strands into shorter lengths.
3   Meanwhile, cut the peppers in half lengthways, carefully removing the stalk ends and seeds. Blanch in boiling water for 3 minutes. Leave upside down to drain.
4   Stir the milk into the soft cheese until smooth, then mix in the eggs and parsley.
5   Stand the pepper halves in a shallow baking dish or tin, propping them upright with foil, if necessary. Divide the fidelini among the halves. Carefully spoon in the cheese mixture, easing it with the point of a knife to flow between the pasta strands. Sprinkle over the Parmesan and bake in the preheated oven for 20–25 minutes until the filling is just set.

051
tonnarelli with tomato & red pesto sauce

PREPARATION TIME 10 minutes COOKING TIME 10 minutes SERVES 6

4 RIPE PLUM TOMATOES, CHOPPED
4 PIECES OF SUN-DRIED TOMATOES,
  DRAINED AND CHOPPED
25g (1oz) PINE NUTS, LIGHTLY TOASTED
3 TBSP EACH OIL FROM THE TOMATOES
  AND EXTRA-VIRGIN OLIVE OIL

SMALL HANDFUL OF BASIL LEAVES, SHREDDED,
  PLUS EXTRA TO GARNISH
SALT AND FRESHLY GROUND BLACK PEPPER
4 TBSP HOME-DRIED BREADCRUMBS
2 GARLIC CLOVES, FINELY CHOPPED
350g (12oz) FRESH TONNARELLI*

1   Put all the tomatoes and the pine nuts in a food processor. With the motor running, slowly pour in 4 tbsp oil to make a chunky mixture. Remove from the processor and add the basil and seasoning.
2   Fry the breadcrumbs and garlic in the remaining oil over a low heat, stirring, until the crumbs are golden; take care the garlic does not burn.
3   Cook and drain the pasta, reserving ½ cup of the cooking water. Toss with the pesto; if it seems too dry, add 2 tbsp of the reserved water. Serve with the breadcrumbs and extra basil sprinkled over.

*   Spaghetti can also be used.

052
mediterranean vegetable & pasta salad

PREPARATION TIME 10 minutes COOKING TIME 10 minutes SERVES 4

225G (8oz) RADIATORI*
6 SUN-DRIED TOMATOES IN OIL, DRAINED
  (OIL RESERVED) AND SLICED
5 TBSP VIRGIN OLIVE OIL
1 TBSP RED WINE VINEGAR
1 GARLIC CLOVE, FINELY CHOPPED
SALT AND FRESHLY GROUND BLACK PEPPER
6 PITTED KALAMATA OLIVES, QUARTERED
150G (5oz) CHERRY PLUM TOMATOES, HALVED

115G (4oz) BABY COURGETTES, SLICED
6 ROAST ARTICHOKE HEARTS IN OIL,
  DRAINED AND SLICED
1 LARGE (OR 2 HALVES) BOTTLED ROASTED
  RED PEPPER IN OIL, CUT INTO STRIPS
LEAVES FROM A SMALL BUNCH OF BASIL, SHREDDED
2–3 HANDFULS OF SMALL CRISP SALAD LEAVES,
  INCLUDING SOME ROCKET

1   Cook and drain the pasta according to the packet instructions. Rinse in cold water and toss immediately
    with 1 tbsp oil from the tomatoes. Leave to cool.
2   Meanwhile, make the dressing by whisking the oil, vinegar, garlic and seasoning together. Toss with
    the pasta, olives, tomatoes, courgettes, artichokes, peppers and basil. Serve on a bed of salad leaves.

*   Fusilli and cavatelli can also be used.

053
potato gnocchi with red pepper
& red pesto sauce

PREPARATION TIME 25 minutes COOKING TIME 30–35 minutes SERVES 4

1 LARGE RED PEPPER, GRILLED, PEELED AND
  CHOPPED (SEE PAGE 67)
1 QUANTITY RED PESTO (SEE PAGE 19)
900G (2LB) FLOURY POTATOES, UNPEELED
50G (2oz/SCANT ¼ CUP) UNSALTED BUTTER, DICED

1 EGG, BEATEN
SALT AND FRESHLY GROUND BLACK PEPPER
225–300G (8–10oz/SCANT 2 CUPS) PLAIN FLOUR
BASIL LEAVES AND OIL-CURED PITTED BLACK OLIVES,
  TO SERVE

1   Put the red pepper and red pesto into a blender and purée together. Set aside.
2   Boil the potatoes until very tender; the time will depend on their size. Drain well and press through a
    potato ricer, or peel and press through a sieve. While still warm, beat in the butter, egg and seasoning.
    Then, using a fork, lightly mix in half the flour. Turn on to a floured surface and lightly knead in enough
    flour to give a soft, smooth, slightly sticky dough.
3   Roll the dough into sausage shapes about 2.5cm (1in) thick. Cut into 2cm (¾in) pieces. Using a lightly
    floured thumb, roll each piece over the back of the tines of a fork, so there are ridges on one side
    and a slight depression on the other. Place the gnocchi on a floured tea towel as they are done.
4   Cook the gnocchi in batches in a large saucepan of gently boiling water for 2–3 minutes per batch
    until they float. Give them a few seconds more before removing with a slotted spoon on to a tea
    towel to drain. Keep warm while cooking the remaining batches. Combine gently with the sauce
    and serve scattered with basil and black olives.

054
fusilli, chicken & fennel salad

PREPARATION TIME 10 minutes, plus cooling time COOKING TIME 10 minutes SERVES 4–6

150G (5oz) FUSILLI

3 TBSP RED PESTO (SEE PAGE 19)

1½ TBSP LEMON JUICE

3 TBSP VIRGIN OLIVE OIL

250G (9oz) COLD SKINLESS ROAST OR
POACHED CHICKEN, SLICED ACROSS THE GRAIN

1 SMALL FENNEL BULB,
FINELY SLICED ACROSS THE BULB

1 PLUMP GARLIC CLOVE, FINELY CHOPPED

5 SPRING ONIONS, INCLUDING SOME GREEN PART,
FINELY CHOPPED

200G (7oz) CHERRY TOMATOES, QUARTERED

2 TBSP MIXED FINELY CHOPPED PARSLEY,
OREGANO AND THYME

PINE NUTS, LIGHTLY TOASTED, AND
FRESHLY GRATED PARMESAN, TO SERVE

1   Cook and drain the pasta according to the packet instructions.
2   Meanwhile, whisk together the pesto, lemon juice and oil. Toss with the hot, drained pasta and leave to cool.
3   Combine the chicken, fennel, garlic, spring onions, tomatoes and herbs. Toss with the cooled pasta and sprinkle over some pine nuts and Parmesan.

44

055
cavatappi with crab & basil

PREPARATION TIME 5 minutes COOKING TIME 10 minutes SERVES 4

225G (8oz) CAVATAPPI
½ SMALL RED CHILLI, SEEDED
  AND FINELY CHOPPED
SMALL BUNCH OF SPRING ONIONS,
  THINLY SLICED ON THE DIAGONAL
SMALL KNOB OF UNSALTED BUTTER

4 TBSP MEDIUM-BODIED DRY WHITE WINE
200G (7oz) FRESH OR FROZEN CRAB MEAT, THAWED
4 TBSP CRÈME FRAÎCHE
SALT AND FRESHLY GROUND BLACK PEPPER
I TBSP SHREDDED BASIL, PLUS A LITTLE EXTRA
  FOR GARNISH

1   Cook and drain the pasta according to the packet instructions, reserving ½ cup of the cooking water.
2   Meanwhile, fry the chilli and spring onions in the butter for I minute. Pour in the wine, bring
    to the boil, lower the heat and stir in the crab meat. Warm through gently, then toss with the
    pasta, crème fraîche and basil. Add a little of the reserved water, if necessary, to moisten.
    Season, and serve lightly garnished with basil.

056
linguine with watercress & capers

PREPARATION TIME 5 minutes COOKING TIME 10 minutes SERVES 4

300G (10oz) LINGUINE*
I TBSP CAPERS
6 ANCHOVY FILLETS, DRAINED
I GARLIC CLOVE

50G (2oz) WATERCRESS LEAVES AND FINE STEMS
6 TBSP VIRGIN OLIVE OIL
SALT AND FRESHLY GROUND BLACK PEPPER
FRESHLY GRATED PARMESAN, TO SERVE

1   Cook and drain the pasta according to the packet instructions, reserving 4 tbsp of the cooking water.
2   Meanwhile, put the capers, anchovies and garlic into a small blender. Mix until well blended. Add the
    watercress and chop finely, then, with the motor running, slowly pour in the olive oil to make
    a smooth paste. Season and add the reserved cooking water. Toss with the pasta and serve
    with freshly grated Parmesan.

*   Spaghetti can also be used.

057
fettuccine with fresh tomatoes & basil

PREPARATION TIME 5–10 minutes COOKING TIME 5 minutes SERVES 4

4 LARGE, WELL-FLAVOURED TOMATOES, ABOUT 550G
  (1¼LB) TOTAL WEIGHT, SEEDED AND CHOPPED
LEAVES FROM A BUNCH OF BASIL, SHREDDED
I GARLIC CLOVE, FINELY CHOPPED
5 TBSP EXTRA-VIRGIN OLIVE OIL

SALT AND FRESHLY GROUND BLACK PEPPER
2-EGG QUANTITY FRESH FETTUCCINE (SEE PAGE 10),
  OR 350G (12oz) DRIED FETTUCCINE
FRESHLY GRATED PARMESAN, TO SERVE

1   Combine the tomatoes, basil and garlic in a bowl. Pour in the oil in a thin, steady stream, stirring.
    Season and set aside.
2   Cook and drain the pasta (see page 14) or according to the packet instructions. Toss with the
    tomato mixture and serve with plenty of freshly grated Parmesan.

058

spaghetti with garlic, parsley & chilli

PREPARATION TIME 5 minutes COOKING TIME 10 minutes SERVES 4–6

400G (14oz) SPAGHETTI
4 GARLIC CLOVES, FINELY CHOPPED
3 TBSP CHOPPED FLAT-LEAF PARSLEY

PINCH OF CRUSHED CHILLI FLAKES
6 TBSP EXTRA-VIRGIN OLIVE OIL

1 Cook and drain the pasta according to the packet instructions, reserving ½ cup of the cooking water.
2 Meanwhile, fry the garlic, parsley and chillies in the oil until the garlic has turned golden. Toss with the pasta, adding enough of the reserved water, if necessary, to moisten.

059

spaghetti with parsley & pine nuts

PREPARATION TIME 5 minutes COOKING TIME 10 minutes SERVES 4

300G (10oz) SPAGHETTI
LEAVES FROM 1 BUNCH OF FLAT-LEAF PARSLEY,
   CHOPPED
40G (1½oz) PINE NUTS

75ML (2½FL OZ/⅓ CUP) VIRGIN OLIVE OIL
1 TBSP BALSAMIC VINEGAR
SALT AND FRESHLY GROUND BLACK PEPPER
FRESHLY GRATED PARMESAN, TO SERVE

1 Cook and drain the pasta according to the packet instructions.
2 Meanwhile, put the parsley in a heatproof bowl. Fry the pine nuts in 1 tbsp of the oil until turning golden. Add to the bowl. Pour the remaining oil into the pan and heat until it is beginning to give off a heat haze. Pour over the parsley, which should sizzle slightly. Toss with the pasta, balsamic vinegar and seasoning. Serve with freshly grated Parmesan.

060

gnocchi, rocket, tomato & black olive salad

PREPARATION TIME 10 minutes COOKING TIME 10 minutes SERVES 4

175G (6oz) GNOCCHI*
HANDFUL OF ROCKET
HANDFUL OF BABY SPINACH LEAVES
4 SPRING ONIONS, SLICED ON THE DIAGONAL
115G (4oz) CHERRY PLUM TOMATOES, HALVED
8 SUN-DRIED TOMATOES IN OIL, DRAINED AND SLICED
10 PITTED KALAMATA OLIVES

DRESSING:
5 SUN-DRIED TOMATOES IN OIL
6 TBSP OIL FROM THE TOMATOES
2 TBSP RED WINE VINEGAR
1 GARLIC CLOVE, CHOPPED
SALT AND FRESHLY GROUND BLACK PEPPER

1 Cook the pasta according to the packet instructions.
2 Meanwhile, put all the dressing ingredients into a blender and process to make a thick dressing. Season.
3 Drain the pasta and toss immediately with the rocket and dressing so the rocket wilts. Then toss with the remaining ingredients.

* Other pasta shapes such as conchiglie can be used.

061
farfalle with rocket, walnuts & dolcelatte

PREPARATION TIME 5 minutes COOKING TIME 10 minutes SERVES 6

400G (14oz) FARFALLE
85G (3oz) ROCKET
200–225G (7–8oz) DOLCELATTE, CRUMBLED

50G (2oz) WALNUT HALVES, LIGHTLY TOASTED
1 TBSP WALNUT OIL
SALT AND FRESHLY GROUND BLACK PEPPER

1   Cook and drain the pasta according to the packet instructions, reserving ½ cup of the cooking water.
2   Toss with the rocket, cheese, walnuts and oil. Season and add enough of the reserved cooking water to moisten, if necessary.

062
tagliatelle with rocket pesto

PREPARATION TIME 5 minutes COOKING TIME 10 minutes SERVES 6

50G (2oz) ROCKET
1 GARLIC CLOVE, CHOPPED
1 TBSP PINE NUTS, LIGHTLY TOASTED
150ML (5FL OZ/SCANT ⅔ CUP) VIRGIN OLIVE OIL

150G (5oz) SOFT GOATS' CHEESE
SALT AND FRESHLY GROUND BLACK PEPPER
2 TBSP FRESHLY GRATED PARMESAN
450G (1LB) TAGLIATELLE

1   Put the rocket, garlic and pine nuts into a blender and mix to a purée, slowly pouring in the oil. Add the cheeses and mix again until just forming a smooth sauce. Do not over-mix. Season.
2   Cook and drain the pasta according to the packet instructions, reserving ½ cup of the cooking water. Toss with the pesto, adding enough of the cooking water, if necessary, to moisten.

063
orecchiette with tomatoes, rocket & pine nuts

PREPARATION TIME 5 minutes COOKING TIME 10 minutes SERVES 6

375G (13oz) ORECCHIETTE
2 TBSP PINE NUTS
3 TBSP VIRGIN OLIVE OIL
500G (1LB 2oz) RIPE WELL-FLAVOURED CHERRY PLUM
   TOMATOES, HALVED

SALT AND FRESHLY GROUND BLACK PEPPER
85G (3oz) ROCKET
50G (2oz) PARMESAN, SHAVED

1   Cook and drain the pasta according to the packet instructions.
2   Meanwhile, fry the pine nuts in 2 tbsp of the oil for 1–2 minutes until they are just turning golden. Add the tomatoes, season and warm through for 1–2 minutes, shaking the pan frequently to avoid breaking up the tomatoes.
3   Toss the pasta with the remaining oil, the rocket and tomato sauce, then most of the Parmesan shavings. Serve with the remaining Parmesan shavings on top.

eliche with tomatoes, black olives & basil

PREPARATION TIME 10 minutes, plus 30 minutes standing COOKING TIME 10 minutes SERVES 4–6

450G (1LB) WELL-FLAVOURED TOMATOES, SEEDED AND
  CUT INTO 5MM (¼IN) CUBES
1 GARLIC CLOVE, FINELY CHOPPED
12 PITTED KALAMATA OLIVES, COARSELY CHOPPED

4 TBSP SHREDDED BASIL
5 TBSP EXTRA-VIRGIN OLIVE OIL
SALT AND FRESHLY GROUND BLACK PEPPER
350G (12OZ) ELICHE

1   Combine the tomatoes, garlic, olives, basil, oil and seasoning, cover and set aside for at least 30 minutes.
2   Cook and drain the pasta according to the packet instructions.
3   Meanwhile, warm the tomato mixture over a low heat, shaking the pan from time to time.
     Toss with the pasta and serve.

spaghetti with goats' cheese, rocket & walnuts

PREPARATION TIME 5 minutes COOKING TIME 10 minutes SERVES 4

275G (9½OZ) SPAGHETTI
40G (1½OZ) WALNUT HALVES, VERY LIGHTLY TOASTED
VIRGIN OLIVE OIL
85G (3OZ) FRESH, SOFT GOATS' CHEESE, CRUMBLED

SMALL HANDFUL OF ROCKET, TORN IN HALF
SALT AND FRESHLY GROUND BLACK PEPPER
PARMESAN SHAVINGS (OPTIONAL)

1   Cook and drain the spaghetti according to the packet instructions.
2   Meanwhile, grind the walnuts coarsely in a blender using a pulse action; do not chop too finely.
3   Toss the spaghetti with a little olive oil, the nuts, cheese, rocket and seasoning, using plenty of
     black pepper. Serve with Parmesan shavings, if liked.

spaghetti with grilled peppers & garlic

PREPARATION TIME 10 minutes COOKING TIME 15 minutes SERVES 4–6

2 LARGE, FLESHY RED PEPPERS, HALVED
  LENGTHWAYS
3 PLUMP GARLIC CLOVES, UNPEELED
5 TBSP EXTRA-VIRGIN OLIVE OIL
5 TBSP PINE NUTS, LIGHTLY TOASTED

SALT AND FRESHLY GROUND BLACK PEPPER
FEW DROPS OF BALSAMIC VINEGAR
375G (13OZ) SPAGHETTI
FRESHLY GRATED PARMESAN, TO SERVE

1   Grill the peppers and garlic until the peppers are charred and blistered and the garlic is soft.
2   When the peppers are cool enough to handle, peel and coarsely chop them and put into a blender.
     Squeeze the garlic flesh from the skins into the blender. Add the oil and pine nuts and pulse until
     just smooth. Season with salt, pepper and balsamic vinegar.
3   Cook and drain the pasta according to the packet instructions, reserving ½ cup of the cooking water.
     Toss thoroughly with the sauce, adding enough reserved water to moisten, if necessary. Serve with Parmesan.

067
green and white tagliatelle
with pine nuts & parmesan

PREPARATION TIME 5 minutes COOKING TIME 10 minutes SERVES 4–6

LEAVES FROM A LARGE BUNCH OF HERBS, SUCH AS
  BASIL, PARSLEY, ROSEMARY, THYME AND OREGANO
1 PLUMP GARLIC CLOVE, COARSELY CHOPPED
450G (1LB) FRESH GREEN AND WHITE TAGLIATELLE
  (PAGLIA E FIENO)*

5 TBSP EXTRA-VIRGIN OLIVE OIL
85G (3OZ) PINE NUTS, LIGHTLY TOASTED
85G (3OZ) PARMESAN, FRESHLY GRATED
SALT AND FRESHLY GROUND BLACK PEPPER

1   Finely chop the herbs and garlic in a food processor. Set aside.
2   Cook and drain the pasta according to the packet instructions.
3   Toss the pasta with the garlic and herb mixture, the oil, pine nuts, Parmesan and seasoning.

*   Plain fettuccine or tagliatelle can also be used.

068
spaghetti with butter & parmesan

PREPARATION TIME 5 minutes COOKING TIME 10 minutes SERVES 4–6

350G (12oz) SPAGHETTI
85G (3oz) UNSALTED BUTTER, DICED

85G (3oz) PARMESAN, FRESHLY GRATED
SALT AND FRESHLY GROUND BLACK PEPPER

1   Cook and drain the pasta according to the packet instructions.
2   Toss with the butter until it has melted, then toss with most of the Parmesan. Season, using plenty of black pepper. Serve with the remaining Parmesan.

069
pasta e piselli (pasta & peas)

PREPARATION TIME 5 minutes COOKING TIME 10 minutes SERVES 4

1 ONION, HALVED AND THINLY SLICED
OLIVE OIL
4 SLICES OF PROSCIUTTO, CUT INTO STRIPS
1 LITRE (1¾ PINTS/4 CUPS) HOT CHICKEN STOCK
150G (5oz) CONCHIGLIETTE OR OTHER SMALL
   DRIED PASTA SHAPES

225G (8oz) PEAS, FRESH OR FROZEN
HANDFUL BASIL LEAVES, SHREDDED
SALT AND FRESHLY GROUND BLACK PEPPER
4 SMALL KNOBS OF UNSALTED BUTTER

1   Fry the onion in a little olive oil until soft but not coloured. Stir in the prosciutto, cook for 1 minute, then pour in the stock. Bring to the boil, add the pasta and cook until al dente, adding fresh peas 4 minutes before the end of the cooking, frozen ones 2 minutes.
2   Add the basil and seasoning and serve with a knob of butter on each portion.

070
warm pasta with mixed peppers & tomatoes

PREPARATION TIME 10 minutes COOKING TIME 10 minutes SERVES 4

5 TBSP VIRGIN OLIVE OIL
½ RED PEPPER, THINLY SLICED
½ YELLOW PEPPER, THINLY SLICED
175G (6oz) YELLOW CHERRY PLUM TOMATOES,
   HALVED
175G (6oz) CHERRY TOMATOES,
   HALVED OR QUARTERED
LEAVES FROM A HANDFUL OF FRESH HERBS SUCH
   AS THYME, PARSLEY, MARJORAM, OREGANO

12 PITTED BLACK OLIVES
3 TBSP CAPERS
2 NARROW STRIPS OF LEMON ZEST,
   CUT INTO FINE SHREDS
SALT AND FRESHLY GROUND BLACK PEPPER
225G (8oz) PASTA SHAPES, SUCH AS
   CONCHIGLIE OR FUSILLI
LEMON JUICE, TO TASTE
4 TBSP FRESHLY GRATED PARMESAN

1   Combine the oil with the peppers, tomatoes, herbs, olives, capers, lemon zest and seasoning. Set aside.
2   Cook and drain the pasta according to the packet instructions. Toss with the salad and add lemon juice to taste. Scatter over the Parmesan and serve warm.

071
trenette with red pesto & ricotta

PREPARATION TIME 5 minutes COOKING TIME 10 minutes SERVES 4–6

400G (14oz) TRENETTE
1 QUANTITY RED PESTO (SEE PAGE 19)

3 TBSP RICOTTA

1   Cook and drain the pasta according to the packet instructions, reserving ½ cup of the cooking water.
2   Meanwhile, combine the red pesto with the ricotta. Toss thoroughly with the pasta, adding enough reserved water to moisten, if necessary.

072
spaghetti with tomatoes, olives & walnuts

PREPARATION TIME 10 minutes COOKING TIME 10 minutes SERVES 4

300G (10oz) SPAGHETTI
85G (3oz) WALNUT HALVES
3 WELL-FLAVOURED PLUM TOMATOES,
   SEEDED AND CHOPPED

16 PITTED KALAMATA OLIVES, COARSELY CHOPPED
SMALL HANDFUL OF BASIL LEAVES, SHREDDED
3 TBSP VIRGIN OLIVE OIL
SALT AND FRESHLY GROUND BLACK PEPPER

1   Cook and drain the spaghetti according to the packet instructions.
2   Meanwhile, lightly toast the walnuts in a heavy dry frying pan, stirring constantly, until they are just fragrant. Break into large pieces.
3   Toss the spaghetti with the walnuts, tomatoes, olives, basil, olive oil and seasoning. Serve warm or at room temperature.

073
spinach & ricotta gnocchi

PREPARATION TIME 10–15 minutes, plus 30 minutes chilling COOKING TIME 15 minutes SERVES 4

400G (14oz) SPINACH
50G (2oz/scant ½ cup) PLAIN FLOUR,
   PLUS EXTRA FOR ROLLING
1 EGG YOLK

100G (3½oz) PARMESAN, FRESHLY GRATED,
   PLUS EXTRA TO SERVE
150G (5oz/scant ⅔ cup) RICOTTA, SIEVED
SALT AND FRESHLY GROUND BLACK PEPPER
70G (2½oz) UNSALTED BUTTER, MELTED

1   Cook the spinach in a large pan, stirring frequently until wilted and tender. Drain, chop finely and squeeze out the surplus moisture. Combine the spinach, flour, egg yolk and two-thirds of the Parmesan. When mixed, lightly but evenly mix in the ricotta and a little salt but plenty of black pepper. Chill for 30 minutes.
2   With floured hands, break off heaped teaspoons of the mixture and form into short lengths about 1–2cm (½–¾in) in diameter.
3   Bring a large pan of water to the boil. Add the gnocchi in batches and simmer gently for about 3 minutes until they have been on the surface for about 30–60 seconds. Using a slotted spoon, transfer to paper towels to drain, then carefully transfer the gnocchi to a shallow baking dish.
4   When all the gnocchi are in the dish, pour over the melted butter and sprinkle with the remaining Parmesan. Place under a preheated grill until the cheese has melted. Serve with extra Parmesan.

074
riccioli with peas & saffron

PREPARATION TIME 5 minutes, plus 20 minutes soaking COOKING TIME 10 minutes SERVES 4

PINCH OF SAFFRON THREADS, CRUSHED
150ML (5FL OZ/SCANT ⅔ CUP) DOUBLE CREAM
225G (8oz) RICCIOLI OR GNOCCHI

225G (8oz) FRESH OR FROZEN PEAS
SMALL KNOB OF UNSALTED BUTTER
FRESHLY GRATED PARMESAN, TO SERVE

1   Soak the saffron in about 1 tbsp of the cream for about 20 minutes.
2   Cook the riccioli according to the packet instructions, adding the peas for the last 4 minutes if fresh,
    2 minutes if frozen. Drain.
3   Meanwhile, gently heat the remaining cream with the butter and saffron cream until the butter has
    melted, stirring occasionally. Warm through completely but do not allow to boil. Season and toss with
    the pasta and peas. Serve sprinkled with freshly grated Parmesan, and accompanied by more Parmesan.

075
trenette with pine nuts & herbs

PREPARATION TIME 5 minutes COOKING TIME 10 minutes SERVES 4

2 GARLIC CLOVES, THINLY SLICED
½ FRESH RED CHILLI, SEEDED AND FINELY SLICED
5 TBSP EXTRA-VIRGIN OLIVE OIL
50G (2oz) PINE NUTS
HANDFUL OF FLAT-LEAF PARSLEY, FINELY CHOPPED

10–14 BASIL LEAVES, SHREDDED
SALT AND FRESHLY GROUND BLACK PEPPER
300G (10oz) FRESH TRENETTE
FRESHLY GRATED PARMESAN, TO SERVE

1   Put the saucepan of water for the pasta on to boil.
2   Meanwhile, fry the garlic and chilli in the oil for 1 minute. Add the pine nuts and parsley and fry for a
    further minute, stirring so the nuts do not burn. Remove from the heat and add the basil and seasoning.
3   Add the pasta to the boiling water, cook and drain, but not too thoroughly. Toss with the pine nuts and
    herb mixture. Serve with freshly grated Parmesan.

076
cavatappi with tomatoes, avocado & basil

PREPARATION TIME 10 minutes COOKING TIME 10 minutes SERVES 4

225G (8oz) CAVATAPPI
1 GARLIC CLOVE, FINELY CRUSHED
VIRGIN OLIVE OIL
3 WELL-FLAVOURED TOMATOES,
  SEEDED AND CHOPPED

1 AVOCADO, PITTED AND QUITE FINELY CHOPPED
4 SPRING ONIONS, THINLY SLICED ON THE DIAGONAL
LEAVES FROM A SMALL BUNCH OF BASIL, SHREDDED
SALT AND FRESHLY GROUND BLACK PEPPER
FRESHLY GRATED PARMESAN, TO SERVE

1   Cook and drain the pasta according to the packet instructions.
2   Meanwhile, fry the garlic in a little oil for 1–2 minutes. Add the tomatoes and heat gently, just to
    warm through. Toss with the pasta, avocado, spring onions, basil and seasoning. Serve warm or cold
    with freshly grated Parmesan.

cavatappi with spinach, raisins & pine nuts

PREPARATION TIME 5 minutes COOKING TIME 10 minutes SERVES 4

25G (1oz) RAISINS

225G (8oz) CAVATAPPI

500G (1LB 2oz) BABY SPINACH

KNOB OF UNSALTED BUTTER

SALT AND FRESHLY GROUND BLACK PEPPER

3–4 TBSP PINE NUTS, LIGHTLY TOASTED

FRESHLY GRATED PARMESAN, TO SERVE

1   Soak the raisins in a little hot water for 3–5 minutes to plump up, then drain.
2   Meanwhile, cook and drain the pasta according to the packet instructions.
3   While the pasta is cooking, cook the spinach in a covered pan, shaking the pan occasionally, until wilted. Drain and press out surplus moisture. Gently reheat with the butter, stirring occasionally. Season and toss with the pasta, raisins and pine nuts. Serve with freshly grated Parmesan.

078

spaghetti with garlic & herb mayonnaise

PREPARATION TIME 5 minutes COOKING TIME 10 minutes SERVES 3–4

225G (8oz) SPAGHETTI
1 GARLIC CLOVE
SALT
4–5 TBSP MAYONNAISE

LEAVES FROM A BUNCH OF MIXED HERBS,
   SUCH AS PARSLEY, THYME, CHIVES, BASIL
FRESHLY GRATED PARMESAN, TO SERVE

1   Cook and drain the pasta according to the pack instructions, reserving ½ cup of the cooking water.
2   Meanwhile, crush the garlic to a paste with a pinch of salt, and then mix into the mayonnaise with the herbs. Toss with the pasta and enough of the reserved water so that it is moist, and serve with freshly grated Parmesan.

079

pennette with tomato & almond sauce

PREPARATION TIME 10 minutes COOKING TIME 10 minutes SERVES 4–6

3 WELL-FLAVOURED PLUM TOMATOES, SEEDED AND
   CHOPPED
25G (1oz) BLANCHED ALMONDS, LIGHTLY TOASTED
6 TBSP EXTRA-VIRGIN OLIVE OIL
4 SUN-DRIED TOMATOES, DRAINED AND CHOPPED

12 BASIL LEAVES, SHREDDED
SALT AND FRESHLY GROUND BLACK PEPPER
350G (12oz) PENNETTE
2 GARLIC CLOVES
4 TBSP DRIED BREADCRUMBS

1   Put the tomatoes, almonds, three-quarters of the oil and the sun-dried tomatoes into small blender. Mix to a nubbly paste. Transfer to a heatproof bowl and stir in the basil and seasoning. Put to warm over a saucepan of gently simmering water.
2   Cook and drain the pasta according to the packet instructions, reserving ½ cup of the cooking water.
3   Meanwhile, fry the garlic and breadcrumbs in the remaining oil in a small frying pan over a low heat until the crumbs are golden; take care the garlic does not burn.
4   Toss the pasta with the tomato mixture, adding enough of the reserved water to moisten if necessary. Serve with the garlic crumbs scattered over.

080

pasta with roast garlic, thyme & crumbled goats' cheese

PREPARATION TIME 5 minutes COOKING TIME 20–25 minutes SERVES 4

1 LARGE HEAD OF PLUMP GARLIC, SEPARATED
   INTO CLOVES
50ML (2FL OZ/SCANT ¼ CUP) EXTRA-VIRGIN
   OLIVE OIL

LEAVES FROM 8 LARGE THYME SPRIGS
225G (8oz) SPAGHETTI
200G (7oz) CRUMBLY GOATS' CHEESE
SALT AND FRESHLY GROUND BLACK PEPPER

1   Lightly crush the garlic cloves to loosen the skins, then remove the skins. Heat the cloves gently in the oil in a small pan for 20–25 minutes until soft and golden; do not allow them to fry and burn because they will taste bitter. Add the thyme leaves after 15 minutes cooking.
2   Meanwhile, cook and drain the pasta according to the packet instructions. Toss with the garlic, oil, thyme, goats' cheese and seasoning.

081

tagliatelle with rocket, pine nuts & thyme

PREPARATION TIME 10 minutes COOKING TIME 10 minutes SERVES 6

2 PLUMP GARLIC CLOVES, CRUSHED
4 TBSP PINE NUTS
EXTRA-VIRGIN OLIVE OIL
15 CHERRY TOMATOES, HALVED
LEAVES FROM 6 THYME SPRIGS

SALT AND FRESHLY GROUND BLACK PEPPER
500G (1LB 2oz) FRESH TAGLIATELLE
LARGE BUNCH OF ROCKET, TORN IN HALF
85G (3oz) PARMESAN, FRESHLY GRATED

1   Fry the garlic and pine nuts in a little oil for 1½ minutes, stirring frequently, until beginning to colour; do not allow to burn. Add the tomatoes and half the thyme and cook, stirring gently, so the tomatoes are warmed through but not broken up. Season.
2   Cook and drain the pasta.
3   Toss the tagliatelle with the rocket, sauce, remaining thyme, 3 tbsp oil and half the cheese. Serve with the remaining cheese.

082

pappardelle with provolone & black olive paste

PREPARATION TIME 5 minutes COOKING TIME 15 minutes SERVES 4

300G (10oz) PAPPARDELLE
VIRGIN OLIVE OIL
5 TBSP BLACK OLIVE PASTE

FRESHLY GROUND BLACK PEPPER
1½ TBSP PINE NUTS
115G (4oz) PROVOLONE, FINELY GRATED

1   Cook and drain the pappardelle according to the packet instructions.
2   Tip the cooked pasta into a flameproof gratin dish. Mix with a little oil, the olive paste and black pepper. Spread out evenly in the dish. Scatter over the pine nuts and provolone, season with black pepper and place under a preheated grill, not too close to the heat, until the cheese is crisp and golden.

083

fettuccine with pesto, ricotta & sun-blush tomatoes

PREPARATION TIME 5 minutes COOKING TIME 5 minutes SERVES 4

10 SUN-BLUSH TOMATOES WITH THEIR OIL,
    CUT INTO STRIPS
2 TBSP VIRGIN OLIVE OIL
2–3 TBSP PESTO (SEE PAGE 18)
4 TBSP RICOTTA

1½ TBSP FRESHLY GRATED PARMESAN
FRESHLY GROUND BLACK PEPPER
350G (12oz) FRESH FETTUCCINE (SEE PAGE 10),
    OR 300G (10oz) DRIED FETTUCCINE

1   Stir the oil from the tomatoes, the olive oil and pesto into the ricotta until smooth, then add the Parmesan and season with black pepper.
2   Cook and drain the pasta (see page 14 or according to the packet instructions), and toss with the ricotta sauce and tomato strips.

084
garlic-flavoured crisp pasta with mozzarella

PREPARATION TIME 5 minutes COOKING TIME 10 minutes SERVES 4–6

300G (10oz) TAGLIATELLE
2 GARLIC CLOVES, SLICED
4 TBSP VIRGIN OLIVE OIL
175G (6oz) BUFFALO MOZZARELLA, GRATED

SMALL HANDFUL OF MIXED CHOPPED HERBS,
    TO SERVE (OPTIONAL)
COARSELY GROUND BLACK PEPPER

1   Cook and drain the pasta according to the packet instructions.
2   Meanwhile, cook the garlic in the oil in a large pan until it smells extremely aromatic. Scoop out
    and discard the garlic.
3   Add the pasta to the oil, toss to coat evenly in oil and fry over a high heat for a few minutes until
    the pasta begins to brown and become crisp. Toss with the mozzarella, and herbs, if liked, so the
    cheese begins to melt. Season with plenty of coarsely ground black pepper.

085
tonnarelli with sage & olive oil

PREPARATION TIME 5 minutes COOKING TIME 5 minutes SERVES 4

LEAVES FROM 1 SMALL BUNCH OF SAGE,
    FINELY SHREDDED
85ML (3FL OZ/⅓ CUP) VIRGIN OLIVE OIL

300G (10oz) FRESH TONNARELLI (SEE PAGE 10)*
SALT AND FRESHLY GROUND BLACK PEPPER
FRESHLY GRATED PARMESAN, TO SERVE

1   Put the sage leaves in a heatproof bowl. Heat the oil in a small pan until it is beginning to give off
    a heat haze. Pour over the sage, which should sizzle slightly.
2   Cook and drain the pasta. Toss with the sage, oil and seasoning. Serve with freshly grated Parmesan.

*   Spaghetti can also be used.

086
tagliatelle with lemon sauce

PREPARATION TIME 5 minutes COOKING TIME 10 minutes SERVES 4

350G (12oz) TAGLIATELLE
JUICE OF 1½–2 LARGE LEMONS*
200ML (7FL OZ/¾ CUP) DOUBLE CREAM
50G (2oz/3½TBSP) UNSALTED BUTTER, DICED

115g (4oz) PARMESAN, FRESHLY GRATED
SALT AND FRESHLY GROUND BLACK PEPPER
SHREDDED BASIL, TO SERVE

1   Cook and drain the pasta according to the packet instructions.
2   Meanwhile, bring the lemon juice, cream and butter to the boil and simmer for about 5 minutes,
    stirring occasionally, until lightly thickened.
3   Toss the pasta with the Parmesan and then with the lemon cream sauce and seasoning.
    Scatter over the basil and serve.

*   The juice from 2 lemons gives quite a tangy flavour, so if you prefer a less sharp sauce,
    use the smaller quantity.

087
conchiglie with gorgonzola & walnuts

PREPARATION TIME 10 minutes COOKING TIME 10 minutes SERVES 4

300G (10oz) CONCHIGLIE
1 TSP FINELY CHOPPED SAGE
SMALL KNOB OF UNSALTED BUTTER
3 TBSP RICOTTA
5 TBSP MILK

115G (4oz) GORGONZOLA, FINELY CHOPPED
SALT AND FRESHLY GROUND BLACK PEPPER
50G (2oz) WALNUT HALVES,
    LIGHTLY TOASTED AND FINELY CHOPPED
FRESHLY GRATED PARMESAN, TO SERVE

1   Cook and drain the pasta according to the packet instructions.
2   Meanwhile, gently heat the sage and butter in a small, heavy saucepan for 1–2 minutes and then add
    the ricotta and milk, stirring until smooth, followed by the Gorgonzola. Continue stirring until smooth
    once more but do not allow it to boil. Season with very little salt but plenty of black pepper.
3   Toss the sauce with the pasta and walnuts. Serve with freshly grated Parmesan.

088
spaghetti with salmon eggs & chives

PREPARATION TIME 5 minutes COOKING TIME 10 minutes SERVES 4

300G (10oz) SPAGHETTI
2 TBSP CRÈME FRAÎCHE
40G (1½oz/2½ TBSP) UNSALTED BUTTER, DICED

65G (2½oz) SALMON EGGS (KETA)
1½ TBSP FINELY SNIPPED CHIVES
SALT AND FRESHLY GROUND BLACK PEPPER

1   Cook and drain the pasta according to the packet instructions, reserving ½ cup of the cooking water.
2   Meanwhile, gently heat the crème fraîche with the butter until warmed through but do not boil.
    Toss with the pasta and then the salmon eggs, chives and seasoning, taking care not to burst
    the eggs. Add enough of the pasta cooking water to moisten, if necessary.

089
trenette with quick spinach
& walnut sauce

PREPARATION TIME 10 minutes COOKING TIME 10 minutes SERVES 4–6

300G (10oz) TRENETTE*
40G (1½oz) BABY SPINACH LEAVES
3 GARLIC CLOVES, CRUSHED
3 HEAPED TBSP WALNUT HALVES,
    LIGHTLY TOASTED

5 TBSP EXTRA-VIRGIN OLIVE OIL
50G (2oz) PECORINO OR PARMESAN,
    FRESHLY GRATED
SALT AND FRESHLY GROUND BLACK PEPPER

1   Cook and drain the pasta according to the packet instructions, reserving ½ cup of the cooking water.
2   Meanwhile, put the spinach, garlic, nuts and oil into a small blender or food processor and pulse
    until just smooth. Transfer to a bowl and stir in the cheese and seasoning. Toss with the pasta,
    adding reserved cooking water to moisten, if necessary.

*   Linguine, tagliatelle, gnocchi rigate or conchiglie rigate can also be used.

090
gnocchi alla romana

PREPARATION TIME 5 minutes, plus 2 hours standing COOKING TIME 25—30 minutes SERVES 4

I CLOVE

I ONION

500ML (17FL OZ/2 CUPS) MILK

I BAY LEAF

85G (3OZ) SEMOLINA

I LARGE EGG YOLK

40G (1½OZ) PARMESAN, FRESHLY GRATED

50G (2OZ/¼ CUP) UNSALTED BUTTER, MELTED

1½ TSP DIJON MUSTARD

SALT AND FRESHLY GROUND BLACK PEPPER

CRISP GREEN SALAD, TO SERVE

1   Stick the clove into the onion. Put into a saucepan with the milk and bay leaf. Bring to the boil slowly,
    cover and leave to infuse for 10 minutes. Strain the milk and return to the rinsed pan. Bring to the boil.
    Over a moderate heat, gradually whisk in the semolina in a thin steady stream. Return to the boil and
    simmer for 3—5 minutes until thick and smooth, stirring constantly.
2   Off the heat, gradually beat in the egg yolk, then add two-thirds of the cheese, half the butter and the
    mustard. Season, using plenty of black pepper. Using a dampened palette knife or back of a spoon, spread
    in a layer approximately 1cm (⅛in) thick on a moistened baking sheet. Brush with the remaining butter.
    Cool and then chill for about 2 hours until firm.
3   Preheat the oven to 230°C/450°F/gas 8.
4   Cut the gnocchi into 5cm (2in) rounds with a plain biscuit cutter. Arrange in a buttered gratin dish
    or individual dishes and sprinkle with the remaining cheese. Bake in the preheated oven for
    15—20 minutes until heated and browned. Serve accompanied by a crisp green salad.

091
spinach & potato gnocchi with fontina

PREPARATION TIME 15 minutes COOKING TIME 20–25 minutes SERVES 4–6

750G (25oz) BAKING POTATOES, CHOPPED
200G (7oz) SPINACH
ABOUT 100G (3½oz/¾ CUP) PLAIN FLOUR
SALT AND FRESHLY GROUND BLACK PEPPER

175G (6oz) FONTINA, THINLY SLICED
2 TBSP MELTED UNSALTED BUTTER
FINELY CHOPPED PARSLEY OR BASIL, TO SERVE

1   Boil the potatoes for about 15 minutes until very tender. Drain thoroughly, then put the pan over a low
    heat to dry the potatoes further. Mash with a potato masher, then press through a mouli-légumes or sieve.
2   Preheat the oven to 220°C/425°F/gas 7.
3   Meanwhile, cook the spinach in a dry pan, stirring frequently until tender and wilted. Drain and then
    squeeze dry. Purée the spinach and work into the potatoes with enough flour to bind the mixture,
    and seasoning.
4   Transfer to a lightly floured surface and knead lightly and briefly; add a little more flour, if necessary,
    to bind the mixture. Divide the dough into 12 pieces and roll each one into a sausage shape about
    1cm (½in) thick. Cut across into 2cm (¾in) lengths. Hold a lightly floured fork in one hand with the
    concave side towards you. Using the thumb of the other hand, roll each length of dough along
    the inside curve of the fork to the tips of the tines, and let it drop on to a tea towel.
5   Cook the gnocchi in batches in simmering water for 1–2 minutes until they float. Remove with
    a slotted spoon and drain on kitchen paper.
6   Lay half the gnocchi in a buttered large shallow baking dish. Cover with half the fontina and pour
    over half the butter. Repeat the layering. Bake in the preheated oven for about 10 minutes until
    the cheese has melted. Scatter over the parsley or basil to serve.

092
olive & triple tomato salad

PREPARATION TIME 10 minutes, plus 1–2 hours standing COOKING TIME about 10 minutes SERVES 4

175G (6oz) PASTA SHAPES, SUCH AS CONCHIGLIE,
   RICCIOLI OR GNOCCHETTI
3 TBSP OIL FROM THE SUN-DRIED TOMATOES
6 SUN-DRIED TOMATOES IN OIL, DRAINED AND SLICED
ABOUT 10 PITTED KALAMATA OLIVES,
   SLICED (OPTIONAL)
225G (8oz) WELL-FLAVOURED CHERRY TOMATOES,
   HALVED

SMALL BUNCH OF SPRING ONIONS,
   FINELY SLICED ON THE DIAGONAL
1 GARLIC CLOVE, COARSELY CHOPPED
2 TSP SUN-DRIED TOMATO PASTE
1½–2 TBSP RED WINE VINEGAR
2 TBSP EXTRA-VIRGIN OLIVE OIL
SALT AND FRESHLY GROUND BLACK PEPPER
SMALL HANDFUL OF BASIL LEAVES, SHREDDED

1   Cook and drain the pasta according to the packet instructions. Toss with 1 tbsp oil, 4 sun-dried tomatoes,
    the olives, cherry tomatoes and spring onions.
2   Meanwhile, put the remaining sun-dried tomato oil and tomatoes, the garlic, tomato paste and vinegar
    into a blender. Mix together briefly then, with the motor running, slowly pour in the olive oil and
    blend just until the fairly thick dressing has emulsified. Season and toss with the salad.
3   Cover the salad and leave in a cool place, preferably not the fridge, for 1–2 hours.
    Toss with the shredded basil before serving.

fish & shellfish

Mussels, clams, prawns, crab, scallops, squid, tuna, sardines and anchovies are the most frequently used fish and seafood in Italian cookery. Many fish and seafood sauces are partnered with spaghetti, linguine and other long pastas, but other types can work just as well. Fish and seafood may be combined in cream-based sauces, or a tomato sauce might be used for a different approach to what is essentially the same dish. For lighter, fresh-tasting dishes, the fish or shellfish will be cooked simply and quickly before being tossed with the pasta. Tagliatelle with Scallops, Red Peppers and Basil is a good example. Salmon, both fresh and smoked, is also becoming popular in dishes such as Green and White Tagliatelle with Smoked Salmon, Spinach and Lemon.

CHAPTER

2

093
fusilli with tuna, olives & garlic

PREPARATION TIME 5 minutes COOKING TIME 20 minutes SERVES 4

3 GARLIC CLOVES, FINELY CHOPPED

VIRGIN OLIVE OIL

3 TBSP CHOPPED MIXED FLAT-LEAF PARSLEY
AND OREGANO

400G CAN CHERRY TOMATOES

375G (13oz) FUSILLI

300G CAN TUNA IN OIL, DRAINED AND FLAKED

16 OIL-CURED PITTED BLACK OLIVES, HALVED

SALT AND FRESHLY GROUND BLACK PEPPER

SMALL KNOB OF UNSALTED BUTTER

FINELY GRATED LEMON ZEST AND
CHOPPED FLAT-LEAF PARSLEY, FOR GARNISH

1   Fry 2 of the garlic cloves in little oil for 1½ minutes. Add the herbs and cook for a further
    30 seconds before stirring in the tomatoes. Simmer gently for 15–20 minutes until thickened.
2   Meanwhile, cook and drain the pasta according to the packet instructions.
3   Add the tuna, olives and seasoning to the sauce, cover and heat gently for about 5 minutes,
    or until the pasta is ready. Carefully stir the butter into the sauce, and then combine
    with the pasta. Serve sprinkled with the remaining garlic, lemon zest and parsley.

094
farfalle with peppers, anchovies & capers

PREPARATION TIME 10 minutes COOKING TIME 10 minutes SERVES 4

350G (12oz) FARFALLE

2 GARLIC CLOVES, FINELY CHOPPED

PINCH OF CRUSHED CHILLI FLAKES

VIRGIN OLIVE OIL

50G CAN ANCHOVIES IN OIL,
DRAINED AND CHOPPED

400G CAN CHERRY TOMATOES

3 RED AND 2 YELLOW PEPPERS, GRILLED,
PEELED AND SLICED (SEE PAGE 67)

2 TBSP CAPERS

SALT AND FRESHLY GROUND BLACK PEPPER

LEMON JUICE, TO TASTE

CHOPPED FLAT-LEAF PARSLEY AND
FRESHLY GRATED PARMESAN, TO SERVE

1   Cook and drain the pasta according to the packet instructions.
2   Meanwhile, fry the garlic and chilli flakes in a little oil for 1 minute. Stir in the anchovies, then stir
    in the tomatoes. Boil for 5 minutes or so until lightly reduced, then add the peppers, capers,
    plus seasoning and lemon juice, to taste. Heat through before tossing with the pasta.
    Sprinkle with parsley and Parmesan, and serve.

salmon ravioli

PREPARATION TIME 45 minutes, plus 30 minutes resting COOKING TIME 8–12 minutes SERVES 4

2-EGG QUANTITY PASTA DOUGH (SEE PAGE 10)
225G (8oz) SALMON FILLET
115G (4oz) PLAICE FILLET
SQUEEZE OF LEMON JUICE
2 TBSP DOUBLE CREAM
2 EGG YOLKS
3 TBSP FRESHLY GRATED PARMESAN
SALT AND FRESHLY GROUND BLACK PEPPER

TO SERVE
50G (2oz/SCANT ¼ CUP) UNSALTED BUTTER
JUICE OF 1 SMALL LEMON
CHOPPED FLAT-LEAF PARSLEY, FOR SPRINKLING

1   While the pasta dough is resting for 30 minutes, lightly poach the salmon
    and plaice together in very gently simmering water with the lemon juice for
    2–3 minutes for the plaice, 3–4 minutes for the salmon, depending on thickness,
    until the flesh just flakes (do not overcook).
2   Remove the plaice with a slotted spoon when it is done, discard any skin and
    bones, and put into a blender. Repeat with the salmon. Add the cream and use
    the pulse button to mix to a nubbly purée. Transfer to a bowl and mix in the
    egg yolks, cheese and seasoning, using a fork. Chill until required.
3   Make the ravioli (see page 11) with the pasta dough and filling.
4   Cook the ravioli in gently boiling water, in batches, for about 4 minutes
    per batch. Drain well.
5   Meanwhile, melt the butter with the lemon juice in a small pan over a low heat.
    Serve poured over with the ravioli and sprinkled with parsley and black pepper.

63

linguine with white clam sauce

PREPARATION TIME 5 minutes COOKING TIME 10 minutes SERVES 4

300G (10oz) LINGUINE
2 GARLIC CLOVES, FINELY CHOPPED
PINCH OF CHILLI FLAKES
VIRGIN OLIVE OIL

900G (2LB) CLAMS
115ML (4FL OZ/SCANT ½ CUP) MEDIUM-BODIED
  DRY WHITE WINE
3 TBSP CHOPPED FLAT-LEAF PARSLEY

1   Cook the linguine until it is almost done (it will finish cooking in the sauce). Drain.
2   Meanwhile, soften the garlic and chilli in a little oil in a large saucepan. Add the clams, pour in the wine, cover the pan and cook for about 2 minutes until the clams open. Discard any that remain closed.
3   Add the pasta and half the parsley, put on the lid and toss the pan over the heat for a minute or so, shaking the pan frequently, until the pasta is tender and coated in the sauce. Serve with the remaining parsley sprinkled over.

spaghetti alla puttanesca

PREPARATION TIME 5 minutes COOKING TIME 15 minutes SERVES 4

2 GARLIC CLOVES, CHOPPED
VIRGIN OLIVE OIL
6 ANCHOVY FILLETS, CHOPPED
2 X 400G CANS CHOPPED PLUM TOMATOES
SALT AND FRESHLY GROUND BLACK PEPPER

450G (1LB) SPAGHETTI
1 TBSP OREGANO
1 TBSP CAPERS, RINSED
14 OIL-CURED PITTED BLACK OLIVES, SLICED

1   Fry the garlic in a little oil for 1 minute, then stir in the anchovy fillets until they have dissolved. Add the tomatoes, bring to the boil and then simmer for about 15 minutes, stirring occasionally, until the sauce has thickened. Season, using plenty of black pepper.
2   Meanwhile, cook and drain the spaghetti according to the packet instructions.
3   Add the oregano, capers and olives to the sauce, and toss with the pasta.

farfalle with hot-smoked salmon & red peppers

PREPARATION TIME 5 minutes COOKING TIME 20 minutes SERVES 4

400G (14oz) FARFALLE
85G (3oz) PINE NUTS
4 TBSP EXTRA-VIRGIN OLIVE OIL
3 LARGE, FLESHY RED PEPPERS, GRILLED, PEELED
  AND SLICED (SEE PAGE 67)

225G (8oz) HOT-SMOKED SALMON, FLAKED
3 TBSP CHOPPED FRESH MIXED PARSLEY, THYME,
  BASIL AND DILL
FRESHLY GROUND BLACK PEPPER

1   Cook and drain the pasta according to the packet instructions.
2   Meanwhile, heat the pine nuts in the oil in a large frying pan until lightly browned. Add the pepper strips and their juices, heat for 1 minute, then add the salmon. After a further minute, remove from the heat and stir in the herbs and black pepper. Toss lightly with the pasta.

099
quick linguine with seafood

PREPARATION TIME 5 minutes COOKING TIME 10 minutes SERVES 4

400G (14oz) LINGUINE
2 PLUMP GARLIC CLOVES, FINELY CHOPPED
EXTRA-VIRGIN OLIVE OIL
4 TBSP DRY MARSALA
600G (1LB 5oz) PREPARED SEAFOOD,
  PREFERABLY FRESH, THAWED IF FROZEN

LEAVES FROM A SMALL BUNCH
  OF FLAT-LEAF PARSLEY, CHOPPED
4 TBSP LOW-FAT CRÈME FRAÎCHE
JUICE OF 1 LEMON
SALT AND FRESHLY GROUND BLACK PEPPER

1 Cook and drain the pasta according to the packet instructions.
2 Meanwhile, fry the garlic in a little oil for 30 seconds. Add the marsala, seafood and half the parsley
   and cook, stirring, until the marsala has reduced by half. Stir in the crème fraîche, and bubble briefly.
   Toss with the pasta, lemon juice and seasoning. Serve sprinkled with the remaining parsley.

100
spaghetti with cherry tomatoes, anchovies & basil

PREPARATION TIME 10 minutes COOKING TIME 10 minutes SERVES 4

400G (14oz) SPAGHETTI
2 GARLIC CLOVES, FINELY CHOPPED
VIRGIN OLIVE OIL
8 ANCHOVY FILLETS, CHOPPED

550G (1¼LB) CHERRY TOMATOES, HALVED
JUICE FROM 1 LEMON
FRESHLY GROUND BLACK PEPPER
LEAVES FROM A BUNCH OF BASIL, SHREDDED

1 Cook and drain the spaghetti according to the packet instructions.
2 Meanwhile, fry the garlic in a little oil for 1 minute. Stir in the anchovy fillets and 3 tbsp water until
   the fillets begin to dissolve, then add the tomatoes, lemon juice and black pepper. Warm through,
   shaking the pan frequently, then toss with the pasta and basil.

101
strozzapreti with fresh tuna, chilli, tomatoes & olives

PREPARATION TIME 10 minutes COOKING TIME 10 minutes SERVES 4

400G (14oz) STROZZAPRETI
450G (1LB) FRESH TUNA, CUT INTO 2.5CM (1IN) CUBES
1 GARLIC CLOVE, THINLY SLICED
1 RED CHILLI, SEEDED AND FINELY CHOPPED
3 TBSP VIRGIN OLIVE OIL

12 CHERRY TOMATOES, QUARTERED OR HALVED
12–14 PITTED KALAMATA OLIVES, SLICED
LEAVES FROM A BUNCH OF FLAT-LEAF PARSLEY,
  FINELY CHOPPED
EXTRA-VIRGIN OLIVE OIL, TO SERVE

1 Cook and drain the pasta according to the packet instructions.
2 Meanwhile, gently cook the tuna, garlic and chilli in a thick-bottomed pan in the virgin olive oil for
   2 minutes; do not let the garlic brown. Add the tomatoes and olives, cover and simmer for 3 minutes.
3 Toss the tuna sauce with the pasta and most of the parsley. Serve with the remaining parsley sprinkled
   over, and a trickle of extra-virgin olive oil.

orecchiette with cauliflower, anchovies & tomatoes

PREPARATION TIME 10 minutes, plus 20 minutes soaking COOKING TIME 25 minutes SERVES 4

450G (1LB) CAULIFLOWER, DIVIDED INTO FLORETS
1 ONION, THINLY SLICED
3 TBSP VIRGIN OLIVE OIL
300G (10oz) CANNED PLUM TOMATOES, CHOPPED
400G (14oz) ORECCHIETTE
4 ANCHOVY FILLETS

PINCH OF CRUSHED CHILLIES
12 PITTED BLACK OLIVES, SLICED
1 TBSP CHOPPED FLAT-LEAF PARSLEY
FRESHLY GROUND BLACK PEPPER
2 TBSP FRESHLY GRATED PECORINO

1   Cook the cauliflower for 3 minutes in a saucepan of water that is large enough for the pasta. Remove with a slotted spoon.
2   Meanwhile, fry the onion in 2 tbsp oil until soft but not coloured. Add the tomatoes and simmer for about 3 minutes. Add the cauliflower, cover and simmer gently for about 10 minutes until tender.
3   Meanwhile, cook and drain the pasta according to the packet instructions.
4   Fry the anchovies and chilli in the remaining oil in a small pan for about 2 minutes. Add to the tomato sauce with the olives and parsley. Toss with the pasta and black pepper, then serve with the pecorino sprinkled over.

spaghetti with tuna, pancetta & tomatoes

PREPARATION TIME 10 minutes, plus 20 minutes soaking COOKING TIME 25 minutes SERVES 4

15G (½oz) DRIED MUSHROOMS
2 GARLIC CLOVES, FINELY CHOPPED
50G (2oz) PANCETTA, CUT ACROSS INTO STRIPS
OLIVE OIL
600G (1LB 5oz) WELL-FLAVOURED TOMATOES, SEEDED
   AND CHOPPED

200G CAN TUNA, DRAINED
SALT AND FRESHLY GROUND BLACK PEPPER
400G (14oz) SPAGHETTI
FINELY CHOPPED FLAT-LEAF PARSLEY, TO SERVE

1   Place the dried mushrooms in a bowl and just cover with boiling water. Soak for 20 minutes. Drain, reserving the water. Chop the mushrooms finely.
2   Fry the garlic and pancetta in a little oil until the pancetta is flecked with brown, but do not allow the garlic to burn. Add the dried mushrooms and the tomatoes and simmer for about 15 minutes until thickened. Add the reserved mushroom liquid and simmer for a further 5 minutes. Gently stir in the tuna so it is not broken up too much, season and heat through.
3   Meanwhile, cook and drain the pasta according to the packet instructions. Toss with the tuna sauce. Sprinkle over the parsley and serve.

104
fusilli lunghi with fresh tuna & roast peppers

PREPARATION TIME 10 minutes COOKING TIME 20 minutes SERVES 4

2–3 FLESHY RED PEPPERS, DEPENDING ON SIZE

300G (10oz) FUSILLI LUNGHI

1 RED ONION, THINLY SLICED

EXTRA-VIRGIN OLIVE OIL

1 PLUMP GARLIC CLOVE, FINELY CHOPPED

350G (12oz) FRESH TUNA,
   CUT INTO 1CM (½IN) CHUNKS

85ML (3FL OZ/SCANT ⅓ CUP) FULL-BODIED DRY
   WHITE WINE

2 TBSP CAPERS

1½ TBSP CHOPPED FRESH FLAT-LEAF PARSLEY

SALT AND FRESHLY GROUND BLACK PEPPER

1   Grill the peppers until they are evenly charred and blistered. When cool enough to handle and working over a bowl to catch any juices, peel off the skins. Thinly slice the flesh.

2   Cook and drain the pasta according to the packet instructions, reserving ½ cup of the cooking water.

3   Meanwhile, fry the onion in a little oil in a large frying pan until soft and golden. Add the garlic and fry for 1 minute. Stir in the tuna for 1 minute until it has changed colour; do not overcook. Add the pepper strips and wine. Bubble until reduced by about half, then add the capers and parsley. Season. Toss with the pasta, adding a little of the reserved water, if necessary.

bucatini with sardines, lemon & fennel

PREPARATION TIME 10 minutes COOKING TIME 10 minutes SERVES 4

400G (14oz) BUCATINI

1 FENNEL BULB, FINELY CHOPPED, FEATHERY
   TOPS RESERVED

2 GARLIC CLOVES, FINELY CHOPPED

2 TBSP VIRGIN OLIVE OIL

8 FRESH SARDINE FILLETS

LEAVES FROM A SMALL BUNCH OF FLAT-LEAF
   PARSLEY, CHOPPED

JUICE OF 1 JUICY LEMON

SALT AND FRESHLY GROUND BLACK PEPPER

1   Cook and drain the pasta following the packet instructions, reserving about ½ cup of the cooking water.
2   Meanwhile, fry the fennel and garlic in the oil, stirring, for about 1 minute. Add the sardine fillets, skin
    side down, and cook for 1 minute. Turn them over and cook for another minute until cooked through.
3   Add the parsley, reserved feathery fennel fronds, lemon juice and seasoning, using plenty of black pepper.
    Toss with the pasta, adding enough of the reserved cooking water to moisten, if necessary.

penne with tuna in tomato & olive sauce

PREPARATION TIME 5 minutes COOKING TIME 10 minutes SERVES 4

1 SMALL ONION, FINELY CHOPPED

4 TBSP VIRGIN OLIVE OIL

2 GARLIC CLOVES, FINELY CHOPPED

400G CAN CHOPPED PLUM TOMATOES

200G CAN TUNA, DRAINED AND FLAKED

12 PITTED BLACK OLIVES, QUARTERED

1 TBSP SALTED CAPERS, RINSED AND DRAINED

SALT AND FRESHLY GROUND BLACK PEPPER

400G (14oz) PENNE

2 TBSP FINELY CHOPPED FLAT-LEAF PARSLEY

1   Fry the onion in the oil until softened, adding the garlic for the last minute. Pour in the tomatoes
    and boil until just thickened. Add the tuna, olives and capers and heat through gently. Season.
2   Meanwhile, cook and drain the pasta according to the packet instructions. Toss with the tuna
    and tomato sauce and parsley.

warm fusilli & seafood salad

PREPARATION TIME 10 minutes COOKING TIME 10 minutes SERVES 4

69

175G (6oz) FUSILLI

3 TBSP VIRGIN OLIVE OIL

1 TBSP RICE WINE VINEGAR

GRATED ZEST AND JUICE OF 1 LEMON

1 GARLIC CLOVE, FINELY CHOPPED (OPTIONAL)

SALT AND FRESHLY GROUND BLACK PEPPER

350G (12oz) MIXED COOKED SEAFOOD, SUCH AS
    PEELED PRAWNS, PEELED TIGER PRAWNS,
    SCALLOPS (QUARTERED, IF LARGE) AND MUSSELS

1 LARGE AVOCADO, SLICED

225G (8oz) MIXED RED AND YELLOW CHERRY
    TOMATOES, HALVED

BUNCH OF SPRING ONIONS, FINELY CHOPPED

50G (2oz) PITTED GREEN OLIVES, SLICED

LEAVES FROM A SMALL BUNCH OF MIXED
    HERBS, SUCH AS PARSLEY, BASIL AND
    MARJORAM, CHOPPED

1   Cook and drain the fusilli according to the packet instructions.
2   Meanwhile, whisk the oil with the vinegar, lemon juice and zest, the garlic and seasoning. Toss with the
    warm fusilli and the remaining ingredients. Serve warm.

spaghetti with prawns, tomatoes & capers

PREPARATION TIME 10 minutes COOKING TIME 10 minutes SERVES 4

1 ONION, CHOPPED

VIRGIN OLIVE OIL

2 GARLIC CLOVES, CRUSHED

500G (1LB 2oz) RIPE WELL-FLAVOURED
    PLUM TOMATOES, CHOPPED

1 TSP OREGANO

350G (12oz) MEDIUM RAW PRAWNS, PEELED

1½ TBSP SALTED CAPERS,
    RINSED AND DRIED

SALT AND FRESHLY GROUND BLACK PEPPER

400G (14oz) SPAGHETTI

1   Fry the onion in a little oil in a large frying pan until soft and beginning to colour. Add the garlic and
    fry for 1–2 minutes. Add the tomatoes and oregano and cook rapidly until the juice has evaporated
    but the tomatoes should not disintegrate.
2   Add the prawns to the sauce and cook over a reduced heat for about 2 minutes, just until they turn
    pink. Remove the pan from the heat and add the capers and seasoning.
3   Meanwhile, cook and drain the pasta according to the pack instructions. Toss with the sauce and serve.

109
spaghetti with flaked sardines & tomatoes

PREPARATION TIME 10 minutes COOKING TIME 15 minutes SERVES 4–5

3 GARLIC CLOVES, FINELY CHOPPED

PINCH OF CRUSHED CHILLI FLAKES

2–3 FRESH SAGE LEAVES, FINELY SHREDDED

2 TBSP VIRGIN OLIVE OIL

500G (1LB 2OZ) WELL-FLAVOURED TOMATOES, SEEDED
  AND CHOPPED

50G CAN ANCHOVY FILLETS IN OIL, DRAINED

115G (4OZ) PITTED OIL-CURED BLACK OLIVES,
  CHOPPED

50G (2OZ) CAPERS, RINSED

2–3 TSP CHOPPED OREGANO

SALT AND FRESHLY GROUND BLACK PEPPER

400G (14OZ) SPAGHETTI

8–12 FRESH SARDINES, DEPENDING ON SIZE

3 TBSP CHOPPED FLAT-LEAF PARSLEY

1   Cook the garlic, chilli and sage in the oil for 1½ minutes. Add the tomatoes, anchovies, olives, capers
    and oregano and simmer for 10 minutes. Season.
2   Meanwhile, cook and drain the pasta according to the packet instructions.
3   While the pasta is cooking, season the sardines and grill for about 2 minutes per side until
    just cooked through. Cool slightly, then remove the flesh from the bones in large pieces.
4   Toss the pasta with the sauce and parsley. Add the sardine flakes and toss gently.

110
black olive pasta with broccoli, capers & anchovies

PREPARATION TIME 5 minutes COOKING TIME 10 minutes SERVES 4

450G (1LB) BROCCOLI FLORETS

1 GARLIC CLOVE, CHOPPED

2 ANCHOVY FILLETS, CHOPPED

EXTRA-VIRGIN OLIVE OIL

25G (1OZ) SMALL CAPERS

FRESHLY GROUND BLACK PEPPER

500G (1LB 2OZ) BLACK OLIVE TAGLIATELLE
  (SEE PAGE 10)

FRESHLY GRATED PARMESAN, TO SERVE

1   Bring enough water for cooking the pasta to the boil. Add the broccoli and cook for 2–3 minutes.
    Remove with a slotted spoon and drain. Cover the pan and keep warm.
2   Cook the garlic and anchovies in a little oil, stirring, for 2 minutes. Add the broccoli and capers
    and cook over a low heat, stirring gently occasionally, for 4–5 minutes. Season with black pepper.
3   Return the water to the boil and cook the pasta. Drain and toss with the broccoli sauce.
    Serve with freshly grated Parmesan.

111
taglioni with mussels, wilted greens & lardons

PREPARATION TIME 10 minutes COOKING TIME 10 minutes SERVES 4

200G (7oz) PANCETTA, CUT ACROSS INTO
  LARDONS (STRIPS)
2 GARLIC CLOVES, FINELY CHOPPED
OLIVE OIL
100ML (3½FL OZ/SCANT ½ CUP) DRY WHITE WINE
LEAVES FROM A SMALL HANDFUL OF FLAT-LEAF
  PARSLEY, CHOPPED

3 SPRING ONIONS, CHOPPED
250G (9oz) COOKED MUSSELS OUT OF THE SHELL
150G (5oz) BABY SPINACH LEAVES
SALT AND FRESHLY GROUND BLACK PEPPER
600G (1LB 5oz) FRESH TAGLIONI

1   Bring a saucepan of water to the boil, for cooking the taglioni.
2   Meanwhile, fry the lardons and garlic in a little oil in a saucepan until lightly browned. Remove with a
    slotted spoon and drain on kitchen paper. Add the wine, parsley and spring onions to the pan and boil
    for 3–4 minutes. Add the pancetta, mussels and spinach and heat until the spinach has wilted. Season.
3   Immediately after adding the spinach to the pan, cook and drain the taglioni. Toss with the mussel
    mixture and serve.

112
linguine with roast red mullet & cherry tomatoes

PREPARATION TIME 5 minutes COOKING TIME 20–25 minutes SERVES 4

425G (15oz) CHERRY TOMATOES, HALVED
VIRGIN OLIVE OIL
SALT AND FRESHLY GROUND BLACK PEPPER
325G (11oz) LINGUINE

2 RED MULLETS, ABOUT 500G (1LB 2oz) EACH,
  FILLETED
1 TBSP FRESH OREGANO
PINCH OF CRUSHED CHILLI FLAKES
16 OIL-CURED PITTED BLACK OLIVES, HALVED

1   Preheat the oven to 200°C/400°F/gas 6.
2   Toss the tomatoes with a little oil and seasoning. Spread in a single layer on a baking sheet and roast
    in the preheated oven for 20–25 minutes.
3   Meanwhile, cook and drain the linguine according to the packet instructions.
4   At the same time, lay the red mullet fillets in a single layer in another dish, sprinkle with the oregano,
    chilli and seasoning, and then trickle over a little oil. Put in the oven for 5 minutes until the flesh flakes.
5   Toss the pasta with the tomatoes and any cooking juices, the olives and 1 tbsp oil. Break the red mullet
    into flakes over the top and toss gently.

113
warm fresh tuna salad niçoise

PREPARATION TIME 10 minutes COOKING TIME 10 minutes SERVES 4

225G (8oz) FARFALLE

200G (7oz) FRENCH BEANS

VIRGIN OLIVE OIL

350G (12oz) FRESH TUNA STEAKS

SALT AND FRESHLY GROUND BLACK PEPPER

1 TBSP BALSAMIC VINEGAR

1 TBSP LEMON JUICE

1 GARLIC CLOVE, FINELY CHOPPED

2 TBSP CHOPPED MIXED HERBS SUCH AS THYME,
    MARJORAM, PARSLEY, BASIL, FENNEL

2½ TBSP CAPERS

7 ANCHOVY FILLETS, CHOPPED

150G (5oz) CHERRY PLUM TOMATOES, HALVED

50G (2oz) PITTED BLACK OLIVES

1   Cook the pasta according to the packet instructions, adding the beans for the last 3 minutes. Drain,
    rinse in cold water and drain thoroughly.
2   Meanwhile, brush the tuna with a little olive oil, season and grill for 3–4 minutes per side until
    still pink in the centre. Cut into bite-sized pieces.
3   While the fish is cooking, whisk together the balsamic vinegar, 6 tbsp oil, the lemon juice,
    garlic, herbs, capers and black pepper until emulsified. Toss with the pasta and beans,
    the anchovies, tomatoes, olives and tuna.

114
spaghetti with cod & pangritata

PREPARATION TIME 10 minutes COOKING TIME 15–20 minutes SERVES 4

115G (4oz) CIABATTA CRUMBS

50G CAN ANCHOVY FILLETS, FINELY CHOPPED,
    OIL RESERVED

115ML (4FL OZ/½ CUP) VIRGIN OLIVE OIL

1 TSP FENNEL SEEDS, CRUSHED

2 GARLIC CLOVES, FINELY CHOPPED

50G (2oz) PINE NUTS, CHOPPED

4 TBSP CHOPPED FLAT-LEAF PARSLEY

350G (12oz) SPAGHETTI

500g (1LB 2oz) COD FILLET

150ML (5FL OZ/SCANT ⅔ CUP) MEDIUM-BODIED DRY
    WHITE WINE

1 BAY LEAF, TORN ACROSS

SALT AND FRESHLY GROUND BLACK PEPPER

LEMON WEDGES, TO SERVE

1   Preheat the oven to 200°C/400°F/gas 6.
2   Mix the breadcrumbs with the anchovies and their oil, the olive oil, fennel seeds, garlic and pine nuts
    in a roasting tin. Bake in the preheated oven for 15–20 minutes, stirring occasionally, until evenly
    browned and crisp; take care that it doesn't burn. Remove from the oven and add the parsley.
3   Meanwhile, cook and drain the pasta according to the packet instructions.
4   Also, poach the fish in the wine, 150ml (5fl oz/⅔ cup) water, the bay leaf and seasoning, for about
    5 minutes, depending on thickness, until the flesh just flakes. Lift the fish from the liquid with
    a fish slice. Discard the bay leaf. Boil the liquid hard until reduced to about 4 tbsp.
5   Meanwhile, discard the fish skin and break the fish into chunks. Toss with the pasta and
    reduced wine. Serve with the crumbs scattered over and accompanied by lemon wedges.

115
green & white tagliatelle with smoked salmon, spinach & lemon

PREPARATION TIME 5 minutes COOKING TIME 10 minutes SERVES 4

400G (14oz) DRIED GREEN AND WHITE TAGLIATELLE
400G (14oz) BABY SPINACH LEAVES
SMALL KNOB OF UNSALTED BUTTER
GRATED ZEST AND JUICE OF 1 LEMON
200G (7oz/1¾ CUP) CRÈME FRAÎCHE

SALT AND FRESHLY GROUND BLACK PEPPER
175G (6oz) SMOKED SALMON TRIMMINGS,
   CUT INTO STRIPS
CHOPPED CHIVES, TO GARNISH

1   Cook the pasta according to the packet instructions, pushing the spinach into the water 30 seconds before the end of the cooking time. Drain.
2   Meanwhile, melt the butter in a small saucepan. Whisk in the lemon zest and juice, the crème fraîche and seasoning and warm through. Toss with the pasta and smoked salmon. Serve garnished with chopped chives.

116
pipe with tuna, lemon & basil

PREPARATION TIME 5 minutes COOKING TIME 10 minutes SERVES 4

400G (14oz) PIPE*
250G (9oz) WELL-FLAVOURED CHERRY TOMATOES
4 TBSP EXTRA-VIRGIN OLIVE OIL
2 TBSP LEMON JUICE
I TBSP CAPERS PACKED IN SALT,
   RINSED AND DRAINED

2 X 200G CANS OF TUNA IN OIL, DRAINED
SALT AND FRESHLY GROUND BLACK PEPPER
½ TSP LEMON ZEST
HANDFUL OF BASIL LEAVES, SHREDDED

1   Cook and drain the pasta according to the packet instructions.
2   Meanwhile, warm the tomatoes in the oil in a large frying pan over a low heat. Just before the pasta
    is ready, gently stir in the lemon juice, capers and tuna, making sure the tuna is not broken up too
    much. Season and heat through.
3   Toss the pasta with the tomato and tuna mixture, the lemon zest and basil.

*   Conchiglie, gnocchi or chifferi can also be used.

117
crab & dill cannelloni

PREPARATION TIME 15 minutes*, plus 1–8 hours standing COOKING TIME 35 minutes* SERVES 4

225G (8oz) MIXED WHITE AND BROWN CRAB MEAT
225G (8oz) RICOTTA
ABOUT 1½ TBSP LEMON JUICE
ABOUT 1 TBSP FINELY GRATED LEMON ZEST
1–2 TBSP CHOPPED DILL, ACCORDING TO THE
   FLAVOUR OF THE DILL

2 LARGE SHALLOTS
SALT AND FRESHLY GROUND BLACK PEPPER
8 CANNELLONI TUBES, ABOUT 7.5CM (3IN) LONG
1 QUANTITY FRESH TOMATO SAUCE (SEE PAGE 18),
   WARMED

1   Combine the crab meat with the ricotta, lemon juice and zest, and dill to taste (the strength of flavour
    can vary quite considerably, especially in bought packets). Holding it over the crab mixture, squeeze
    the shallots through a garlic press to extract the juice. Stir in, with seasoning. Cover and leave in
    a cool place for 1–8 hours.
2   Preheat the oven to 190°C/375°F/gas 5.
3   Cook, drain and rinse the cannelloni tubes, even if using the no-pre-cook type (see page 15).
    Spread on a tea towel to dry.
4   Spoon or pipe the crab filling into the tubes and place in an oiled shallow baking dish.
    Pour over the sauce and bake for about 25 minutes until heated through.

*   Assumes the tomato sauce is already made.

118
bucatini with melting onion & anchovy sauce

PREPARATION TIME 10 minutes COOKING TIME 25–35 minutes SERVES 4

550G (1LB 4OZ) LARGE ONIONS, VERY THINLY SLICED
  ON A MANDOLIN OR IN A FOOD PROCESSOR
VIRGIN OLIVE OIL
SALT AND FRESHLY GROUND BLACK PEPPER
3 TBSP DRY MARSALA

200G (7OZ) BUCATINI
2 TBSP CAPERS
6–8 ANCHOVY FILLETS IN OIL
2 TBSP CHOPPED FLAT-LEAF PARSLEY,
  PLUS EXTRA TO SERVE

1 Cook the onions in a little oil in a heavy-based pan for about 5 minutes. Season and add the marsala. Cover the onions closely with a disc of greaseproof paper. Put a lid on the pan and cook very gently for 20–30 minutes until the onions are almost melting; if they become too dry, add a few drops of water. Uncover and stir for 1–2 minutes.

2 Meanwhile, cook and drain the pasta according to the packet instructions.

3 Add the capers to the sauce and stir in the anchovies until dissolved. Season and add the parsley. Toss with the pasta. Serve with extra parsley scattered over.

119
salmon shells with pesto & tomato sauce

PREPARATION TIME 5 minutes, plus standing time COOKING TIME 30 minutes SERVES 4

200G CAN SALMON, DRAINED
100G (3½OZ/SCANT ½ CUP) RICOTTA
2–3 TSP LEMON ZEST
SALT AND FRESHLY GROUND BLACK PEPPER
115G (4OZ) LARGE CONCHIGLIE,
  ABOUT 7.5CM (3IN) LONG
2 TBSP PESTO (SEE PAGE 18)

2 WELL-FLAVOURED TOMATOES, SEEDED AND
  CHOPPED

WHITE SAUCE
35G (1¼OZ/1¼ TBSP) UNSALTED BUTTER
35G (1¼OZ/2 TBSP) PLAIN FLOUR
425ML (15FL OZ/1¾ CUPS) MILK

1 Combine the salmon with the ricotta, lemon zest and seasoning. Cover and leave overnight if time allows, to allow the flavour to develop.

2 Preheat the oven to 190°C/375°F/gas 5.

3 Cook and drain the conchiglie according to the packet instructions, and leave upside down.

4 Divide the salmon mixture among the shells and place, open side up, in a shallow baking dish. Cover tightly and place in the preheated oven for 15–20 minutes to warm through.

5 While the shells are in the oven, make a simple white sauce (see page 17) with the butter, flour and milk. Stir in the pesto and tomatoes. Pour over the shells and serve.

120
seafood cannelloni

PREPARATION TIME 10 minutes COOKING TIME 35 minutes SERVES 4

225G (8oz) FRESH LASAGNE SHEETS (SEE PAGE 10)

2 SHALLOTS, FINELY CHOPPED

OLIVE OIL

2 GARLIC CLOVES, FINELY CHOPPED

1 TBSP CHOPPED MIXED OREGANO, PARSLEY AND
 TARRAGON

500G (1LB 2oz) MIXED MONKFISH AND SALMON, CUT
 INTO SMALL PIECES, AND LARGE PRAWNS,
 CHOPPED

2 WELL-FLAVOURED TOMATOES, PEELED,
 SEEDED AND VERY FINELY CHOPPED

4 TBSP FRESH BREADCRUMBS

SALT AND FRESHLY GROUND BLACK PEPPER

450G (1LB) SPINACH

15G (½oz/3 TSP) UNSALTED BUTTER

1 QUANTITY FRESH TOMATO SAUCE (SEE PAGE 18)
 OR WINTER TOMATO SAUCE (SEE PAGE 19)

4 TBSP FRESHLY GRATED PARMESAN

1 Preheat the oven to 190°C/375°F/gas 5.
2 Cook and drain the lasagne sheets (see page 15) and spread on a tea towel to dry.
3 Meanwhile, fry the shallots in a little oil until soft. Add the garlic and fry for 1 minute. Stir in the herbs, seafood, tomatoes, and three quarters of the breadcrumbs. Season and remove from the heat.
4 Cook the spinach in a covered pan, stirring occasionally, until wilted and tender. Drain, chop coarsely and squeeze out as much water as possible. Heat in a small pan with the butter and seasoning for 2–3 minutes, stirring frequently.
5 Divide the seafood mixture and the spinach among the lasagne sheets. Roll them up and place seam side down in an oiled shallow baking dish that they just fit in. Pour over the tomato sauce, sprinkle over the remaining breadcrumbs and the Parmesan.
6 Bake in the preheated oven for about 30 minutes until the top is golden.

121
smoked fish raviolini

PREPARATION TIME 45 minutes, plus resting time COOKING TIME 20 minutes SERVES 4

2-EGG QUANTITY PASTA DOUGH (SEE PAGE 10)

550G (1LB 4oz) SMOKED COD OR HADDOCK FILLET

OLIVE OIL, FOR BRUSHING

2 SHALLOTS, FINELY CHOPPED

SMALL KNOB OF UNSALTED BUTTER

115G (4oz/SCANT ½ CUP) RICOTTA, SIEVED

2 EGG YOLKS

2 TBSP FINELY CHOPPED
 FLAT-LEAF PARSLEY

FRESHLY GROUND BLACK PEPPER

TO SERVE

50G (2oz/SCANT ¼ CUP) UNSALTED BUTTER

JUICE OF 1 SMALL LEMON

1 Wrap the dough in clingfilm and leave to rest for 30 minutes.
2 Meanwhile, brush the fish lightly with oil and grill, skin side up, for 5–10 minutes until the flesh flakes when tested with a fork; the time will depend on the thickness of the fish. Discard the skin and any bones, and flake the fish into a bowl.
3 While the fish is cooking, fry the shallots in the butter until soft but not coloured. Add to the fish with the ricotta, egg yolks, parsley and black pepper. Using a fork, combine the ingredients.
4 Make raviolini with the dough and filling (see page 11).
5 Cook the raviolini in batches in a large saucepan of gently boiling water for about 3 minutes per batch. Remove with a slotted spoon and drain thoroughly.
6 Meanwhile, melt the butter with the lemon juice. Pour over the raviolini to serve.

122
smoked fish pie

PREPARATION TIME 15 mins, plus Tomato Sauce preparation COOKING TIME 45 mins SERVES 6

625G (1LB 6OZ) SPINACH

SMALL KNOB OF UNSALTED BUTTER

675G (1½LB) SMOKED HADDOCK FILLET,
   SKINNED AND CUBED

1 QUANTITY GRILLED TOMATO SAUCE
   (SEE PAGE 18)

2 TBSP CHOPPED MIXED HERBS SUCH
   AS BASIL, OREGANO, THYME AND FENNEL

350G (12OZ) CHIFFERI RIGATE OR
   CURVED MACARONI RIGATE

2 TBSP FRESHLY GRATED PARMESAN

1 TBSP FRESH BREADCRUMBS

CHEESE SAUCE

25G (1OZ) BUTTER

3 TBSP PLAIN FLOUR

300ML (10FL OZ/1½ CUPS) MILK

40G (1½OZ) PARMESAN, FRESHLY GRATED

1   Cook the spinach in a covered pan without adding any water, until wilted. Drain and squeeze out the surplus moisture. Heat through with the butter, then spread in the bottom of a 2.5 litre (4¾ pint/10 cup) baking dish. Scatter the haddock evenly over the top. Mix the tomato sauce with the herbs and spoon over the haddock.

2   Meanwhile, cook and drain the pasta according to the packet instructions.

3   While the pasta is cooking, make the cheese sauce (see page 17) and mix with the pasta. Pile evenly over the tomato sauce. Sprinkle with the Parmesan and breadcrumbs. Bake for 25–30 minutes in an oven preheated to 190°C/375°F/Gas 5, until golden.

cod, prawn & leek lasagne

PREPARATION TIME 15 minutes COOKING TIME 45 minutes SERVES 6

450G (1LB) COD FILLET, SKINNED

1 BAY LEAF, TORN ACROSS

1 SLICE EACH OF CARROT, FENNEL AND ONION

300ML (10FL OZ/SCANT 1¼ CUPS) MEDIUM-BODIED DRY WHITE WINE

ABOUT 700ML (24FL OZ/2¾ CUPS) FISH STOCK

200G (7OZ) SPINACH LASAGNE

450G (1LB) SLIM LEEKS, SLICED

1 GARLIC CLOVE, CHOPPED

115G (4OZ/SCANT ½ CUP) UNSALTED BUTTER

85G (3OZ/SCANT ¾ CUP) PLAIN FLOUR

115G (4OZ/SCANT ½ CUP) RICOTTA

150ML (5FL OZ/SCANT ⅔ CUP) LOW-FAT CRÈME FRAÎCHE

1 TBSP CHOPPED DILL

SALT AND FRESHLY GROUND BLACK PEPPER

225G (8OZ) PEELED COOKED PRAWNS

4 TBSP FRESHLY GRATED PARMESAN

LEMON WEDGES, TO SERVE

1 Put the cod, bay leaf, vegetable slices and half the wine in a saucepan. Cover with water and poach for about 5 minutes until tender. Lift out the fish and flake, discarding any skin and bones. Strain the cooking liquid and make up to 1 litre (1¾ pints/4 cups) with fish stock.

2 Preheat the oven to 200°C/400°F/gas 6.

3 Meanwhile, cook, drain and rinse the lasagne, even if using the no-pre-cook type (see page 15). Spread on a tea towel to dry.

4 Cook the leeks and garlic in 50g (2oz/scant ¼ cup) of the butter in a covered pan until tender. Remove with a slotted spoon. Add the remaining butter to the pan, then continue to make a white sauce with the flour, reserved cooking liquid and wine (see page 17). Off the heat, stir in the ricotta and crème fraîche, dill and seasoning.

5 Spoon a little sauce into a large shallow baking dish. Cover with a layer of lasagne sheets followed by some of the fish, prawns and leeks. Then some more sauce. Continue the layering, ending with sauce. Scatter over the Parmesan.

6 Bake in the preheated oven for about 30 minutes. Leave to stand for 5 minutes before serving with lemon wedges.

124

scallop & prawn lasagne

PREPARATION TIME 10 minutes COOKING TIME 30 minutes SERVES 4

3 SHALLOTS, FINELY CHOPPED

PINCH OF CHILLI FLAKES

OLIVE OIL

1 TBSP CHOPPED FLAT-LEAF PARSLEY

225G (8OZ) PEELED MEDIUM PRAWNS, HALVED OR
   QUARTERED ACROSS

115G (4OZ) SKINNED SEA BASS, COD OR
   HADDOCK FILLET

225G (8OZ) SCALLOPS, SHUCKED, QUARTERED OR
   COARSELY CHOPPED, DEPENDING ON SIZE

2-EGG QUANTITY OF PASTA DOUGH (SEE PAGE 10),
   CUT INTO LASAGNE SHEETS

2 TBSP FRESHLY GRATED PARMESAN (OPTIONAL)

LEMON WEDGES, TO SERVE

BÉCHAMEL SAUCE

225ML (8FL OZ/SCANT 1 CUP) MEDIUM-BODIED DRY
   WHITE WINE

350ML (12FL OZ/1½ CUPS) MILK

1 BAY LEAF AND 2 PARSLEY SPRIGS

1 ONION SLICE AND 1 CLOVE

50G (2OZ/SCANT ¼ CUP) UNSALTED BUTTER

4 TBSP PLAIN FLOUR

SALT AND FRESHLY GROUND BLACK PEPPER

1   Preheat the oven to 200°C/400°F/gas 6. Make the béchamel sauce (see page 17).

2   Fry the shallots and chilli in a little oil until the shallots are soft and lightly coloured. Add the parsley, prawns and sea bass, cod or haddock and cook fairly briskly for about 1 minute. Add the scallops and cook for a further minute.

3   Cook, drain and rinse the lasagne, even if using the no-pre-cook type (see page 15). Spread on a tea towel to dry.

4   Spread a little of the béchamel sauce over the bottom of a shallow baking dish and cover with a layer of pasta. Stir the fish mixture into the remainder and use to coat the pasta in a fairly thin layer. Repeat the layering, ending with a layer of sauce. Sprinkle over the Parmesan, if using.

5   Bake in the preheated oven for 15–20 minutes until golden on top. Remove from the oven and leave for 5 minutes before serving with lemon wedges.

125

smoked fish & mushroom cannelloni

PREPARATION TIME 10 minutes COOKING TIME 45 minutes SERVES 6

675G (1½LB) SMOKED HADDOCK FILLET

1 BOUQUET GARNI OF 2 TARRAGON SPRIGS, A BAY
   LEAF AND 2 THYME SPRIGS

3 GARLIC CLOVES

ABOUT 725ML (1¼ PINTS/SCANT 3 CUPS) MILK

225G (8OZ) DRIED LASAGNE SHEETS

85G (3OZ/SCANT ⅓ CUP) UNSALTED BUTTER

50G (2OZ/SCANT ½ CUP) PLAIN FLOUR

2 TBSP CHOPPED FLAT-LEAF PARSLEY

GRATED ZEST AND JUICE OF 1 LEMON

115G (4OZ) BUTTON CHESTNUT/BROWN-CAP
   MUSHROOMS, FINELY CHOPPED

3 TBSP FRESHLY GRATED PARMESAN

LEMON WEDGES, TO SERVE

1   Put the haddock, bouquet garni, garlic and 570ml (1 pint/scant 2½ cups) milk into a saucepan. Cover and poach the fish for about 10 minutes until it just flakes when tested with the tip of a knife. Remove the fish and flake it, discarding any skin and bones. Strain the milk and add more milk to make it up to 570ml (1 pint/scant 2½ cups).

2   Preheat the oven to 190°C/375°F/gas 5.

3   Meanwhile, cook, drain and rinse the lasagne, even if using the no-pre-cook type (see page 15). Spread on a tea towel to dry.

4   While the lasagne sheets are cooking, make a white sauce (see page 17) with the butter, flour and milk. Off the heat, add the parsley and lemon zest and juice.

5   Mix one-quarter of the sauce with the fish and mushrooms. Divide among the lasagne sheets then carefully roll up each one from a shorter end. Place seam side down in an oiled shallow baking dish. Spoon the remaining sauce evenly over the cannelloni and sprinkle with the Parmesan.

6   Bake in the preheated oven for about 30 minutes. Serve with lemon wedges.

riccioli with prawns & asparagus

PREPARATION TIME 10 minutes COOKING TIME 15 minutes SERVES 4

350G (12oz) SLIM ASPARAGUS

1 GARLIC CLOVE, CRUSHED

VIRGIN OLIVE OIL

450G (1LB) MEDIUM RAW PRAWNS, PEELED

SALT AND FRESHLY GROUND BLACK PEPPER

400G (14oz) RICCIOLI*

SMALL KNOB OF UNSALTED BUTTER

FRESHLY GRATED PARMESAN (OPTIONAL)

1   Blanch the asparagus in salted boiling water for 3–4 minutes until just tender. Drain (reserve the water),
    rinse in cold water and drain well. Cut the asparagus into 4cm (1½in) lengths.
2   Stir-fry the garlic and asparagus in a little oil in a large non-stick frying pan for 2–3 minutes.
    Add 115ml (4fl oz/scant ½ cup) reserved asparagus cooking water. Boil until reduced by half.
    Add the prawns and cook gently for 2–3 minutes, stirring, until they have just turned pink
    and the sauce is still slightly runny. If necessary, add a little more asparagus water. Season.
3   Meanwhile, cook and drain the pasta according to the packet instructions. Toss with the
    butter and asparagus and prawns. Serve with freshly grated Parmesan, if liked.

*   Radiatori, fusilli or eliche can also be used.

127

smoked mussel & pimento pasta salad

PREPARATION TIME 10 minutes COOKING TIME 10 minutes SERVES 4

300G (10oz) CONCHIGLIE

115G (4oz) FRENCH BEANS, HALVED ACROSS

6 TBSP VIRGIN OLIVE OIL, PLUS EXTRA
    FOR BRUSHING

ABOUT 1 TBSP BALSAMIC VINEGAR, TO TASTE

1 GARLIC CLOVE, FINELY CHOPPED

½–1 RED CHILLI, SEEDED AND FINELY CHOPPED

SALT AND FRESHLY GROUND BLACK PEPPER

1 AVOCADO, CHOPPED

5 SPRING ONIONS, FINELY CHOPPED

2 X 105G CANS SMOKED MUSSELS, DRAINED

1½ TBSP CAPERS

1½ BOTTLED ROAST PIMENTOS (RED PEPPERS)
    IN OIL, DRAINED AND THINLY SLICED

LEAVES FROM A SMALL HANDFUL OF FLAT-LEAF
    PARSLEY, CHOPPED

LEMON WEDGES, TO SERVE

1   Cook and drain the pasta according to the packet instructions, adding the beans 3–4 minutes before
    the end. Rinse under running cold water.
2   Meanwhile, whisk the oil with the vinegar, garlic and chilli. Season.
3   Toss the pasta and beans with the dressing and remaining ingredients. Serve cold but not chilled,
    with lemon wedges.

linguine with mussels & courgettes

PREPARATION TIME 10 minutes COOKING TIME 10 minutes SERVES 4

400G (14oz) LINGUINE
2 SHALLOTS, FINELY CHOPPED
1 GARLIC CLOVE, FINELY CHOPPED
PINCH OF CRUSHED CHILLI FLAKES
VIRGIN OLIVE OIL

450G (1LB) SMALL COURGETTES,
  CUT INTO 1CM (½IN) PIECES
5 TBSP DRY WHITE VERMOUTH
725G (1¾LB) MUSSELS
LEAVES FROM A SMALL BUNCH OF BASIL, SHREDDED
SALT AND FRESHLY GROUND BLACK PEPPER

1   Cook the pasta for 1 minute less than usual, and then drain, reserving ½ cup of the cooking water.
2   Meanwhile, fry the shallots, garlic and chilli in a little oil for about 1 minute in a pan that is large enough to hold all the mussels and cooked pasta. Add the courgettes and fry until softened and flecked with gold.
3   Pour in the vermouth, bring to the boil, then add the mussels. Cover and cook for 3–4 minutes until they open; discard any that remain closed. Add the linguine, toss to mix, scatter over the basil and add a little of the reserved water, if necessary, to moisten. Season, cover and heat together for 1 minute.

FISH & SHELLFISH

81

cavatappi with prawns, mushrooms & tomatoes

PREPARATION TIME 10 minutes COOKING TIME 10 minutes SERVES 4

400G (14oz) CAVATAPPI
1 ONION, THINLY SLICED
VIRGIN OLIVE OIL
2 GARLIC CLOVES, CRUSHED
350G (12oz) MIXED OYSTER AND SHIITAKE
  MUSHROOMS, HALVED OR QUARTERED IF LARGE

175ML (6FL OZ/SCANT ¾ CUP) MEDIUM-BODIED DRY
  WHITE WINE
4 RIPE WELL-FLAVOURED PLUM TOMATOES, CHOPPED
500G (1LB 2oz) LARGE RAW PRAWNS, PEELED
2 TBSP CHOPPED FLAT-LEAF PARSLEY
SALT AND FRESHLY GROUND BLACK PEPPER

1   Cook and drain the pasta according to the packet instructions.
2   Meanwhile, fry the onion in a little oil in a large frying pan until soft but not coloured. Add the garlic and fry for 1 minute. Add the mushrooms and cook until tender and there is no spare liquid. Add the wine and bubble the liquid until reduced by half.
3   Add the tomatoes and prawns and simmer very gently for 2–3 minutes until the prawns have just turned pink. Add the parsley and seasoning. Toss with the pasta.

130
taglioni with prawns & spinach

PREPARATION TIME 5 minutes COOKING TIME 10 minutes SERVES 4

375G (13OZ) TAGLIONI
VIRGIN OLIVE OIL
2 GARLIC CLOVES, FINELY CHOPPED
250G (9OZ) LARGE RAW PRAWNS, PEELED

225G (8OZ) BABY SPINACH LEAVES
3 TBSP SHREDDED BASIL
SALT AND FRESHLY GROUND BLACK PEPPER

1 Cook and drain the taglioni according to the packet instructions.
2 Meanwhile, heat about 4 tbsp oil with the garlic, then add the prawns and stir-fry for 2–3 minutes
   until they change colour; take care not to overcook. Toss with the taglioni, spinach, basil, seasoning
   and a further 4 tbsp oil. Serve.

131
tagliatelle with mussels & pesto

PREPARATION TIME 10 minutes COOKING TIME 10 minutes SERVES 4

1 SHALLOT, FINELY CHOPPED
2 GARLIC CLOVES, THINLY SLICED
2 SPRIGS OF FLAT-LEAF PARSLEY
4 TBSP DRY WHITE VERMOUTH

1KG (2¼LB) MUSSELS
400G (14OZ) TAGLIATELLE
1–1½ QUANTITIES PESTO (SEE PAGE 18)

1 Put the shallot, garlic, parsley, vermouth and mussels into a large pan over a fairly high heat, cover.
   Bring to the boil, then cook for 3–4 minutes, shaking the pan occasionally, until the shells open; discard
   any that remain closed. Remove the shells from half of the mussels. Strain off and reserve the liquid.
2 Meanwhile, cook and drain the pasta, reserving ½ cup of the cooking water.
3 At the same time, warm the pesto over a very low heat. Add all the mussels and heat gently.
   Toss with the pasta, adding the reserved liquid, as necessary, to moisten.

132
fidelini with lobster,
basil & wilted tomatoes

PREPARATION TIME 15 minutes COOKING TIME 10 minutes SERVES 4

375G (13OZ) FIDELINI
1 GARLIC CLOVE, FINELY CHOPPED
4 TBSP VIRGIN OLIVE OIL
450G (1LB) WELL-FLAVOURED CHERRY TOMATOES,
   QUARTERED

675–900G (1½–2LB) FRESH LOBSTER,
   SHELLED AND CUT INTO SMALL PIECES
2 TBSP DRY WHITE VERMOUTH
2 TBSP SHREDDED BASIL
SALT AND FRESHLY GROUND BLACK PEPPER

1 Cook and drain the fidelini according to the packet instructions, reserving ½ cup of the cooking water.
2 Meanwhile, fry the garlic in the oil for about 2 minutes. Add the tomatoes and lobster and cook,
   stirring occasionally, for 2–3 minutes until the tomatoes are just beginning to collapse.
3 Pour in the vermouth, add the basil and bubble for 1–2 minutes. Season and toss
   with the pasta, adding enough of the reserved cooking water to moisten, if necessary.

black spaghettini with scallops, white wine & parsley

PREPARATION TIME 5 minutes COOKING TIME 10 minutes SERVES 4

I GARLIC CLOVE, FINELY CHOPPED
OLIVE OIL
15G (½OZ/I TBSP) UNSALTED BUTTER
8 LARGE SCALLOPS, HALVED HORIZONTALLY,
  SHUCKED

115ML (4FL OZ/½ CUP) MEDIUM-BODIED DRY
  WHITE WINE
2 TBSP CHOPPED FLAT-LEAF PARSLEY
SALT AND FRESHLY GROUND BLACK PEPPER
450G (ILB) FRESH BLACK SPAGHETTINI

1. Put the water for the pasta on to boil. Fry the garlic in little oil and the butter in a wide frying pan for about 2 minutes until softened. Over a high heat, add the scallops and fry quickly on both sides until they have just turned opaque and remain tender. Remove from the pan.
2. Add the wine, parsley and seasoning to the pan and boil until slightly reduced. Lower the heat and return the scallops to the pan; do not allow them to boil otherwise they will toughen.
3. About 2 minutes before the scallops are ready, cook and drain the pasta according to the packet instructions. Toss with the scallops and sauce.

134
haddock, spinach & pasta al forno

PREPARATION TIME 15 minutes* COOKING TIME 45 minutes SERVES 6

625G (1LB 6OZ) SPINACH

SMALL KNOB OF UNSALTED BUTTER

675G (1½LB) SMOKED HADDOCK FILLET,
  SKINNED AND CUBED

1 QUANTITY GRILLED TOMATO SAUCE (SEE PAGE 18)

2 TBSP CHOPPED MIXED HERBS
  SUCH AS BASIL, OREGANO, THYME, FENNEL

350G (12OZ) CHIFFERI RIGATE OR
  CURVED MACARONI RIGATE

2 TBSP FRESHLY GRATED PARMESAN

1 TBSP FRESH BREADCRUMBS

CHEESE SAUCE
25G (1OZ/2 TBSP) BUTTER

3 TBSP PLAIN FLOUR

300ML (10FL OZ/SCANT 1¼ CUPS) MILK

40G (1½OZ) PARMESAN,
  FRESHLY GRATED

1   Preheat the oven to 190°C/375°F/gas 5.
2   Cook the spinach in a covered pan, shaking the pan occasionally, until wilted. Drain and squeeze out
     surplus moisture. Heat through with the butter, then spread in the bottom of a baking dish. Scatter
     the haddock evenly over the top. Mix the tomato sauce with the herbs and spoon over the haddock.
3   Cook and drain the pasta according to the packet instructions.
4   While the pasta is cooking, make the cheese sauce (see page 17) and mix with the pasta.
     Pile evenly over the tomato sauce. Sprinkle with the Parmesan and breadcrumbs.
5   Bake in the preheated oven for 25–30 minutes until golden.

*   Assumes the tomato sauce is already made.

135
mediterranean seafood & pasta salad

PREPARATION TIME 15 minutes, plus cooling time COOKING TIME 15 minutes SERVES 4

225ML (8FL OZ/⅞ CUP) MEDIUM-BODIED DRY
  WHITE WINE

1 GARLIC CLOVE

1 SHALLOT, QUARTERED

1 BAY LEAF

1 LEMON, SLICED

4 TBSP EXTRA-VIRGIN OLIVE OIL

1½ TBSP LEMON JUICE

SALT AND FRESHLY GROUND BLACK PEPPER

225G (8OZ) RAW KING PRAWNS, PEELED

125G (4½OZ) SCALLOPS, SHUCKED, HALVED
  OR QUARTERED ACCORDING TO SIZE

125G (4½OZ) COOKED SHELLED MUSSELS

200G (7OZ) BLACK LINGUINE

2 RED PEPPERS, GRILLED, PEELED
  AND CHOPPED (SEE PAGE 67)

1 TBSP CAPERS

LEAVES FROM A SMALL BUNCH OF
  FLAT-LEAF PARSLEY, CHOPPED

2 HANDFULS OF CRISP SALAD LEAVES

1 LEMON, CUT INTO WEDGES

1   Put the wine, garlic, shallot, bay leaf and lemon slices into a saucepan, cover and bring to the boil.
     Remove from the heat and leave to infuse for 10 minutes.
2   Meanwhile, make the dressing by whisking the oil with the lemon juice and seasoning.
3   Return the liquid to a gentle simmer, add the prawns and poach for about 2 minutes until they
     turn pink. Using a slotted spoon, transfer to the bowl of dressing. Poach the scallops for 1–1½ minutes
     until they change colour. Add to the prawns. Dunk the mussels into the poaching liquid to warm them,
     and add to the other seafood. Set aside.
4   Strain the poaching liquid, return to the pan and add enough water for cooking the pasta. Bring to
     the boil, then cook and drain the pasta according to the packet instructions. Toss with the seafood
     mixture and leave to cool.
5   Toss the cooled pasta and seafood with the red pepper, capers and parsley and pile on to a bed
     of salad leaves. Serve with lemon wedges.

136
pizza macaroni pie

PREPARATION TIME 20 minutes COOKING TIME 35 minutes SERVES 4–6

175G (6oz) MACARONI

1 SMALL ONION, FINELY CHOPPED

3 GARLIC CLOVES, SLICED

570ML (1 PINT/SCANT 2½ CUPS) MILK

40G (1½oz/2 TBSP) UNSALTED BUTTER

40G (1½oz/4 TBSP) PLAIN FLOUR

SALT AND FRESHLY GROUND BLACK PEPPER

ABOUT 1½ TBSP SUN-DRIED TOMATO PASTE

85G (3oz) PARMESAN, FRESHLY GRATED

150G (5oz) BUFFALO MOZZARELLA,
   THINLY SLICED

3–4 RIPE TOMATOES, THINLY SLICED

ABOUT 12 PITTED BLACK OLIVES, SLICED

50G CAN OF ANCHOVIES,
   DRAINED AND HALVED LENGTHWAYS

HERBES DE PROVENCE, FOR SPRINKLING

40G (1½oz) FRESH BREADCRUMBS

OLIVE OIL

1   Preheat the oven to 180°C/350°F/gas 4.
2   Cook the macaroni for 2 minutes less than usual, and then drain.
3   Meanwhile, simmer the onion and garlic with enough milk to just cover, until tender. Purée, unless you prefer to have pieces of onion.
4   Make a white sauce (see page 17) with the butter, flour and the remaining milk. Season and add the tomato paste, Parmesan and macaroni.
5   Spoon evenly into an oiled shallow 1.75 litre (3 pint) baking dish. Interleave the mozzarella and tomatoes over the top, adding the olives and anchovies and a sprinkling of herbes de Provence and black pepper. Sprinkle the breadcrumbs around the edge of the dish and trickle over a little oil.
6   Bake in the preheated oven for 25 minutes.

seafood tossed with spaghetti, lemon & rocket

PREPARATION TIME 5 minutes COOKING TIME 10 minutes SERVES 4

500G (1LB 2OZ) FRESH SPAGHETTI

650G (1LB 7OZ) GOOD-QUALITY MARINATED
   SEAFOOD SALAD*

100G (3½OZ) ROCKET

GRATED ZEST AND JUICE OF 1 LEMON

4 TBSP CHOPPED PARSLEY

3 TBSP PINE NUTS, LIGHTLY TOASTED

FRESHLY GROUND BLACK PEPPER

1   Cook and drain the pasta according to the packet instructions.

2   Return to the hot pan, toss in the seafood salad and return the pan to a moderate heat. Heat for 2–3 minutes, tossing occasionally, until piping hot. Add the rocket with the lemon zest and juice and parsley. When it has wilted, serve sprinkled with the toasted pine nuts and black pepper.

*   If prepared marinated seafood salad is not available, toss 650g (1lb 7oz) cooked mixed seafood with a few tablespoons of virgin olive oil, a dash of white wine vinegar and a small handful of chopped mixed herbs.

linguine with red clam sauce

PREPARATION TIME 5 minutes COOKING TIME 30 minutes SERVES 4

1 SMALL ONION, FINELY CHOPPED

2 GARLIC CLOVES, CRUSHED

VIRGIN OLIVE OIL

400G CAN CHERRY TOMATOES

900G (2LB) CLAMS

175ML (6FL OZ/SCANT ¾ CUP) MEDIUM-BODIED DRY
   WHITE WINE

350G (12OZ) LINGUINE

HANDFUL OF FLAT-LEAF PARSLEY, CHOPPED

1   Fry the onion and garlic in a little oil in a frying pan until translucent and soft. Add the tomatoes, bring to the boil, then simmer for 15–20 minutes until thickened to a sauce.

2   Meanwhile, put the clams and wine in a large, heavy casserole, cover and cook over a high heat, shaking the pan occasionally for about 5 minutes until the shells open; discard any that remain closed. Using a slotted spoon, transfer the clams to a bowl.

3   Strain off the cooking juices. Boil until reduced by half, then add to the tomato sauce.

4   Meanwhile, cook and drain the linguine according to the packet instructions. Toss with the sauce, clams and parsley.

quick tagliatelle with prawns & red pesto

PREPARATION TIME 10 minutes COOKING TIME 10 minutes SERVES 4

350G (12oz) TAGLIATELLE
3 GARLIC CLOVES, THINLY SLICED
PINCH OF DRIED CHILLI FLAKES
VIRGIN OLIVE OIL
350G (12oz) RAW TIGER PRAWNS, PEELED
2 TBSP RED PESTO (SEE PAGE 19)

ZEST AND JUICE OF 1 LEMON
1 TBSP CAPERS, RINSED (OPTIONAL)
4 TBSP MIXED CHOPPED BASIL
 AND FLAT-LEAF PARSLEY
SALT AND FRESHLY GROUND BLACK PEPPER

1   Cook and drain the pasta according to the packet instructions.
2   Meanwhile, cook the garlic and chilli in a little oil until softened. Add the prawns and cook, stirring, for 2–3 minutes until they turn pink. Remove the pan from the heat immediately to avoid overcooking and toughening the prawns.
3   Toss the tagliatelli with 1–2 tbsp oil, the red pesto, lemon zest and juice, capers (if using), the herbs, prawns and seasoning. Serve straight away.

FISH & SHELLFISH

87

tonnarelli with prawns, clams & rocket

PREPARATION TIME 5 minutes COOKING TIME 10 minutes SERVES 4

375G (13oz) TONNARELLI
3 GARLIC CLOVES, FINELY CHOPPED
PINCH OF DRIED CHILLI FLAKES
VIRGIN OLIVE OIL
150ML (5FL OZ/SCANT ⅔ CUP) MEDIUM-BODIED DRY
 WHITE WINE

900G (2LB) CLAMS
250G (9oz) COOKED MEDIUM PRAWNS, PEELED
100G (3½oz) ROCKET
EXTRA-VIRGIN OLIVE OIL, TO SERVE

1   Cook and drain the pasta according to the packet instructions, giving it 1 minute less than usual; reserve ½ cup of the cooking water.
2   Meanwhile, fry the garlic and chilli in a little oil in a large frying pan for about 2 minutes. Pour in the wine, then add the clams. Cook for about 2 minutes until they open; discard any that remain closed. Add the prawns and rocket.
3   Add the pasta to the pan, adding the reserved cooking water, if necessary, to moisten and heat together for about a minute. Serve with extra-virgin olive oil trickled over.

141
seafood linguine en papillote

PREPARATION TIME 5 minutes COOKING TIME 35 minutes SERVES 4–6

500G (1LB 2OZ) LINGUINE

2 GARLIC CLOVES, CRUSHED

OLIVE OIL

400G CAN CHERRY TOMATOES

2 TBSP SUN-DRIED TOMATO PASTE

SALT AND FRESHLY GROUND BLACK PEPPER

675G (1½LB) COOKED MIXED SEAFOOD,
SUCH AS PEELED PRAWNS, MUSSELS,
HALVED TIGER PRAWNS, CANNED TUNA

175G (6OZ) COOKED CLAMS

1½–2 TBSP CAPERS

LEAVES FROM A SMALL BUNCH OF
FLAT-LEAF PARSLEY, CHOPPED

1   Preheat the oven to 190°C/375°F/gas 5. Lightly oil 4–6 35cm (14in) square pieces of greaseproof paper.
2   Cook the linguine for 1 minute less than usual, then drain well.
3   Meanwhile, fry the garlic in a little oil for 1 minute. Stir in the canned tomatoes, tomato paste
    and seasoning. Simmer for 5 minutes. Toss with the pasta, seafood, capers and parsley.
4   Place one portion in the centre of each of the pieces of greaseproof paper. Fold the edges loosely
    over the pasta mixture and twist the edges together to seal tightly. Place on a baking sheet
    and bake in the preheated oven for 20–25 minutes until hot throughout.

142
rotelle with tuna & rocket

PREPARATION TIME 10 minutes COOKING TIME 10 minutes SERVES 4

350G (12oz) ROTELLE*
2 X 200G CANS TUNA IN OIL
I RED ONION, CHOPPED

GRATED ZEST AND JUICE OF I LEMON
50G (2oz) PITTED GREEN OLIVES, SLICED
100G (3½oz) ROCKET

1   Cook and drain the pasta according to the packet instructions.
2   Meanwhile, drain the oil from the tuna into a frying pan and fry the onion until tender. Add the
    flaked tuna, lemon zest and juice, olives and two-thirds of the rocket. Season and warm through.
    Toss with the pasta and remaining rocket.

*   Conchiglie, fusilli, farfalle or gnocchi can also be used.

143
fettuccine with smoked salmon, dill & ricotta

PREPARATION TIME 5 minutes COOKING TIME 10 minutes SERVES 4

400G (14oz) FETTUCCINE
3 EGGS
85G (3oz/SCANT ⅓ CUP) RICOTTA
SALT AND FRESHLY GROUND BLACK PEPPER

2 TBSP CHOPPED DILL
115G (4oz) SMOKED SALMON, CUT INTO STRIPS
SALMON EGGS (KETA), TO SERVE (OPTIONAL)

1   Cook the pasta according to the packet instructions.
2   Meanwhile, work the eggs into the ricotta, using a fork. Season with a pinch of salt, if liked
    (the smoked salmon will make the dish quite salty) and plenty of black pepper.
3   Drain the pasta well and immediately and quickly toss with the eggs and ricotta to make a creamy
    sauce (place over a very low heat if necessary). Then toss lightly with the dill and smoked salmon.
    Serve garnished with salmon eggs, if liked.

144
penne with cauliflower, anchovies & garlic

PREPARATION TIME 5 minutes COOKING TIME 10 minutes SERVES 4

500G (1LB 2oz) CAULIFLOWER, DIVIDED
  INTO FLORETS
450G (1LB) DRIED PENNE
2 LARGE GARLIC CLOVES, FINELY CHOPPED
PINCH OF CRUSHED CHILLI FLAKES

4 ANCHOVY FILLETS, CHOPPED
6 TBSP EXTRA-VIRGIN OLIVE OIL
2 TBSP CHOPPED FLAT-LEAF PARSLEY
SALT AND FRESHLY GROUND BLACK PEPPER

1   Boil the cauliflower until tender. Drain well.
2   Meanwhile, cook and drain the pasta following the packet instructions.
3   While the pasta is cooking, fry the garlic, chilli and anchovies in the oil in a large frying pan, stirring
    occasionally until the anchovies have dissolved and the garlic is golden; do not allow it to burn.
    Add the cauliflower. Using a fork, stir thoroughly so it is coated in the oil, quickly breaking it
    up and reducing some to a purée. Toss thoroughly with the pasta, parsley and seasoning.

145
cavatelli with crab, avocado & fresh tomatoes

PREPARATION TIME 10 minutes COOKING TIME 10 minutes SERVES 4

350G (12oz) CAVATELLI*
2 GARLIC CLOVES, FINELY CHOPPED
PINCH OF CHILLI FLAKES
2 TBSP VIRGIN OLIVE OIL
4 VINE-RIPENED TOMATOES, SEEDED AND CHOPPED
175G (6oz) FRESH OR FROZEN MIXED WHITE
  AND BROWN CRAB MEAT

2 TBSP FINELY CHOPPED FLAT-LEAF PARSLEY, PLUS
  EXTRA FOR GARNISH
2 TBSP LEMON JUICE
1 AVOCADO, DICED
SMALL BUNCH OF SLIM SPRING ONIONS,
  FINELY CHOPPED
SALT AND FRESHLY GROUND BLACK PEPPER

1   Cook and drain the pasta according to the packet instructions.
2   Meanwhile, fry the garlic and chilli in the oil for 1 minute, then add the tomatoes, crab meat, parsley
     and lemon juice and heat gently until just warmed through.
3   Toss with the pasta, avocado, spring onions and seasoning. Serve sprinkled with flat-leaf parsley.

*   Radiatori, fusilli, riccioli or taglioni can also be used.

146
prawn & pasta al forno

PREPARATION TIME 10 minutes COOKING TIME 50 minutes SERVES 4

ABOUT 225G (8oz) LEEKS, THINLY SLICED

450G (1LB) WELL-FLAVOURED TOMATOES, QUARTERED

OLIVE OIL

SALT AND FRESHLY GROUND BLACK PEPPER

300G (10oz) PENNE RIGATE OR RIGATONI

115G (4oz) PEELED COOKED PRAWNS

1½ TBSP COARSELY CHOPPED
  FLAT-LEAF PARSLEY

85ML (3FL oz/⅓ CUP) VEGETABLE OR FISH STOCK

150ML (5FL oz/SCANT ⅔ CUP) DOUBLE CREAM

85G (3oz) BUFFALO MOZZARELLA, GRATED

2 TBSP PARMESAN, FRESHLY GRATED

1 THICK SLICE CRUSTLESS BREAD, MADE
  INTO CRUMBS

1   Preheat the oven to 200°C/400°F/gas 6.
2   Spread leeks and tomatoes in a small roasting tin and trickle over a little oil. Season and stir together. Roast in the preheated oven for 30 minutes.
3   Meanwhile, cook and drain the pasta according to the packet instructions, giving it 1 minute less than usual. Tip into the roasting tin with the prawns and parsley and stir in the stock. Season and trickle over the cream. Sprinkle over the cheese and breadcrumbs and return to the oven for 15–20 minutes until the top is crisp and golden.

147
orecchiette with smoked mussels, spinach & cashews

PREPARATION TIME 5 minutes COOKING TIME 10 minutes SERVES 4

250G (9oz) PASTA SHELLS

3 PLUMP GARLIC CLOVES, FINELY CHOPPED

350G (12oz) BABY SPINACH

115ML (4FL oz/SCANT ½ CUP) VIRGIN OLIVE OIL

2 X 105G CANS OF SMOKED MUSSELS, DRAINED

1 RED PEPPER, GRILLED, PEELED AND SLICED
  (SEE PAGE 67)

50G (2oz) CASHEW NUTS, LIGHTLY TOASTED

FRESHLY GROUND BLACK PEPPER

LEMON WEDGES, TO SERVE

1   Cook and drain the pasta according to the packet instructions.
2   Meanwhile, stir-fry the garlic and spinach in the oil in a deep frying pan or wok set over a high heat for 1 minute.
3   Gently stir in the mussels, red pepper, nuts and season with black pepper. Heat briefly until warmed through, shaking the pan occasionally, then toss with the pasta. Serve with lemon wedges.

roast vegetable, seafood & pasta salad

PREPARATION TIME 15 minutes, plus cooling time COOKING TIME 30–40 minutes SERVES 4–6

I COURGETTE, CUT INTO 4cm (1½in) CHUNKS

I SMALL AUBERGINE, CUT INTO 4cm (1½in) CHUNKS

I FENNEL BULB, CUT INTO 4cm (1½in) PIECES

I ONION, CUT INTO 4cm (1½in) CHUNKS

I RED PEPPER, CUT INTO 4cm (1½in) CHUNKS

3 GARLIC CLOVES, CHOPPED

I SPRIG OF ROSEMARY

2 SPRIGS OF THYME

VIRGIN OLIVE OIL

4 RIPE TOMATOES, QUARTERED

275G (9oz) PASTA SHAPES

225G (8oz) PREPARED MIXED SEAFOOD

50G (2oz) PITTED BLACK OLIVES

1 Preheat the oven to 200°C/400°F/gas 6.
2 Put the vegetables, except the tomatoes, in a large roasting tin with the garlic and herbs. Trickle over a little oil, stir together to coat the vegetables and spread them out. Roast in the top of the preheated oven for 30–40 minutes until tender and charred in patches, adding the tomatoes after 15 minutes. Discard the herbs.
3 About 15 minutes before the vegetables are ready, cook and drain the pasta according to the packet instructions. Combine with the vegetables, seafood and olives. Serve warm.

green fettuccine & lobster with vodka cream sauce

PREPARATION TIME 5 minutes COOKING TIME 10 minutes SERVES 4

2 GARLIC CLOVES, FINELY CHOPPED

4 LARGE SPRING ONIONS, CHOPPED

2 TBSP VIRGIN OLIVE OIL

1–2 TBSP SUN-DRIED TOMATO PASTE

2 TBSP VODKA

175ML (6FL OZ/¾ CUP) DOUBLE CREAM

ABOUT 300G (10oz) COOKED LOBSTER

MEAT, CHOPPED

350G (12oz) GREEN FETTUCCINE

SALT AND FRESHLY GROUND BLACK PEPPER

CHOPPED FRESH DILL, TO SERVE

1 Fry the garlic and spring onions in the oil in a frying pan for 2 minutes. Stir in the tomato paste until it is amalgamated with the oil, then stir in the vodka and bring to the boil. Add the cream and simmer until beginning to thicken slightly. Add the lobster and remove from the heat if pasta is not ready.
2 Meanwhile, cook and drain the pasta according to the packet instructions, reserving ½ cup of the cooking water.
3 If necessary, just before the pasta is cooked, reheat the sauce over a low heat, stirring gently occasionally, until warmed through. Season and toss with the pasta, adding enough of the reserved cooking water to moisten, if necessary. Serve sprinkled with dill.

seafood spaghetti with saffron

PREPARATION TIME 10 minutes COOKING TIME 20 minutes SERVES 4–6

2 LEEKS, THINLY SLICED
1 ONION, FINELY CHOPPED
2 GARLIC CLOVES, FINELY CHOPPED
VIRGIN OLIVE OIL
350G (12oz) DRIED SPAGHETTI
200ML (7FL oz/¾ CUP) MEDIUM-BODIED
  DRY WHITE WINE

150ML (5FL oz/SCANT ⅔ CUP) CRÈME FRAÎCHE
4 TBSP CHOPPED FLAT-LEAF PARSLEY,
  PLUS EXTRA TO GARNISH
LARGE PINCH OF SAFFRON THREADS, CRUSHED
225G (8oz) LARGE PRAWNS, PEELED
900G (2LB) MUSSELS
175G (6oz) SCALLOPS, SHUCKED

1 Fry the leeks, onion and garlic in a little olive oil for 3–4 minutes. Cover and cook gently for about 10 minutes until very soft.
2 Cook and drain the spaghetti according to the packet instructions.
3 Meanwhile, add the wine, crème fraîche, parsley and saffron to the vegetables. Bubble for a few minutes, and then add all the prawns and mussels. Re-cover the pan and cook, shaking the pan frequently, for about 3 minutes until the mussels have opened; discard any that remain closed. Add the scallops and poach for about 2 minutes. Toss with the pasta and serve with plenty of parsley sprinkled over.

FISH & SHELLFISH

93

puffed spinach & anchovy bake

PREPARATION TIME 15 minutes COOKING TIME 50 minutes SERVES 4

175G (6oz) PASTA
350G (12oz) SPINACH
4 EGGS, SEPARATED
2 X 50G CANS ANCHOVY FILLETS, DRAINED AND
  QUITE FINELY CHOPPED
ABOUT 2 TSP WHOLEGRAIN MUSTARD

WHITE SAUCE
25G (1oz/1½ TBSP) UNSALTED BUTTER
3 TBSP PLAIN FLOUR
300ML (10FL oz/SCANT 1¼ CUPS) MILK

1 Preheat the oven to 190°C/375°F/gas 5.
2 Cook and drain the pasta according to the packet instructions, but allowing 2 minutes less than usual.
3 Meanwhile, cook the spinach in a covered pan until wilted. Drain well and squeeze dry.
4 Make a simple white sauce (see page 17) with the butter, flour and milk. Off the heat, stir in the egg yolks, spinach, anchovies, pasta and mustard to taste.
5 Whisk the egg whites until stiff but not dry. Stir 2 spoonfuls into the sauce, then gently fold in the remainder in 3 batches. Transfer to an oiled baking dish.
6 Bake in the preheated oven for about 40 minutes.

152
tagliarini with crab & fennel

PREPARATION TIME 10 minutes COOKING TIME 10 minutes SERVES 4

I FENNEL BULB, VERY THINLY SLICED CROSSWAYS
    USING A MANDOLINE OR FOOD PROCESSOR
2 TSP FENNEL SEEDS, CRUSHED
I GARLIC CLOVE, FINELY CHOPPED
SMALL KNOB OF UNSALTED BUTTER
300G (10oz) TAGLIARINI

225G (8oz) FRESH MIXED WHITE AND
    BROWN CRAB MEAT
GRATED ZEST AND JUICE OF I LEMON
SALT AND FRESHLY GROUND BLACK PEPPER
1½ TBSP CHOPPED FRESH HERB FENNEL

1   Cook the sliced fennel, fennel seeds and garlic in a little butter and 2 tbsp water in a covered heavy
    pan, shaking the pan occasionally, until the fennel is tender. If necessary, add a little dry white wine
    or water to prevent sticking.
2   Meanwhile, cook and drain the pasta according to the packet instructions, reserving a little of the
    cooking water.
3   While the pasta is cooking, stir the crab and lemon zest and juice into the fennel and heat
    gently to warm though. Season.
4   Combine the crab sauce with the pasta, adding a little of the cooking water, if necessary,
    to moisten. Serve with the herb fennel scattered over.

153
fusilli lunghi with prawns,
fennel & tomatoes

PREPARATION TIME 10 minutes COOKING TIME 20 minutes SERVES 4

I GARLIC CLOVE, FINELY CHOPPED
VIRGIN OLIVE OIL
2 LARGE FENNEL BULBS (ABOUT 350G/12oz TOTAL),
    THINLY SLICED CROSSWAYS, FEATHERY
    TOPS RESERVED
4 TBSP MEDIUM-BODIED DRY WHITE WINE
400G (14oz) FUSILLI LUNGHI

450G (1LB) WELL-FLAVOURED PLUM TOMATOES,
    PEELED, SEEDED AND CHOPPED
I TSP OREGANO
350G (12oz) MEDIUM RAW PRAWNS, PEELED
SALT AND FRESHLY GROUND BLACK PEPPER
FRESHLY GRATED PARMESAN TO SERVE (OPTIONAL)

1   Cook the garlic in a little oil in a large frying pan until just beginning to change colour. Stir in the
    fennel, then add the wine. Cover the pan and cook gently for about 15 minutes until the fennel is tender.
2   Meanwhile, cook and drain the pasta according to the packet instructions.
3   When the fennel is tender, uncover the pan and boil until the liquid has evaporated. Add the tomatoes
    and oregano and cook until the tomato liquid has almost evaporated. Stir in the prawns and cook
    for about 2–3 minutes until they just turn to pink. Season and toss with the pasta. Serve with
    the reserved feathery tops sprinkled over, and accompanied by Parmesan, if liked.

crab in conchiglie with red pesto sauce

PREPARATION TIME 10 minutes COOKING TIME 30 minutes SERVES 4

20 LARGE CONCHIGLIE

2 SHALLOTS, FINELY CHOPPED

1 GARLIC CLOVE, FINELY CHOPPED

SMALL KNOB OF UNSALTED BUTTER

2 TBSP DRY WHITE VERMOUTH

450G (1LB) FRESH MIXED WHITE AND
   BROWN CRAB MEAT

15G (½oz) FRESH BASIL LEAVES, FINELY SHREDDED

SALT AND FRESHLY GROUND BLACK PEPPER

5 TBSP RED PESTO (SEE PAGE 19)

5 TBSP SINGLE CREAM

2–3 TBSP FRESH BREADCRUMBS

3 TBSP FRESHLY GRATED PARMESAN

VIRGIN OLIVE OIL

1   Preheat the oven to 220°C/425°F/gas 7.
2   Cook the conchiglie according to the packet instructions but giving them 1 minute less than usual. Drain, rinse in cold water and drain thoroughly. Leave upside down to drain on a cloth.
3   Fry the shallots and garlic in the butter until softened but not coloured. Add the vermouth and boil until almost evaporated. Remove from the heat and gently stir in the crab, basil and seasoning. Divide among the pasta shells and place upright in a single layer in a shallow baking dish.
4   Stir the pesto into the cream. Add black pepper and pour around the shells. Sprinkle over the breadcrumbs and cheese. Trickle over a little oil and bake in the preheated oven for 15 minutes. Uncover and bake for a further 5 minutes.

taglioni with seared scallops, pancetta & tomatoes

PREPARATION TIME 10 minutes COOKING TIME 10 minutes SERVES 4

85G (3oz) PANCETTA, CUBED

2 GARLIC CLOVES, CRUSHED AND COARSELY CHOPPED

5 LARGE, RIPE, WELL-FLAVOURED PLUM TOMATOES,
   CORED, SEEDED AND COARSELY CHOPPED

LEAVES FROM A LARGE HANDFUL OF
   FLAT-LEAF PARSLEY, CHOPPED

LEAVES FROM A FEW SPRIGS OF TARRAGON, CHOPPED

SALT AND FRESHLY GROUND BLACK PEPPER

12–20 SCALLOPS, DEPENDING ON SIZE, SHUCKED

400G (14oz) TAGLIONI

1   Fry the pancetta in a large non-stick frying pan until lightly coloured and then add the garlic. Cook for 2 minutes. Stir in the tomatoes, cook for 2–3 minutes and add the herbs and seasoning. Draw the pan partly off the heat so the sauce cooks very gently.
2   Season the scallops, then sear in a hot ridged grill pan, or a heated heavy frying pan for about 1½ minutes, undisturbed. Turn them over and cook for a further 1–2 minutes so they remain tender and juicy.
3   While the scallops are cooking, cook and drain the taglioni according to the packet instructions. Toss with the sauce and serve topped with the scallops.

156
fettuccine with tiger prawns, tomatoes & basil

PREPARATION TIME 10 minutes COOKING TIME 5 minutes SERVES 4

675G (1½LB) WELL-FLAVOURED PLUM TOMATOES,
    QUARTERED LENGTHWAYS
EXTRA-VIRGIN OLIVE OIL
2 TBSP FINELY SHREDDED BASIL,
    PLUS EXTRA TO SERVE
ABOUT 1 TBSP BALSAMIC VINEGAR

SALT AND FRESHLY GROUND BLACK PEPPER
500G (1LB 2OZ) HEADLESS RAW TIGER PRAWNS,
    PEELED
2 PLUMP GARLIC CLOVES, CRUSHED
450G (1LB) FRESH FETTUCCINE

1   Cut away the tomato 'cores', if tough. Scoop the seeds and juice into a sieve set over a bowl. When all the juice has drained through, discard the seeds. Dice the flesh and add to the bowl with 1 tbsp oil, the basil, and vinegar and seasoning to taste, and warm through over a saucepan of simmering water, stirring occasionally.
2   Stir-fry the prawns in some oil in a large non-stick frying pan for 2 minutes. Add the garlic and stir-fry until the prawns turn pink. Remove immediately from the heat.
3   While the prawns are cooking, cook and drain the pasta according to the packet instructions. Toss with the prawns, tomatoes and juices. Serve sprinkled with finely shredded basil.

157

conchiglie with seafood sauce

PREPARATION TIME 10 minutes COOKING TIME 20 minutes SERVES 4–6

2 ONIONS, CHOPPED
200ML (7FL OZ/1¾ CUP) MEDIUM-BODIED
   DRY WHITE WINE
900G (2LB) MUSSELS
2 GARLIC CLOVES, FINELY CHOPPED
OLIVE OIL
115G (4OZ) BROWN-CAP MUSHROOMS, SLICED

PINCH OF CRUSHED CHILLI FLAKES
450G (1LB) RAW PRAWNS, PEELED
115G (4OZ) SCALLOPS, SHUCKED
400G (14OZ) CONCHIGLIE
LEAVES FROM A SMALL BUNCH OF
   FLAT-LEAF PARSLEY, CHOPPED

1   Put 1 onion and the wine into a large pan, bring to the boil and add the mussels. Cover and simmer for about 4 minutes until the shells open; discard any that remain closed. Remove the mussels from the shells; reserve the liquid.
2   Meanwhile, fry the remaining onion and the garlic in a little oil until soft. Add the mushrooms and chilli and cook until the moisture has evaporated.
3   Strain in the liquid from the mussels. Boil until reduced to 225ml (8fl oz/scant 1 cup). Add the prawns, cook for 1 minute, then add the scallops and cook gently for a further 2 minutes or so until they turn white and the prawns turn pink. Add the mussels and reheat gently.
4   Meanwhile, cook and drain the pasta according to the packet instructions. Toss with the shellfish sauce and the parsley.

158

tagliatelle with scallops,
red peppers & basil

PREPARATION TIME 10 minutes COOKING TIME 10 minutes SERVES 4

8 LARGE SCALLOPS, SHUCKED
2 LARGE RED PEPPERS, QUARTERED LENGTHWAYS
4 TBSP VIRGIN OLIVE OIL
450G (1LB) TAGLIATELLE

½ JUICY LEMON
SMALL HANDFUL OF BASIL LEAVES, SHREDDED
SALT AND FRESHLY GROUND BLACK PEPPER

1   Separate the corals from the scallops. Slice the bodies in half horizontally. Set corals and slices aside.
2   Lay the peppers skin-side up on a baking sheet or grill rack and grill until the skin is charred and blackened. Working over a bowl, peel off the skins and slice the flesh. Combine the flesh with any juices that are in the bowl and 2 tbsp oil in a small saucepan and warm through gently.
3   Meanwhile, cook and drain the pasta according to the packet instructions.
4   Just before the pasta is ready, cook the scallops and corals on a preheated hot ridged grill pan (or preheated very hot grill) for 1 minute per side until the flesh has just become opaque. Take care not to overcook the scallops. Squeeze lemon juice over them.
5   Toss the red pepper, basil, remaining oil and seasoning with the pasta and serve with the scallops on top.

159
linguine with seafood, saffron & tomatoes

PREPARATION TIME 10 minutes COOKING TIME 20 minutes SERVES 4

2 SHALLOTS, FINELY CHOPPED

2 GARLIC CLOVES, FINELY CHOPPED

PINCH OF CRUSHED CHILLI FLAKES

SMALL KNOB OF UNSALTED BUTTER

175ML (6FL OZ/SCANT ¾ CUP) MEDIUM-BODIED
    DRY WHITE WINE

400G CAN CHOPPED PLUM TOMATOES

PINCH OF SAFFRON THREADS, CRUSHED

675G (1½LB) MUSSELS

400G (14OZ) LINGUINE

225G (8OZ) LARGE RAW PRAWNS, PEELED

175G (6OZ) FRESH SCALLOPS, SHUCKED

3 TBSP CHOPPED FLAT-LEAF PARSLEY

SALT AND FRESHLY GROUND BLACK PEPPER

1   Fry the shallots, garlic and chilli flakes in a little butter in a large saucepan until softened. Add the wine and boil until almost evaporated.

2   Stir in the tomatoes and saffron and simmer for 15 minutes. Add the mussels. Cover the pan and simmer for 3–4 minutes, shaking the pan occasionally, until the mussels open; discard any that remain closed. Remove the mussels from the pan and remove some or all of the top shells, if liked.

3   Cook and drain the linguine according to the packet instructions.

4   Meanwhile, add the prawns to the pan and poach gently for 1½ minutes, then add the scallops and cook for a further 1½–2 minutes or so until the prawns have just turned pink and the scallops just become white; take care not overcook. Return the mussels to the pan, add the parsley and seasoning and warm through. Toss with the pasta and sauce.

*   Squid could be used, if preferred; remove the tentacles to cook separately, and thinly slice the bodies. Add with the prawns.

160
tagliatelle & tiger prawns with red pepper sauce

PREPARATION TIME 5 minutes COOKING TIME 20 minutes SERVES 4

4 PLUMP RED PEPPERS

6 UNPEELED WHOLE GARLIC CLOVES

SALT AND FRESHLY GROUND BLACK PEPPER

400G (14OZ) TAGLIATELLE

VIRGIN OLIVE OIL, FOR FRYING

450G (1LB) TIGER PRAWNS

1 TBSP BALSAMIC VINEGAR

LEAVES FROM A SMALL BUNCH OF
    FLAT-LEAF PARSLEY, CHOPPED

1   Grill the peppers and garlic until peppers have blackened, blistered and softened, and the garlic cloves have softened. Remove the papery skins from the garlic and put the cloves in a blender or food processor. Holding the peppers over a bowl to catch the juices, peel off the skins and discard the seeds and cores. Add the peppers and any juices in the bowl to the blender or food processor and mix to a nubbly purée. Season and set aside.

2   Cook and drain the pasta according to the packet instructions.

3   Meanwhile, heat a little oil in a large frying pan, add the prawns and fry quickly until they have just turned colour; take care not to overcook. Pour in the red pepper sauce, add the balsamic vinegar and parsley and heat through gently. Toss with the pasta, and serve.

161
shellfish spaghetti with
sun-blush tomatoes

PREPARATION TIME 10 minutes COOKING TIME 15 minutes SERVES 4–6

1 SHALLOT, FINELY CHOPPED

4 GARLIC CLOVES, SLICED

PINCH OF CHILLI FLAKES

4 TBSP VIRGIN OLIVE OIL

150ML (5FL OZ/SCANT ⅔ CUP) MEDIUM-BODIED
  DRY WHITE WINE

12 PEELED RAW MEDITERRANEAN PRAWNS, WITH
  HEADS AND TAILS LEFT ON

450G (1LB) SQUID, SLICED BUT TENTACLES
  LEFT WHOLE

900G (2LB) MUSSELS

400G (14OZ) SPAGHETTI

12 SUN-BLUSH TOMATOES

SALT AND FRESHLY GROUND BLACK PEPPER

SHREDDED BASIL LEAVES, TO SERVE

1 Fry the shallots, garlic and chilli in a little oil in saucepan until soft but not coloured. Pour in the wine and bubble for 2 minutes. Add the prawns, cover and cook gently for 2 minutes. Add the squid, cook for 1–2 minutes until the prawns have changed colour and the squid is just cooked. Remove them both with a slotted spoon.

2 Add the mussels to the pan, cover and cook for 3–4 minutes, shaking the pan frequently, until the shells open; discard any that remain closed. Strain off and reserve the liquid.

3 Meanwhile, cook the spaghetti according to the packet instructions, but giving it 1 minute less than normal. Drain and return to the pan. Add the reserved liquid, the prawns, mussels, squid and sun-blush tomatoes, plus any cooking juices. Toss lightly and heat through for 1 minute. Season. Serve with plenty of basil scattered over.

FISH & SHELLFISH

162
crab & prawn ravioli

PREPARATION TIME 45 minutes COOKING TIME 4–8 minutes SERVES 4

2-EGG QUANTITY OF PASTA (SEE PAGE 10)
225G (8oz) MIXED COOKED FRESH WHITE CRAB
  AND PEELED PRAWNS
50G (2oz) RICOTTA, SIEVED
2 SPRING ONIONS, FINELY CHOPPED

SALT AND FRESHLY GROUND BLACK PEPPER
50G (2oz/SCANT ¼ CUP) UNSALTED BUTTER
JUICE OF 1 SMALL LEMON
CHOPPED FENNEL, FOR SPRINKLING

1 While the pasta is resting, mix the crab and prawns with the ricotta, the spring onions and seasoning.
2 Make the ravioli with the pasta dough and filling (see page 11).
3 Cook the ravioli in gently boiling water, in batches, for about 4 minutes per batch. Drain well.
4 Meanwhile, melt the butter with the lemon juice in a small pan over a low heat.
   Serve with the butter poured over the ravioli and sprinkled with fennel.

163
conchiglie with prawn sauce

PREPARATION TIME 10 minutes COOKING TIME 10 minutes SERVES 4

400G (14oz) CONCHIGLIE
2 GARLIC CLOVES, FINELY CHOPPED
1 SMALL RED PEPPER, SEEDED AND FINELY CHOPPED
4 SPRING ONIONS, CHOPPED

OLIVE OIL
550G (1LB 4oz) MEDIUM RAW PRAWNS, PEELED
LEAVES FROM A SMALL BUNCH OF FLAT-LEAF
  PARSLEY, FINELY CHOPPED

1 Cook and drain the pasta according to the packet instructions, reserving ½ cup of the cooking water.
2 Meanwhile, fry the garlic, red pepper and spring onions in a little oil in a large frying pan for a couple
   of minutes. Stir in the prawns and cook for 2–3 minutes until they turn pink. Toss with the pasta and
   parsley, adding enough cooking water, if necessary, to moisten and serve.

164
spaghetti with squid, tomatoes & herbs

PREPARATION TIME 10 minutes COOKING TIME 10 minutes SERVES 4

400G (14oz) SPAGHETTI
3 GARLIC CLOVES, THINLY SLICED
5 TBSP VIRGIN OLIVE OIL
350G (12oz) PREPARED SQUID, TENTACLES DETACHED,
  BODIES THINLY SLICED

225G (8oz) WELL-FLAVOURED CHERRY TOMATOES,
  QUARTERED
2 TBSP LEMON JUICE
2 TBSP MIXED FINELY CHOPPED FLAT-LEAF PARSLEY,
  OREGANO AND BASIL
SALT AND FRESHLY GROUND BLACK PEPPER

1 Cook and drain the pasta according to the packet instructions.
2 Meanwhile, fry the garlic in 3 tbsp of the oil until turning golden. Add the squid and cook quickly for
   2–3 minutes until just turning opaque, stirring. Scoop out into a covered bowl.
3 Add the tomatoes to the pan and warm gently, shaking the pan occasionally so the tomatoes do not
   break up too much. Add the lemon juice, herbs and seasoning, and return the squid to the pan.
   Toss with the pasta and remaining oil, then serve.

165

fettuccine with scallops, buttered pine nuts & shredded lettuce

PREPARATION TIME 5 minutes COOKING TIME 10 minutes SERVES 2

200G (7oz) FETTUCCINE

1 GARLIC CLOVE, CRUSHED, WITH A PINCH OF SALT

50G (2oz) OF UNSALTED BUTTER, DICED

3 TBSP PINE NUTS

12 QUEEN SCALLOPS

FRESHLY GROUND BLACK PEPPER

OUTER LEAVES OF 2 SMALL SOFT LETTUCES,
    TORN INTO WIDE STRIPS

LEMON WEDGES, TO SERVE (OPTIONAL)

1   Cook and drain the pasta according to the packet instructions.
2   Meanwhile, fry the garlic in the butter for 1 minute. Stir in the scallops and pine nuts and cook for
    1–2 minutes until the scallops start to turn opaque. Season lightly with pepper and toss in the lettuce.
3   Drain the pasta and toss with the scallops, lettuce and pine nuts. Serve with lemon wedges, if liked.

166

linguine with squid, basil & chilli

PREPARATION TIME 10 minutes COOKING TIME 5 minutes SERVES 4

300G (10oz) CLEANED SQUID

3 GARLIC CLOVES, THINLY SLICED

1 RED CHILLI, SEEDED AND FINELY CHOPPED

VIRGIN OLIVE OIL

1–2 TSP LEMON JUICE

SALT AND FRESHLY GROUND BLACK PEPPER

450G (1LB) FRESH LINGUINE

3 TBSP SHREDDED BASIL LEAVES

1   Remove and reserve the tentacles from the squid. Slice the bodies into rings. Stir-fry the tentacles
    and rings, the garlic and chilli in a little oil in a large frying pan over a high heat for about
    3 minutes until the squid has turned white. Toss with the lemon juice and seasoning.
2   Meanwhile, cook and drain the linguine. Toss with the squid and basil and serve.

167

spaghetti with swordfish, lemon, capers & rocket

PREPARATION TIME 10 minutes COOKING TIME 10 minutes SERVES 4

400G (14oz) SPAGHETTI

3 GARLIC CLOVES, THINLY SLICED

PINCH OF CRUSHED CHILLI FLAKES

4 TBSP VIRGIN OLIVE OIL

350G (12oz) SWORDFISH STEAKS, CUT ACROSS INTO
    STRIPS ABOUT 2CM (¾IN) WIDE

LEAVES FROM A BUNCH OF FLAT-LEAF PARSLEY,
    FINELY CHOPPED

1 TBSP CAPERS

1 TBSP LEMON JUICE

SALT AND FRESHLY GROUND BLACK PEPPER

1   Cook and drain the pasta according to the packet instructions.
2   Meanwhile, fry the garlic and chilli in the oil for 2 minutes. Add the swordfish strips and parsley and cook
    quickly for about 2 minutes on each side, until the fish is just cooked through; take care not to overcook.
    Add the capers and lemon juice and seasoning and toss with the pasta.

168

bucatini with squid, prawns, lemon, parsley & garlic

PREPARATION TIME 10 minutes COOKING TIME 10 minutes SERVES 4

400G (14oz) BUCATINI

3 GARLIC CLOVES, THINLY SLICED

4 TBSP VIRGIN OLIVE OIL

350G (12oz) PREPARED SQUID, TENTACLES DETACHED,
   BODIES THINLY SLICED

12 LARGE RAW PRAWNS, PEELED

GRATED ZEST AND JUICE OF ½ LEMON

SMALL HANDFUL OF FLAT-LEAF PARSLEY
   LEAVES, CHOPPED

SALT AND FRESHLY GROUND BLACK PEPPER

1   Cook and drain the pasta according to the packet instructions.

2   Meanwhile, fry the garlic in 3 tbsp oil until turning golden. Scoop out with a slotted spoon into a covered bowl. Add the squid in batches to the pan and cook for 1–2 minutes per batch, stirring until it has just changed colour. Scoop out and add to the garlic. Fry the prawns until they just turn pink.

3   Add the lemon zest and juice and return the squid and any juices that have collected. Warm through gently and briefly. Toss with the pasta, remaining oil, parsley and seasoning.

169

taglioni with crab sauce

PREPARATION TIME 10 minutes COOKING TIME 10 minutes SERVES 4

300G (10oz) TAGLIONI

1 GARLIC CLOVE, FINELY CHOPPED

PINCH OF CHILLI FLAKES

GRATED ZEST OF 1 LEMON

5 SPRING ONIONS, THINLY SLICED DIAGONALLY

VIRGIN OLIVE OIL

225ML (8FL OZ/SCANT 1 CUP) MEDIUM-BODIED
   DRY WHITE WINE

85G (3oz) FRESH OR FROZEN BROWN CRAB
   MEAT, THAWED

225G (8oz) FRESH OR FROZEN MIXED CRAB
   MEAT, THAWED

1–2 TSP LEMON JUICE

SALT AND FRESHLY GROUND BLACK PEPPER

2½ TBSP FINELY CHOPPED FLAT-LEAF PARSLEY, PLUS
   EXTRA TO GARNISH

1   Cook and drain the pasta according to the packet instructions, reserving ½ cup of the cooking water.

2   Meanwhile, cook the garlic, chilli flakes, lemon zest and spring onions gently in a little oil for 1½ minutes.

3   Pour in the wine and boil, uncovered, until most of the wine has evaporated. Stir in the crab meat and lemon juice and seasoning to taste. Warm through briefly. Toss with the pasta and parsley, adding enough of the reserved water to moisten, if necessary. Sprinkle parsley over and serve.

170

tuna & broccoli bake

PREPARATION TIME 10 minutes COOKING TIME 35 minutes SERVES 4

225G (8oz) FUSILLI

175G (6oz) BROCCOLI, DIVIDED INTO SMALL FLORETS

115G (4oz) TALEGGIO OR FONTINA, GRATED

200G CAN OF TUNA, DRAINED AND FLAKED

1 LARGE (OR 2 HALVES) GRILLED RED PEPPER IN
   OIL, DRAINED AND SLICED

570ML (1 PINT/SCANT 2½ CUPS) MILK

3 LARGE EGGS, BEATEN

SALT AND FRESHLY GROUND BLACK PEPPER

2 TBSP FRESH BREADCRUMBS

1   Preheat the oven to 180°C/350°F/gas 4.
2   Cook and drain the pasta according to the packet instructions but giving it 1 minute less than usual; add the broccoli for the last 2–3 minutes.
3   Combine the pasta and broccoli with half of the cheese, then tip half of the mixture into an oiled baking dish. Scatter over the tuna and red pepper. Cover with the remaining pasta mixture.
4   Beat the milk with the eggs and seasoning. Pour into the dish; it should flow through the pasta, but if not, ease the pasta apart. Scatter over the remaining cheese and the breadcrumbs, making sure any protruding broccoli is covered.
5   Bake in the preheated oven for about 25 minutes until just set and golden.

171

cavatelli with mussels, tomatoes & chilli

PREPARATION TIME 5 minutes COOKING TIME 15 minutes SERVES 4

4 TBSP MEDIUM-BODIED DRY WHITE WINE

900G (2LB) MUSSELS

2 GARLIC CLOVES, FINELY CHOPPED

1 SMALL CHILLI, SEEDED AND FINELY CHOPPED

3 TBSP VIRGIN OLIVE OIL

300G (10oz) WELL-FLAVOURED CHERRY TOMATOES

LEAVES FROM A SMALL BUNCH OF FLAT-LEAF
   PARSLEY, CHOPPED

SALT AND FRESHLY GROUND BLACK PEPPER

400G (14oz) CAVATELLI

1   Put the wine and mussels in a large saucepan, cover and cook over a medium heat for 3–4 minutes, shaking the pan frequently, until the shells open; discard any that remain closed. Remove the shells from half of the mussels. Strain off and reserve the liquid.
2   Meanwhile, fry the garlic and chilli in the oil in a large frying pan for about 2 minutes until soft but not coloured. Halve some of the tomatoes, then add all the tomatoes to the pan and fry until beginning to soften but still retain their shape. Add the parsley, all the mussels and the reserved cooking liquid, and seasoning. Heat through gently.
3   Meanwhile, cook and drain the pasta according to the packet instructions. Toss with the mussel sauce.

meat & poultry

Meat sauces for pasta tend to come from the mid to north of Italy, especially from the region of Emilia-Romagna, the source of abundant supplies of hams, pancetta, salami and fresh sausages. And, of course, there's the well-known Bolognese sauce, or ragù alla Bolognese to give it its correct name. Contrary to the norm outside Italy, the rich, intensely flavoured sauce should be served with tagliatelle, not spaghetti. This chapter also features plenty of lasagne recipes, such as chicken with leek and sausage with aubergine. As well as the popular beef-filled version of cannelloni, there is a lighter recipe using pork and spinach and ricotta, plus a version with a chicken and prosciutto filling. Meat, particularly cured meats, are often combined with vegetables, as in Tagliatelle with Parma Ham, Peas and Lemon.

172

tagliolini with meatballs & tomato sauce

PREPARATION TIME 10 minutes*, plus soaking time COOKING TIME 35 minutes* SERVES 4

1 SLICE STALE FIRM WHITE BREAD, CRUSTS REMOVED
2 TBSP MILK
1 ONION, FINELY CHOPPED
1 GARLIC CLOVE, FINELY CHOPPED
OLIVE OIL
350G (12oz) LEAN MINCED BEEF
1 EGG, BEATEN

2 TBSP FRESHLY GRATED PARMESAN,
      PLUS EXTRA, TO SERVE (OPTIONAL)
4 TBSP CHOPPED FLAT-LEAF PARSLEY
SALT AND FRESHLY GROUND BLACK PEPPER
PLAIN FLOUR
FRESH TOMATO SAUCE (SEE PAGE 18) OR WINTER
      TOMATO SAUCE (SEE PAGE 19), WARMED
400G (14oz) TAGLIOLINI

1   Crumble the bread into the milk and leave to soak for 10 minutes.
2   Meanwhile, fry the onion and garlic in a little oil until very soft and pale gold. Remove to paper towels
    to drain and cool.
3   Put the beef into a large bowl and break it up. Squeeze the milk from the breadcrumbs and add
    the soaked crumbs to the beef with the onion, garlic, egg, Parmesan, half the parsley and seasoning.
    Combine thoroughly. With floured hands, form into walnut-sized balls.
4   Fry the balls in oil, in batches, if necessary, so the pan is not crowded, until golden. Pour in the warmed
    sauce, turn over gently a few times so they are well coated and cook together gently for 15–20 minutes.
5   Meanwhile, cook and drain the pasta. Toss with the meatballs and sauce, and serve with the Parmesan.

*   Assumes the sauce is already made.

173

prosciutto & basil frittata
with roast tomatoes

PREPARATION TIME 5 minutes COOKING TIME 15–20 minutes SERVES 4

250G (9oz) CHERRY TOMATOES

I TBSP BALSAMIC VINEGAR

VIRGIN OLIVE OIL

SALT AND FRESHLY GROUND BLACK PEPPER

85G (3oz) MACARONI

150ML (5FL OZ/SCANT ⅔ CUP) SINGLE OR
   WHIPPING CREAM

4 EGGS

LEAVES FROM A BUNCH OF BASIL, SHREDDED

3 SLICES PROSCIUTTO, SHREDDED

85G (3oz) FONTINA OR TALEGGIO,
   FINELY CHOPPED

SMALL BUNCH OF ROCKET

1　Preheat the oven to 200°C/400°F/gas 6.
2　Put the tomatoes in a roasting tin and stir with the balsamic vinegar, a little oil, and seasoning. Spread in a single layer. Roast in the preheated oven for 15–20 minutes until softened. Stir a couple of times.
3　Meanwhile, cook the pasta according to the packet instructions, and drain well.
4　Combine the cream, eggs and basil briefly in a blender, add to the cooked pasta with the prosciutto and seasoning and stir together.
5　Heat a little oil in a large non-stick frying pan. Pour in the prosciutto mixture to make an even layer and cook slowly until the frittata is set most of the way through but still creamy on top.
6　Scatter the cheese over evenly and place under a preheated grill until golden. Slide the frittata onto a large plate. Serve topped with the roast tomatoes and any pan juices, and the rocket.

174

sardinian ragù

PREPARATION TIME 10 minutes COOKING TIME 2 hours SERVES 4

450G (I LB) LEAN SHOULDER OF LAMB, CUT INTO
   2CM (¾IN) CUBES

SEASONED FLOUR

OLIVE OIL

I LARGE ONION, CHOPPED

4 GARLIC CLOVES, CHOPPED

LEAVES FROM I SMALL SPRIG OF ROSEMARY, FINELY
   CHOPPED

175ML (6FL OZ/SCANT ¾ CUP) FULL-BODIED DRY
   WHITE WINE

I BOUQUET GARNI

I TSP GROUND CINNAMON

SALT AND FRESHLY GROUND BLACK PEPPER

85G (3oz) PITTED GREEN OLIVES

300G (10oz) GARGANELLI

1　Preheat the oven to 180°C/350°F/gas 4.
2　Toss the lamb in seasoned flour to coat lightly, then fry in batches in a little oil in a heavy flameproof casserole dish until evenly browned. Remove with a slotted spoon.
3　Add the onion to the pan, and more oil, if necessary, and fry until browned. Add the garlic and rosemary, fry for I minute, then stir in the wine to dislodge the sediment. Add the bouquet garni, cinnamon, seasoning, fried lamb and enough water to just cover the meat. Cover and heat until the liquid bubbles at the edges.
4　Cook the casserole in the preheated oven for 1½–2 hours until the lamb is very tender. Stir in the olives 10 minutes before the end. If there is too much liquid, uncover the casserole towards the end of the cooking; if the casserole is too dry, stir in a little more wine or water.
5　Meanwhile, cook and drain the pasta according to the packet instructions. Toss with the lamb ragù.

175
tortiglioni with lamb ragù

PREPARATION TIME 10 minutes, plus soaking time COOKING TIME 2–2½ hours SERVES 4

15G (½oz) DRIED PORCINI

I ONION, CHOPPED

I CARROT, FINELY CHOPPED

OLIVE OIL

3 GARLIC CLOVES, FINELY CHOPPED

2 TSP FENNEL SEEDS, LIGHTLY CRUSHED

I SPRIG OF ROSEMARY

350G (12oz) MINCED LEAN LAMB

115ML (4FL OZ/SCANT ½ CUP) RED WINE

400G CAN CHOPPED TOMATOES

3 TBSP CHOPPED OREGANO

SALT AND FRESHLY GROUND BLACK PEPPER

400G (14oz) TORTIGLIONI*

FRESHLY GRATED PARMESAN, TO SERVE

1 Soak the porcini in about 115ml (4fl oz/scant ½ cup) boiling water for 15 minutes.
2 Meanwhile, cook the onion and carrot in a little oil in a large frying pan until softened and lightly coloured, adding the garlic about 2 minutes before the end.
3 Stir in the fennel seeds and rosemary for 1 minute. Increase the heat, add the lamb and cook until lightly browned, stirring to break it up. Stir in the wine. Bubble very gently until reduced by half.
4 Lift the mushrooms from the liquid (reserve the liquid) and chop them.
5 Add the tomatoes, oregano and mushrooms to the lamb and strain in the mushroom liquid. Cook, uncovered, over a very low heat for at least 1½ hours, preferably 2 hours, stirring occasionally, until the lamb is very tender and the sauce no longer watery. If necessary, add a little more wine or water during cooking. Discard the rosemary. Season.
6 Cook and drain the pasta according to the packet instructions, and toss with the sauce. Serve with grated Parmesan.

* Rigatoni can also be used.

176
sedani with tomatoes, sausages & mushrooms

PREPARATION TIME 10 minutes COOKING TIME 40 minutes SERVES 4

I ONION, FINELY CHOPPED

VIRGIN OLIVE OIL

150G (5oz) CHESTNUT/BROWN-CAP
   MUSHROOMS, SLICED

2 PLUMP GARLIC CLOVES, FINELY CHOPPED

250G (9oz) FRESH ITALIAN (OR FRENCH) SAUSAGES,
   SKINNED AND CRUMBLED

PINCH OF CHILLI FLAKES

1–1¼ TSP DRIED OREGANO

400G CAN CHERRY TOMATOES

I TBSP SUN-DRIED TOMATO PASTE

115ML (4FL OZ/SCANT ½ CUP) DOUBLE CREAM
   (OPTIONAL)

SALT AND FRESHLY GROUND BLACK PEPPER

300G (10oz) SEDANI OR OTHER LARGE PASTA TUBES

CHOPPED PARSLEY AND FRESHLY GRATED PARMESAN,
   TO SERVE

1 Fry the onion in a little oil in a large frying pan until soft. Add the mushrooms and garlic and fry briskly until the mushrooms have browned.
2 Stir in the sausages to break them up, and cook until lightly browned. Add the chilli, oregano, tomatoes and tomato paste. Simmer gently for 15–20 minutes until thickened, stirring occasionally. Stir in the cream, if using, and heat through gently. Season.
3 Meanwhile, cook and drain the pasta according to the packet instructions. Toss with the sauce, sprinkle with parsley and serve accompanied by Parmesan.

pappardelle with steak & mushrooms

PREPARATION TIME 10 minutes COOKING TIME 15 minutes SERVES 4

1 ONION, HALVED AND THINLY SLICED

50G (2OZ) UNSALTED BUTTER

1 GARLIC CLOVE, FINELY CHOPPED

225G (8OZ) MIXED MUSHROOMS, WILD IF POSSIBLE,
   HALVED, QUARTERED OR SLICED,
   ACCORDING TO SIZE

450G (1LB) SIRLOIN STEAK,
   CUT ACROSS THE GRAIN INTO STRIPS

2 TBSP DRY MARSALA

3 TBSP CRÈME FRAÎCHE

SALT AND FRESHLY GROUND BLACK PEPPER

LEMON JUICE

450G (1LB) FRESH PAPPARDELLE

SMALL HANDFUL OF MIXED FLAT-LEAF
   PARSLEY AND TARRAGON, CHOPPED

1. Fry the onion in half the butter until soft and lightly coloured, adding the garlic for the last 2 minutes. Add the mushrooms and cook, stirring frequently, until lightly browned and tender. Remove the vegetables with a slotted spoon and keep warm.

2. Add the remaining butter to the cooking juices and fry the steak strips briskly, keeping them moving, for 2–3 minutes until sealed on the outside but still pink in the centre.

3. Add the marsala to the pan and boil until almost evaporated. Stir the crème fraîche into the pan, return the mushrooms and bring to the boil. Simmer gently to thicken slightly. Season, adding lemon juice, to taste.

4. Cook the pappardelle according to the packet instructions and drain, reserving ½ cup of the cooking water. Toss the pasta with the meat and mushroom sauce; include some of the reserved water, if necessary, to moisten. Serve sprinkled with parsley and tarragon.

MEAT & POULTRY

178
tagliatelle with steak & onions

PREPARATION TIME 10 minutes COOKING TIME 15 minutes SERVES 4

2 LARGE RED ONIONS, THICKLY SLICED
VIRGIN OLIVE OIL
200ML (7FL OZ/SCANT ¾ CUP) HALF-FAT CRÈME FRAÎCHE
250G (9oz) TAGLIATELLE

2 X 200G (7oz) STEAKS
SALT AND FRESHLY GROUND BLACK PEPPER
LEAVES FROM A SMALL HANDFUL OF FLAT-LEAF
    PARSLEY, CHOPPED

1   Cook the onions, stirring frequently, in a little oil in large heavy non-stick frying pan for
    8–10 minutes until softened and golden. Stir in the crème fraîche and heat through gently.
2   Meanwhile, cook and drain the pasta according to the packet instructions, reserving ½ cup
    of the cooking water.
3   At the same time, season the steaks and cook on a hot ridged grill pan for 2–3 minutes
    per side until browned but still pink inside. Remove to a plate and leave to rest.
4   Cut the steaks into strips across the grain. Add to the onions, with any juices that have
    collected on the plate, and the parsley. Season. After a minute or so, toss with the pasta,
    and enough of the reserved water, if necessary to moisten.

179
fettuccine with mushrooms, pancetta & wine

PREPARATION TIME 10 minutes COOKING TIME 10 minutes SERVES 4

400G (14oz) FETTUCCINE
115G (4oz) PANCETTA, CUT INTO STRIPS
SMALL KNOB OF UNSALTED BUTTER
1 GARLIC CLOVE, VERY THINLY SLICED
350G (12oz) CHESTNUT/BROWN-CAP
    MUSHROOMS, SLICED

5 TBSP MEDIUM-BODIED DRY WHITE WINE
115ML (4FL OZ/SCANT ½ CUP) DOUBLE CREAM
SALT AND FRESHLY GROUND BLACK PEPPER
4 TBSP FRESHLY GRATED PARMESAN, PLUS EXTRA
    TO SERVE

1   Cook and drain the pasta according to the packet instructions, reserving ½ cup of the cooking water.
2   Meanwhile, fry the pancetta in the butter in a large frying pan until crisp. Add the garlic and
    mushrooms and fry for about 5 minutes, until lightly coloured, stirring frequently.
3   Pour in the wine, bubble until just evaporated, then add the cream and simmer gently for a couple of
    minutes until lightly thickened. Season. Toss with the pasta and Parmesan, adding reserved water,
    as necessary, to moisten.

180
sedani with beef ragù

PREPARATION TIME 10 minutes COOKING TIME 20 minutes SERVES 4

350G (12oz) RUMP STEAK, CUT ACROSS INTO
  5CM (2IN) STRIPS
OLIVE OIL
1 ONION, FINELY CHOPPED
2 GARLIC CLOVES, THINLY SLICED
400G CAN CHOPPED PLUM TOMATOES

1 TSP DRIED OREGANO
14 PITTED BLACK OLIVES, SLICED
2 TBSP CAPERS
1 TBSP FLAT-LEAF PARSLEY
SALT AND FRESHLY GROUND BLACK PEPPER
400G (14oz) SEDANI*

1 Fry the steak in a little oil in a large frying pan for about 3 minutes, until browned.
Remove with a slotted spoon.
2 Add the onion to the pan, fry until soft and lightly browned, adding the garlic 2 minutes before the
end of cooking. Stir in the tomatoes and oregano. Simmer over a fairly high heat, stirring occasionally,
for about 10 minutes until thickened. Add the olives, capers and parsley. Season.
3 Meanwhile, cook and drain the pasta according to the packet instructions. Toss with the beef sauce.

* Penne rigate, macaroni rigate or strozzapreti can also be used.

181
bucatini with prosciutto, radicchio, capers & lemon

PREPARATION TIME 10 minutes COOKING TIME 10 minutes SERVES 4

400G (14oz) BUCATINI*
9 THIN SLICES OF PROSCIUTTO, CUT ACROSS INTO
  THIN SLICES
VIRGIN OLIVE OIL
2 GARLIC CLOVES, FINELY CHOPPED

1 HEAD OF RADICCHIO, THINLY SLICED
2 TBSP CAPERS
JUICE OF 1 LEMON, OR TO TASTE
SALT AND FRESHLY GROUND BLACK PEPPER
FRESHLY GRATED PARMESAN, TO SERVE

1 Cook and drain the pasta according to the packet instructions, reserving ½ cup of the cooking water.
2 Meanwhile, fry the prosciutto in olive oil until golden. Add the garlic, radicchio and capers. As soon
as the radicchio wilts, add the lemon juice and remove from the heat. Season lightly with salt
but plenty of black pepper. Toss with the pasta, adding reserved cooking water to moisten.
Serve with freshly grated Parmesan.

* Tagliatelle can also be used.

182
tonnarelli with pork & mushrooms

PREPARATION TIME 10 minutes COOKING TIME 10 minutes SERVES 4

300G (10oz) PORK, CUT ACROSS
  INTO 2.5CM (1IN) WIDE STRIPS
VIRGIN OLIVE OIL
225G (8oz) BROWN-CAP/CHESTNUT
  MUSHROOMS, SLICED

2 GARLIC CLOVES, FINELY CHOPPED
2–3 TSP THYME
2 TBSP LEMON JUICE
SALT AND FRESHLY GROUND BLACK PEPPER
400G (14oz) TONNARELLI

1   Fry the pork strips in some olive oil in a large pan for about 4 minutes, stirring frequently, until they
    have changed colour.
2   Add the mushrooms, garlic and thyme and continue to cook stirring frequently, until the mushrooms are
    tender and the pork is cooked. Stir in the lemon juice and seasoning, using plenty of black pepper.
3   Meanwhile, cook and drain the pasta according to the packet instructions. Toss with the sauce
    and 2–3 tbsp virgin olive oil.

183
penne with chorizo, rocket & tomatoes

PREPARATION TIME 5 minutes COOKING TIME 10 minutes SERVES 2

175G (6oz) PENNE
125G (4½oz) PIECE OF CHORIZO, CHOPPED
OLIVE OIL
250G (9oz) CHERRY OR BABY PLUM TOMATOES,
  HALVED LENGTHWAYS

2 TSP BALSAMIC VINEGAR
2 TBSP TAPENADE
50G (2oz) ROCKET
FRESHLY GROUND BLACK PEPPER

1   Cook the penne according to the packet instructions.
2   Meanwhile, fry the chorizo in a little olive oil in a non-stick frying pan for 2–3 minutes.
    Add the tomatoes and vinegar and cook until the tomatoes are just beginning to collapse.
3   Drain the penne and stir in the tapenade, then the rocket, chorizo mixture and black pepper.

184
tagliatelle with chicken & sage

PREPARATION TIME 10 minutes COOKING TIME 10 minutes SERVES 4

400G (14oz) TAGLIATELLE

2 SHALLOTS, FINELY CHOPPED

KNOB OF UNSALTED BUTTER

325G (11oz) CHICKEN BREAST,
 CUT ACROSS INTO STRIPS

1 GARLIC CLOVE, CUT INTO THIN SLIVERS

8 SMALL SAGE LEAVES, SHREDDED

4 TBSP MEDIUM-BODIED DRY WHITE WINE

SALT AND FRESHLY GROUND BLACK PEPPER

FRESHLY GRATED PARMESAN, TO SERVE

1   Cook and drain the pasta according to the packet instructions, reserving ½ cup of the cooking water.
2   Meanwhile, fry the shallots in the butter until transparent. Add the chicken and fry until golden on
    the outside and just cooked through, but do not overcook. Add the garlic and sage for the final
    2 minutes or so of cooking. Pour in the wine and bubble for a couple of minutes. Season.
3   Toss the chicken mixture with the pasta and enough of the reserved water to moisten.
    Serve with plenty of grated Parmesan.

185
tagliatelle alla bolognese

PREPARATION TIME 5 minutes COOKING TIME 10 minutes* SERVES 4

3-EGG QUANTITY TAGLIATELLE (SEE PAGE 10) OR
 400G (14oz) DRIED TAGLIATELLE

1 QUANTITY RAGÙ (SEE PAGE 16)

50G (2oz) PARMESAN, FRESHLY GRATED

1   Put on a large saucepan of water for cooking fresh pasta, or cook and drain dried pasta according
    to the packet instructions.
2   Meanwhile, reheat the sauce over a low heat, stirring frequently and adding a little water,
    if necessary, to prevent the sauce sticking.
3   Cook and drain fresh pasta. Toss with the ragù and Parmesan.

*   Assumes that the sauce is already made.

186
cavatappi with pork ragù

PREPARATION TIME 10 minutes COOKING TIME 30 minutes SERVES 4

1 SMALL ONION, FINELY CHOPPED
OLIVE OIL
2 GARLIC CLOVES, FINELY CHOPPED
225G (8oz) BROWN-CAP/CHESTNUT MUSHROOMS,
  SLICED
350G (12oz) PORK, CUT INTO QUITE SMALL PIECES
50G (2oz) PROSCIUTTO, CHOPPED

150ML (5FL OZ/SCANT ⅔ CUP) MEDIUM-BODIED DRY
  WHITE WINE
2 TBSP CHOPPED FLAT-LEAF PARSLEY
SALT AND FRESHLY GROUND BLACK PEPPER
375G (13oz) CAVATAPPI*
FRESHLY GRATED PARMESAN, TO SERVE

1   Fry the onion in a little oil until soft. Add the garlic and mushrooms, cook for 2 minutes, then stir in the pork and prosciutto. Cook, stirring, until lightly browned.
2   Add the wine, bubble for a couple of minutes, then add the parsley. Cover and simmer gently for about 20 minutes. Season.
3   Meanwhile, cook and drain the pasta according to the packet instructions. Toss with the ragù and serve with freshly grated Parmesan.

*   Conchiglie, bucatini or tagliatelle can also be used.

187
penne with sausages & mushrooms

PREPARATION TIME 10 minutes COOKING TIME 15 minutes SERVES 4

1 ONION, FINELY CHOPPED
2 GARLIC CLOVES, FINELY CHOPPED
PINCH OF CHILLI FLAKES
250G (9oz) GOOD-QUALITY SPICY FRESH ITALIAN (OR
  FRENCH) SAUSAGES, SKINS REMOVED
VIRGIN OLIVE OIL
350G (12oz) BROWN-CAP/CHESTNUT
  MUSHROOMS, CHOPPED

1 TBSP THYME
SALT AND FRESHLY GROUND BLACK PEPPER
400G (14oz) PENNE
40G (1½oz) UNSALTED BUTTER, DICED
LEAVES FROM A SMALL HANDFUL OF
  FLAT-LEAF PARSLEY
50G (2oz) PARMESAN, FRESHLY GRATED,
  PLUS EXTRA TO SERVE

1   Fry the onion, garlic, chilli and sausagemeat in a little oil until lightly browned, stirring frequently to break up the sausagemeat. Add the mushrooms and thyme and cook until the liquid from the mushrooms has evaporated but do not let them become too dry. Season.
2   Meanwhile, cook and drain the penne according to the packet instructions, reserving ½ cup of the cooking water.
3   Off the heat, add the butter to the mushrooms, then toss with the pasta, parsley and Parmesan, and enough of the reserved cooking water to moisten.

188
elicoidali, sausages & peppers al forno

PREPARATION TIME 10 minutes COOKING TIME 35—40 minutes SERVES 4

325G (11oz) ELICOIDALI*
1 CHILLI, SEEDED AND SLICED INTO RINGS
450ML (16FL OZ/1¾ CUPS) PASSATA
150G (5oz) DRAINED GRILLED RED AND YELLOW
   PEPPERS SLICES IN OIL

150G (5oz) BUFFALO MOZZARELLA, TORN INTO PIECES
5 TBSP BASIL LEAVES, TORN
SALT AND FRESHLY GROUND BLACK PEPPER
250G (9oz) WELL-FLAVOURED ITALIAN (OR FRENCH)
   SAUSAGES, SKINS REMOVED

1   Preheat the oven to 200°C/400°F/gas 6.
2   Cook and drain the pasta according to the packet instructions, but giving it 1—2 minutes
    less than normal. Reserve about 4 tbsp of the cooking water.
3   Stir the reserved cooking water into the passata, then gently combine with the pasta, peppers,
    cheese, basil and seasoning.
4   Using damp hands, form the sausagemeat into 12 golf ball-sized balls. Gently stir into the pasta.
    Transfer to a large gratin dish and bake in the preheated oven for 25—30 minutes until
    the sausage balls are cooked and the cheese is bubbling.

*   Penne rigate can also be used.

115

189
strozzapreti with sausages, onions & peppers

PREPARATION TIME 10 minutes COOKING TIME 35 minutes SERVES 4—6

400G (14oz) WELL-FLAVOURED ITALIAN (OR
   FRENCH) SAUSAGES
1 LARGE ONION, HALVED LENGTHWAYS AND SLICED
VIRGIN OLIVE OIL

2 EACH RED AND YELLOW PEPPERS, GRILLED,
   PEELED AND SLICED (SEE PAGE 67)
SALT AND FRESHLY GROUND BLACK PEPPER
400G (14oz) STROZZAPRETI
2 TBSP SHREDDED BASIL

1   Preheat the oven to 180°C/350°F/gas 4.
2   Put the sausages into a shallow baking dish, pour a little water around them and
    bake in the preheated oven for 25 minutes.
3   Meanwhile, fry the onion in some oil until soft and brown.
    Stir in the peppers and seasoning. Remove from the heat.
4   Slice the sausages while they are still in the dish, using a knife and fork or scissors.
    Stir in the onion and peppers and return to the oven for 10 minutes.
5   During this time, cook and drain the pasta according to the packet instructions.
    Toss with the sausage mixture and the basil.

190
orecchiette with cauliflower, chorizo & black olives

PREPARATION TIME 10 minutes COOKING TIME 10 minutes SERVES 4

400g (14oz) ORECCHIETTE
I SMALL-MEDIUM CAULIFLOWER, DIVIDED
  INTO FLORETS
I ONION, CHOPPED

200g (7oz) PIECE OF CHORIZO, CHOPPED
OLIVE OIL
24 OIL-CURED PITTED BLACK OLIVES, HALVED
CHOPPED FLAT-LEAF PARSLEY, TO SERVE

1   Cook and drain the pasta according to the packet instructions.
2   Meanwhile, boil the cauliflower until just tender. Drain, reserving about ½ cup of the cooking water.
    About 1 minute before the pasta is cooked, add half of the cauliflower, to warm through.
3   While the cauliflower is cooking, fry the onion and chorizo in a little olive oil until the onion is soft
    and transparent. Stir in the remaining cauliflower for 2–3 minutes. Toss with the pasta and olives
    and add enough reserved cooking water, if necessary, to moisten. Serve sprinkled with parsley.

191

tagliatelle with parma ham, peas & lemon

PREPARATION TIME 10 minutes COOKING TIME 10 minutes SERVES 4

300G (10oz) TAGLIATELLE

2 SHALLOTS, FINELY CHOPPED

SMALL KNOB OF UNSALTED BUTTER

150G (5oz) SHELLED FRESH, OR FROZEN, PEAS

200G (7oz/¾ CUP) CRÈME FRAÎCHE

4 TBSP MILK OR SINGLE CREAM

FINELY GRATED ZEST AND JUICE OF I LEMON, PLUS
  EXTRA LEMON ZEST TO SERVE

3 TBSP FRESHLY GRATED PARMESAN

8 SLICES OF PARMA HAM, CUT INTO STRIPS

2 TBSP SHREDDED BASIL

SALT AND FRESHLY GROUND BLACK PEPPER

PARMESAN SHAVINGS, TO SERVE

1   Cook and drain the pasta according to the packet instructions.
2   Meanwhile, soften the shallots in the butter, without browning. Add the peas, crème fraîche, milk or cream
    and lemon zest and juice. Heat through gently.
3   Toss with the pasta, Parmesan, Parma ham, basil and seasoning, using not too much salt but plenty
    of black pepper. Sprinkle with lemon zest and serve topped with Parmesan shavings.

192

mediterranean chicken & pasta al forno

PREPARATION TIME 15 minutes COOKING TIME I hour SERVES 4

350G (12oz) SKINLESS, BONELESS CHICKEN THIGHS,
  THICKLY SLICED ACROSS

VIRGIN OLIVE OIL

I SMALL ONION, CHOPPED

2 GARLIC CLOVES, FINELY CHOPPED

I TBSP THYME LEAVES

70ML (2½FL OZ/¼ CUP) DRY WHITE VERMOUTH

400G CAN CHOPPED PLUM TOMATOES

275ML (9½FL OZ/SCANT 1¼ CUPS) PASSATA

2 TBSP SUN-DRIED TOMATO PASTE

SALT AND FRESHLY GROUND BLACK PEPPER

200G (7oz/¾ CUP) RICOTTA

5 TBSP PESTO (SEE PAGE 18)

115G (4oz) CONCHIGLIE*

50G (2oz) PITTED BLACK OLIVES

WHITE SAUCE

25G (1oz/1½ TBSP) UNSALTED BUTTER

3 TBSP PLAIN FLOUR

425ML (15FL OZ/1¾ CUPS) MILK

1   Fry the chicken thighs in a little oil, turning frequently, until just cooked; take care not to overcook.
    Remove with a slotted spoon.
2   Fry the onion in the oil until softened, then add the garlic and thyme and fry for 2 minutes.
    Pour in the vermouth. Bubble for a couple of minutes or so, then add the tomatoes, passata
    and sun-dried tomato paste. Simmer for 15–20 minutes until reduced by about one third. Season.
3   Meanwhile, make the simple white sauce (see page 17), and leave to simmer gently for 10–15 minutes.
    Off the heat, whisk the ricotta and pesto into the white sauce.
4   Preheat the oven to 200°C/400°F/gas 6.
5   While the sauce is cooking, cook and drain the pasta according to packet instructions but for 1½ minutes
    less than usual. Combine with the chicken, olives and tomato sauce. Transfer to a large, shallow baking
    dish. Spoon the white sauce over and bake in the oven for about 30 minutes until golden.
    Leave to stand for 5 minutes before serving.

*   Other pasta shapes such as farfalle, fusilli or macaroni can also be used.

193
vermicelli, chorizo & mozzarella torta

PREPARATION TIME 5 minutes COOKING TIME 20 minutes SERVES 4

300G (10oz) VERMICELLI

3–4 TBSP OLIVE OIL

200G (7oz) BUFFALO MOZZARELLA, VERY
   THINLY SLICED

8–12 BASIL LEAVES

100G (3½oz) CHORIZO, VERY FINELY SLICED

PINCH OF CHILLI FLAKES

SALT AND FRESHLY GROUND BLACK PEPPER

3 LARGE EGGS, BEATEN

GRILLED RED PEPPERS (SEE PAGE 67), TO SERVE
   (OPTIONAL)

1   Cook and drain the vermicelli according to the packet instructions. Rinse under running cold water
   and leave to cool.

2   Pour a little oil into a large frying pan, preferably non-stick, and spread an even layer of half the
   vermicelli on the base. Top with the mozzarella, basil leaves, chorizo and then the remaining vermicelli.

3   Season the eggs and add the chilli flakes. Pour over the vermicelli in the pan, prodding the pasta with
   a fork to allow the eggs to seep through to the base. Cook over a medium heat for 8 minutes until
   the underneath is golden.

4   Put a large plate over the top. Flip the pan over so the torta falls on to the plate. Add a little more
   oil to the pan and slide the torta back in. Cook for a further 5–6 minutes until the other side is
   golden. Flip out of the pan on to a warmed serving plate. Serve in large wedges, accompanied by
   grilled peppers, if liked.

194
penne rigate with sausages al forno

PREPARATION TIME 10 minutes COOKING TIME 30 minutes SERVES 4–6

350G (12oz) LAGUENGA OR OTHER FRESH
  ITALIAN SAUSAGES
OLIVE OIL
1 ONION, FINELY CHOPPED
2 GARLIC CLOVES, CHOPPED
115ML (4FL OZ/SCANT ½ CUP) MEDIUM-BODIED DRY
  WHITE WINE
2 X 400G CANS CHOPPED TOMATOES

6 SUN-DRIED TOMATOES IN OIL, DRAINED AND SLICED
12 PITTED BLACK OLIVES, SLICED
2 TBSP CHOPPED FRESH OREGANO
2 TBSP CHOPPED FLAT-LEAF PARSLEY
SALT AND FRESHLY GROUND BLACK PEPPER
400G (14oz) PENNE RIGATE
175G (6oz) MOZZARELLA, GRATED
50G (2oz) PARMESAN, SHAVED

1   Preheat the oven to 200°C/400°F/gas 6.
2   Fry the sausages in a little oil in a large frying pan until lightly browned. Remove and slice.
3   Fry the onion and garlic in the pan until softened and lightly coloured. Pour in the wine, bubble until reduced by about two-thirds, then stir in the tomatoes. Add the sausage slices, sun-dried tomatoes and olives and cook, uncovered, for about 15 minutes until just lightly reduced. Add the herbs and seasoning.
4   Meanwhile, cook the pasta according to the packet instructions but giving it about 2 minutes less than usual, then drain.
5   Tip the pasta into a large oiled baking dish and stir in the tomato mixture. Scatter over the mozzarella and then the Parmesan. Bake in the preheated oven for about 15 minutes until bubbling. Leave to stand for 5 minutes before serving.

195
tonnarelli with meatballs
& grilled tomato sauce

PREPARATION TIME 15 minutes*, plus 30 minutes chilling COOKING TIME 10 minutes* SERVES 4

85G (3oz) CRUSTLESS BREAD, CRUMBLED
2 TBSP MILK
225G (8oz) MINCED PORK
115G (4oz) MORTADELLA, FINELY CHOPPED
1 GARLIC CLOVE, FINELY CHOPPED
2 TBSP FINELY CHOPPED FLAT-LEAF PARSLEY
1 EGG, BEATEN

2 TBSP FRESHLY GRATED PARMESAN,
  PLUS EXTRA TO SERVE
SALT AND FRESHLY GROUND BLACK PEPPER
OLIVE OIL
400G (14oz) TONNARELLI**
1 QUANTITY GRILLED TOMATO SAUCE
  (SEE PAGE 18), WARMED

1   Soak the bread in the milk for a few minutes until it is no longer dry. Combine with the pork, mortadella, garlic, parsley, egg, Parmesan and seasoning. With wet hands, break off walnut-sized pieces and roll into balls. Cover and chill for 30 minutes, to firm up.
2   Fry the balls in batches in a large frying pan in a little oil for 4–5 minutes per batch, until browned and crisp, turning the balls over a couple of times.
3   Meanwhile, cook and drain the pasta according to the packet instructions. Toss with the meatballs and warmed sauce. Serve sprinkled with Parmesan.

*   Assumes sauce is already made.
**   Bucatini, spaghetti or bigoli can also be used.

196
light tagliatelle alla bolognese

PREPARATION TIME 5 minutes COOKING TIME 40–50 minutes SERVES 4

1 LARGE ONION, CHOPPED
OLIVE OIL
2 GARLIC CLOVES, CHOPPED
225G (8OZ) LEAN MINCED BEEF
115G (4OZ) RED LENTILS
450ML (16FL OZ/1¾ CUPS) BEEF OR VEGETABLE STOCK
400G CAN CHOPPED TOMATOES

2–3 TBSP SUN-DRIED TOMATO PASTE
1–1½ TBSP DIJON MUSTARD
2–3 TSP HERBES DE PROVENCE
SALT AND FRESHLY GROUND BLACK PEPPER
250G (9OZ) TAGLIATELLE
FRESHLY GRATED PARMESAN, TO SERVE (OPTIONAL)

1   Fry the onion in a little oil in a heavy pan or flameproof casserole until soft and golden, adding the garlic for the final 2 minutes of cooking.
2   Stir in the meat to break it up and cook, stirring occasionally, until it has changed colour. Add the lentils, stock, tomatoes, tomato paste, mustard, herbs and seasoning. Heat just to simmering point, then cook very gently for 30–40 minutes until the beef is tender. Add a little more liquid if it becomes too dry.
3   About 10 minutes before the sauce is ready, cook and drain the tagliatelle, according to the packet instructions. Toss lightly with the sauce, and serve with freshly grated Parmesan, if liked.

197
spiced chicken tortellini

PREPARATION TIME 55–65 minutes COOKING TIME 15–20 minutes SERVES 4

150G (5OZ) SKINLESS CHICKEN BREAST, CUT INTO
   1CM (½IN) PIECES
VIRGIN OLIVE OIL
50G (2OZ) SPICY SALAMI, FINELY CHOPPED
150G (5OZ/SCANT ⅔ CUP) RICOTTA
1 EGG YOLK

50G (2OZ) PARMESAN, FRESHLY GRATED
SALT AND FRESHLY GROUND BLACK PEPPER
2-EGG QUANTITY PASTA DOUGH (SEE PAGE 10)
175ML (6FL OZ/SCANT ¾ CUP) SINGLE CREAM
2–3 TSP PESTO (SEE PAGE 18), TO TASTE

1   Cook the chicken in a little oil over a fairly low heat, stirring, until just cooked through. Using a slotted spoon, transfer to paper towels to drain.
2   Chop the chicken finely in a food processor using the pulse button; do not reduce to a paste. Tip into a bowl and mix with the salami, ricotta, egg yolk, Parmesan and seasoning.
3   Make tortellini with the pasta dough and filling (see page 11). Bring a large saucepan of water to the boil for the tortellini.
4   Meanwhile, warm the cream and pesto, to taste, in a small pan over a low heat.
5   Cook the tortellini, in batches, if necessary, in gently simmering water for 4–5 minutes. Drain well and serve with the pesto sauce.

penne with chicken, leeks & gorgonzola

PREPARATION TIME 10 minutes COOKING TIME 15 minutes SERVES 4

115G (4oz) SLIM LEEKS, THINLY SLICED
2 GARLIC CLOVES, FINELY CHOPPED
SMALL KNOB OF UNSALTED BUTTER
2 SKINLESS CHICKEN BREASTS,
    CUT ACROSS INTO THIN STRIPS
150ML (5FL OZ/SCANT ⅔ CUP) MEDIUM-BODIED DRY
    WHITE WINE

150ML (5FL OZ/SCANT ⅔ CUP) CRÈME FRAÎCHE
SALT AND FRESHLY GROUND BLACK PEPPER
400G (14oz) PENNE
85G (3oz) GORGONZOLA, DICED
FRESHLY GRATED PARMESAN,
    TO SERVE

1   Fry the leeks and garlic in the butter until soft. Add the chicken and continue cooking, stirring occasionally, until the chicken changes colour.
2   Pour in the wine, boil until reduced by half, then add the crème fraîche and bubble until slightly thickened. Season.
3   Meanwhile, cook and drain the penne according to the packet instructions. Toss with the Gorgonzola and sauce; return to a low heat if the cheese does not start to melt. Serve with freshly grated Parmesan.

MEAT & POULTRY

bigoli with lamb, tomatoes & olives

PREPARATION TIME 10 minutes COOKING TIME 25 minutes SERVES 4

300G (10oz) LEAN LAMB, SUCH AS FILLET END OF
    LEG, CUT ACROSS INTO 1CM (½IN) WIDE STRIPS
VIRGIN OLIVE OIL
2 GARLIC CLOVES, FINELY CHOPPED
1 TSP DRIED OREGANO
400G CAN CHOPPED TOMATOES

10 PITTED KALAMATA OLIVES, CHOPPED
2 TBSP CAPERS
2 TBSP CHOPPED FLAT-LEAF PARSLEY
SALT AND FRESHLY GROUND BLACK PEPPER
400G (14oz) BIGOLI*

1   Fry the lamb in a little olive oil in a large frying pan for about 3–4 minutes until evenly browned, adding the garlic and oregano for the last 1½–2 minutes.
2   Stir in the tomatoes, olives and capers. Heat until just simmering, then simmer very gently for about 15 minutes, stirring occasionally, until the sauce has thickened slightly and the lamb is tender. Add the parsley and seasoning.
3   Meanwhile, cook and drain the pasta according to the packet instructions. Toss with the sauce.

*   Penne can also be used.

200

chicken & leek lasagne

PREPARATION TIME 10 minutes COOKING TIME 1 hour SERVES 6–8

1 LITRE (1¾ PINTS/4 CUPS) GOOD CHICKEN STOCK
150ML (5FL OZ/⅔ CUP) DRY WHITE VERMOUTH
450G (1LB) BONELESS, SKINLESS CHICKEN LEGS (OR
    BREASTS, IF PREFERRED)
BOUQUET GARNI OF 3 THYME SPRIGS, 1 BAY LEAF
    TORN ACROSS AND 2 SAGE LEAVES
200G (7OZ) SPINACH LASAGNE
450g (1LB) LEEKS, THICKLY SLICED
2 GARLIC CLOVES, FINELY CHOPPED

150G (5OZ/⅔ CUP) UNSALTED BUTTER
100G (3½OZ/¼ CUP) PLAIN FLOUR
85G (3OZ) PARMESAN, FRESHLY GRATED
175G (6OZ) FONTINA, GRATED
150G (5OZ/⅔ CUP) RICOTTA
150ML (5FL OZ/SCANT ⅔ CUP) SINGLE CREAM
SALT AND FRESHLY GROUND BLACK PEPPER
3 TBSP PINE NUTS

1   Combine the stock and vermouth. Poach the chicken legs in the stock-vermouth mixture with the bouquet
    garni in a covered pan for about 10 minutes, until lightly cooked. Lift out with a slotted spoon and
    cut into bite-sized pieces. Reserve the liquid and bouquet garni.
2   Cook the lasagne, even if using the no pre-cook type (see page 15), and spread on a tea towel to dry.
3   Preheat the oven to 200°C/400°F/gas 6.
4   Meanwhile, fry the leeks and garlic in 50g (2oz/⅓ cup) of the butter, over a fairly low heat until
    tender and pale gold in colour. Remove with a slotted spoon.
5   Add the remaining butter to the pan and make a simple white sauce (see page 17) with the flour
    and reserved liquid. Discard the bouquet garni. Off the heat, whisk in two-thirds of the Parmesan,
    three-quarters of the fontina, the ricotta and cream. Season, using plenty of black pepper.
6   Spoon a little of the sauce into a large shallow baking dish. Cover with a layer of lasagne, followed
    by chicken, leeks, a sprinkling of Parmesan and then sauce. Continue layering to finish with lasagne,
    sauce and the last of the Parmesan and fontina. Sprinkle over the pine nuts. Bake in the preheated
    oven for about 35 minutes until golden. Leave to stand for 10 minutes before serving.

201

cavatappi with pancetta,
peppers & tomatoes

PREPARATION TIME 10 minutes COOKING TIME 15 minutes SERVES 4

1 ONION, FINELY CHOPPED
VIRGIN OLIVE OIL
85G (3OZ) PANCETTA, CUT INTO STRIPS
1 GARLIC CLOVE, FINELY CHOPPED
PINCH OF CHILLI FLAKES
1 TSP OREGANO
4 TBSP CHOPPED FLAT-LEAF PARSLEY

1 LARGE RED PEPPER, SLICED
450G (1LB) WELL-FLAVOURED PLUM TOMATOES,
    PEELED, SEEDED AND CHOPPED
2 TBSP CAPERS
85G (3OZ) PITTED GREEN OLIVES, QUARTERED
350G (12OZ) CAVATAPPI
50G (2OZ) PARMESAN, FRESHLY GRATED

1   Fry the onion in a little oil until soft and golden. Add the pancetta, garlic, chilli, oregano and half
    the parsley. Cook until the pancetta is crisp but not brown.
2   Add the pepper, cook for 5–6 minutes until tender, then add the tomatoes and cook for a further
    5 minutes, stirring occasionally, until they are no longer watery. Stir in the remaining parsley,
    the capers and olives.
3   Meanwhile, cook and drain the pasta according to the packet instructions.
    Toss with the Parmesan and vegetable sauce.

202
chicken-stuffed pasta shells

PREPARATION TIME 15 minutes COOKING TIME 35 minutes SERVES 4

225G (8oz) BUTTON BROWN-CAP/CHESTNUT
  MUSHROOMS, SLICED
1 ONION, FINELY CHOPPED
175G (6oz) COURGETTES, FINELY CHOPPED
1 RED PEPPER, FINELY CHOPPED
115G (4oz) SKINLESS CHICKEN BREAST,
  FINELY CHOPPED
15G (½oz) FRESH BREADCRUMBS
2 TBSP CHOPPED FLAT-LEAF PARSLEY
SALT AND FRESHLY GROUND BLACK PEPPER
3 TBSP CHICKEN STOCK
16 LARGE PASTA SHELLS, ABOUT 5.5CM (2¼IN) LONG

RED PEPPER AND TOMATO SAUCE
2 LARGE RED PEPPERS (ABOUT 225G/8oz EACH)
1 GARLIC CLOVE, CHOPPED
2 SPRING ONIONS, CHOPPED
350G (12oz) WELL-FLAVOURED TOMATOES,
  SEEDED AND CHOPPED
LEAVES FROM A SMALL BUNCH OF BASIL,
  SHREDDED

1   Fry the mushrooms, onion, courgettes and pepper in a little oil over a moderate heat, stirring occasionally,
    until softened. Mix in the chicken and cook for a further 5 minutes. Add the breadcrumbs, parsley and
    seasoning, and moisten with chicken stock. Bring to the boil and set aside.
2   Cook the pasta shells according to packet instructions but for 1 minute less than usual, and drain well.
3   Meanwhile, make the sauce by cooking the peppers, garlic, spring onions and tomatoes for 15–20 minutes
    until thickened. Purée until almost smooth. Add the basil and seasoning.
4   Preheat the oven to 220°C/425°F/gas 7.
5   Fill the pasta shells with the chicken mixture and arrange in a single layer in a shallow baking dish. Pour
    the sauce around, cover and bake in the preheated oven for 15 minutes or so until heated through.

203
garganelle with chicken & watercress sauce

PREPARATION TIME 10 minutes COOKING TIME 10 minutes SERVES 4

2 SHALLOTS, FINELY CHOPPED

350G (12OZ) BONELESS CHICKEN,
   CUT INTO 1CM (½IN) STRIPS

VIRGIN OLIVE OIL

LEAVES FROM A BUNCH OF MIXED HERBS, CHOPPED

3–4 TBSP BALSAMIC VINEGAR, TO TASTE

SALT AND FRESHLY GROUND BLACK PEPPER

400G (14OZ) GARGANELLE

175G (6OZ) WATERCRESS, COARSE STALKS DISCARDED

1 GARLIC CLOVE, CHOPPED

JUICE OF ½ LEMON

3 TOMATOES, SEEDED AND CHOPPED

1   Fry the shallots and chicken in a little olive oil in a large non-stick frying pan for 3–4 minutes. Add the herbs and balsamic vinegar and cook for 2–3 minutes, stirring, until the chicken is cooked through and flecked in pale gold. Season.

2   Meanwhile, cook and drain the pasta according to the packet instructions, reserving ½ cup of the cooking water.

3   While the pasta is cooking, blanch the watercress in boiling water for 30 seconds. Drain well and purée with the garlic and 4 tbsp virgin olive oil. Season and add lemon juice to taste.

4   Shortly before the pasta is ready, add the tomatoes to the chicken and heat gently. Toss with the pasta and watercress sauce. Add some of the reserved cooking water, to moisten, if necessary.

204
bucatini with sausages & pancetta

PREPARATION TIME 10 minutes COOKING TIME 25 minutes SERVES 4

115G (4oz) PANCETTA, CHOPPED

OLIVE OIL

1 ONION, CHOPPED

1 FLESHY RED PEPPER, CHOPPED

2 GARLIC CLOVES, CHOPPED

175G (6oz) TASTY FRESH ITALIAN (OR FRENCH)
   SAUSAGES, SKINNED AND CRUMBLED

400G CAN CHOPPED PLUM TOMATOES

2 TBSP CHOPPED MIXED PARSLEY,
   SAGE AND THYME, PLUS EXTRA TO SERVE

400G (14oz) BUCATINI

FRESHLY GRATED PARMESAN, TO SERVE

1   Fry the pancetta in a little oil until browned. Remove with a slotted spoon and drain on kitchen paper.
2   Fry the onion in the oil until beginning to colour, adding the red pepper towards the end. Stir in the garlic for 1 minute, then add the sausage meat, stirring to break it up. Cook, stirring, for 3–4 minutes then add the tomatoes, pancetta and herbs. Simmer gently, stirring occasionally, for about 15 minutes until lightly thickened.
3   Meanwhile, cook and drain the pasta according to the packet instructions. Toss the pasta with the sauce and serve with the Parmesan.

205
tagliatelle with bresaola, peas & leeks

PREPARATION TIME 10 minutes COOKING TIME 10 minutes SERVES 4

400G (14oz) TAGLIATELLE

1 SMALL LEEK, HALVED LENGTHWAYS,
   THEN THINLY SLICED

SMALL KNOB OF UNSALTED BUTTER

225G (8oz) SMALL FROZEN PEAS, THAWED

115G (4oz) BRESAOLA SLICES,
   CUT ACROSS INTO STRIPS

SALT AND FRESHLY GROUND BLACK PEPPER

4 TBSP FRESHLY GRATED PARMESAN, PLUS EXTRA
   TO SERVE

1   Cook and drain the pasta according to the packet instructions, reserving ½ cup of the cooking water.
2   Meanwhile fry the leek in the butter until soft. Add the peas and bresaola and cook for about 2 minutes, until warmed through. Season, using plenty of pepper. Toss with the pasta and Parmesan, adding reserved water as necessary. Serve with additional Parmesan.

206
taglioni with parma ham, peas & parsley

PREPARATION TIME 10 minutes COOKING TIME 15 minutes SERVES 4

400G (14oz) TAGLIONI

175G (6oz) FROZEN PEAS

4 SLICES PARMA HAM, CUT ACROSS INTO STRIPS

70G (2½oz) UNSALTED BUTTER, DICED

2 TBSP FINELY CHOPPED FLAT-LEAF PARSLEY

50G (2oz) PARMESAN, FRESHLY GRATED

SALT AND FRESHLY GROUND BLACK PEPPER

1   Cook and drain the pasta according to the packet instructions, adding the peas for the last 2–3 minutes.
2   Toss with the Parma ham, butter, parsley, most of the Parmesan and seasoning. Serve with the remaining Parmesan.

207
conchiglie with chicken, cherry tomato & herb sauce

PREPARATION TIME 10 minutes, plus 1 hour marinating COOKING TIME 20 minutes SERVES 4

350G (12oz) SKINLESS CHICKEN, CUT INTO
 BITE-SIZED PIECES
4 TBSP DRY ITALIAN VERMOUTH
1 TSP FINELY CHOPPED ROSEMARY
LEAVES FROM 3 SPRIGS OF THYME
SALT AND FRESHLY GROUND BLACK PEPPER
1 ONION, FINELY CHOPPED

100G (3½oz) PIECE OF SALAMI, CHOPPED
OLIVE OIL
400G CAN CHERRY TOMATOES
1 TBSP BALSAMIC VINEGAR
PINCH OF CHILLI FLAKES
300G (10oz) CONCHIGLIE
FRESHLY GRATED PARMESAN, TO SERVE (OPTIONAL)

1　Stir the chicken with the vermouth, herbs and black pepper. Cover and set aside for 1 hour.
2　Fry the onion and salami in a little oil until the onion is tender and pale gold. Scoop the chicken from the vermouth and fry quickly, stirring, until the colour has changed. Stir in the vermouth, tomatoes, vinegar and chilli flakes. Simmer gently for about 15 minutes until the chicken is cooked through and the sauce slightly thickened. Season.
3　About 10 minutes before the chicken is done, cook and drain the pasta according to the packet instructions. Toss with the sauce, and serve with a little freshly grated Parmesan, if liked.

208
pasta with pork, spinach & lemon

PREPARATION TIME 10 minutes COOKING TIME 15 minutes SERVES 4

400G (14oz) PORK FILLET
VIRGIN OLIVE OIL
2 GARLIC CLOVES, FINELY CHOPPED
300ML (10FL OZ/SCANT 1¼ CUPS) MEDIUM-BODIED
 DRY WHITE WINE
1 TBSP FINELY CHOPPED ROSEMARY
115ML (4FL OZ/SCANT ½ CUP) DOUBLE CREAM

675G (1½LB) BABY SPINACH
400G (14oz) FRESH PAPPARDELLE
JUICE OF 1½ LARGE OR 2 SMALL LEMONS, TO TASTE
85G (3oz) PARMESAN, FRESHLY GRATED,
 PLUS EXTRA TO SERVE
SALT AND FRESHLY GROUND BLACK PEPPER

1　Cover the pork with clingfilm and flatten with a meat bat, rolling pin or the bottom of a heavy pan. Cut into thick strips, then fry quickly in a little oil in a large, heavy frying pan until browned. Remove and keep warm.
2　Fry the garlic for 1 minute, then add the wine and rosemary and boil until reduced by at least half. Pour in the cream and heat through gently. Return the pork to the pan.
3　Meanwhile, put the pan of water for the pasta on to boil. Cook the spinach in a large pan, stirring or shaking the pan occasionally, until wilted and excess water has evaporated.
4　Cook and drain the pasta. Toss with the spinach, pork and cooking juices, the lemon juice, Parmesan and seasoning. Serve with additional Parmesan.

chicken & walnut cannelloni

PREPARATION TIME 15 minutes COOKING TIME 35 minutes SERVES 4

12 CANNELLONI TUBES

175G (6oz) COOKED SKINLESS CHICKEN, MINCED

50G (2oz) WALNUT HALVES, LIGHTLY TOASTED AND
  FINELY CHOPPED

115G (4oz) RICOTTA

115G (4oz/SCANT ½ CUP) COTTAGE CHEESE, SIEVED

2–3 TSP FINELY CHOPPED FLAT-LEAF PARSLEY

SALT AND FRESHLY GROUND BLACK PEPPER

½ QUANTITY FRESH TOMATO SAUCE (SEE PAGE 18)
  OR WINTER TOMATO SAUCE (SEE PAGE 19)

25G (1oz) PARMESAN, FRESHLY GRATED

BÉCHAMEL SAUCE

25G (1oz/1½ TBSP) BUTTER

3 TBSP PLAIN FLOUR

425ML (15FL OZ/1¾ CUPS) MILK

1 Preheat the oven to 180°C/350°F/gas 4.
2 Cook and drain the cannelloni tubes according to the packet instructions.
3 Meanwhile, make the béchamel sauce (see page 17).
4 Combine the chicken with all but 1 tbsp walnuts, the ricotta, cottage cheese, parsley and seasoning.
   Divide among the cannelloni tubes.
5 Spread a little of the tomato sauce in the bottom of a large gratin dish. Lay the filled tubes on top and
   cover with the remaining sauce. Scatter over the Parmesan and reserved walnuts. Cover and bake in the
   preheated oven for 15 minutes, then uncover and bake for a further 20 minutes until the top is browned.

MEAT & POULTRY

127

chicken & spinach pasticcio

PREPARATION TIME 15 minutes COOKING TIME 45 minutes SERVES 4–6

500G (1LB 2oz) SPINACH

115G (4oz) TAGLIATELLE

500G (1LB 2oz) BONELESS SKINLESS CHICKEN LEGS,
  QUITE FINELY CHOPPED

OLIVE OIL

2 PLUMP GARLIC CLOVES, CHOPPED

PINCH OF CHILLI FLAKES

1½ TBSP SUN-DRIED TOMATO PASTE

85G (3oz) PARMESAN, FRESHLY GRATED

BÉCHAMEL SAUCE

25G (1oz/1½ TBSP) UNSALTED BUTTER

3 TBSP PLAIN FLOUR

570ML (1 PINT/SCANT 1½ CUPS) MILK

1 Preheat the oven to 200°C/400°F/gas 6.
2 Cook the spinach in a covered pan until wilted, shaking the pan occasionally. Drain and squeeze out
   surplus moisture.
3 Meanwhile, cook and drain the pasta according to the packet instructions, but for 1 minute less than the
   recommended time.
4 While the pasta is cooking, fry the chicken in a little oil for 2–3 minutes, add the garlic and chilli flakes
   and fry for a further 2 minutes, stirring in the tomato paste just before the end. Spoon evenly into a
   large, shallow baking dish. Cover with the spinach.
5 While the chicken is cooking, make the béchamel sauce (see page 17). Gently combine with the
   pasta and pour over the spinach. Sprinkle the cheese over the top and bake in the preheated
   oven for 20–25 minutes until golden brown. Leave to stand for 5 minutes before serving.

211
lumache with prosciutto, rocket & capers

PREPARATION TIME 10 minutes COOKING TIME 10–15 minutes SERVES 4

400G (14oz) LUMACHE

2 SHALLOTS, FINELY CHOPPED

2 GARLIC CLOVES, FINELY CHOPPED

LEAVES FROM 2 SMALL SPRIGS OF SAGE,
    FINELY SHREDDED

OLIVE OIL

115G (4oz) PROSCIUTTO, CUT ACROSS INTO STRIPS

400G CAN CHERRY TOMATOES

400G CAN CHICKPEAS, DRAINED AND RINSED

FRESHLY GROUND BLACK PEPPER

2 HANDFULS OF YOUNG ROCKET

85G (3oz) FETA, CRUMBLED

1   Cook and drain the lumache according to the packet instructions.
2   Meanwhile, fry the shallots, garlic and sage in a little oil for about 4 minutes until the shallots are soft
    and translucent. Add the prosciutto halfway through the cooking.
3   Add the tomatoes and chickpeas, bring to the boil, then simmer for about 10 minutes until the sauce
    has thickened slightly. Season with black pepper (the salt in the prosciutto and feta should make extra
    salt unnecessary). Toss with the pasta, rocket and feta.

212
strappiozi with sausages,
mixed peppers & tomatoes

PREPARATION TIME 10 minutes COOKING TIME 10 minutes SERVES 4

175G (6oz) GOOD-QUALITY FRESH ITALIAN (OR
    FRENCH) SAUSAGES, CUT INTO 1CM (½IN) SLICES

VIRGIN OLIVE OIL

1 SMALL ONION, THINLY SLICED

1 PLUMP RED PEPPER, SLICED

1 PLUMP YELLOW OR ORANGE PEPPER, SLICED

2 LARGE RIPE WELL-FLAVOURED TOMATOES, SEEDED
    AND CHOPPED

SALT AND FRESHLY GROUND BLACK PEPPER

400G (14oz) STRAPPIOZI

25G (1oz) PARMESAN, FRESHLY GRATED, PLUS EXTRA
    TO SERVE

1   Fry the sausages in a little oil until browned. Remove to paper towels to drain. Fry the onion in the oil
    until pale golden brown. Add the peppers and cook until softened but not coloured.
2   At the same time, in another pan, cook the tomatoes in a little oil for about 10 minutes. Add to the
    peppers, with the sausages, and cook together, stirring frequently for 1 minute. Season.
3   Meanwhile, cook and drain the pasta according to the packet instructions. Toss with the sausage sauce
    and Parmesan, and serve with additional Parmesan.

213
agnolotti with asparagus & parma ham

PREPARATION TIME 5 minutes COOKING TIME 15 minutes SERVES 6

675G (1½LB) ASPARAGUS
130ML (4½FL OZ/½ CUP) CRÈME FRAÎCHE
SALT AND FRESHLY GROUND BLACK PEPPER
2 SHALLOTS, FINELY CHOPPED
15G (½OZ/3 TSP) UNSALTED BUTTER

85G (3OZ) PARMA HAM, CUT ACROSS INTO STRIPS
1 QUANTITY HERB AND CHEESE AGNOLOTTI (SEE
PAGE 12), OR BOUGHT FILLED PASTA SHAPE
FRESH SHAVINGS OF PARMESAN, TO SERVE

1   Cut off the asparagus tips and reserve. Cook the remaining stems in boiling water until just tender.
    Drain well, pat dry and purée with a little of the crème fraîche, then mix in the remaining crème
    fraîche and season.
2   Fry the shallots in the butter until soft but not coloured. Add the Parma ham for a couple of minutes,
    then stir in the asparagus purée and warm through very gently.
3   Cook the agnolotti, in batches if necessary, in simmering water, adding the asparagus tips for the final
    2–3 minutes. Drain well and combine with the asparagus purée. Serve sprinkled with Parmesan.

214
conchiglie with broccoli, walnuts & pancetta

PREPARATION TIME 10 minutes COOKING TIME 15 minutes SERVES 4

450G (1LB) BROCCOLI FLORETS
350G (12OZ) CONCHIGLIE
200G (7OZ) PANCETTA, SLICED ACROSS
VIRGIN OLIVE OIL
2 PLUMP GARLIC CLOVES, CHOPPED

50G (2OZ) WALNUT HALVES, LIGHTLY TOASTED AND
CHOPPED
SALT AND FRESHLY GROUND BLACK PEPPER
FRESHLY GRATED PARMESAN, TO SERVE

1   Bring enough water to the boil for cooking the pasta. Add the broccoli and boil for 3–4 minutes until
    just tender. Remove with a slotted spoon. Cook the pasta in the water according to the packet instructions.
2   Meanwhile, fry the pancetta in a little oil until crisp. Add the garlic, cook for 1 minute, then stir in the
    broccoli, walnuts and seasoning. Stir gently for 2–3 minutes to warm through.
3   Drain the pasta, reserving some of the cooking water. Toss the pasta with the broccoli sauce and enough
    cooking water to moisten. Sprinkle over some freshly grated Parmesan, and serve with extra Parmesan.

215
campanelli with chicken, prosciutto & basil

PREPARATION TIME 10 minutes COOKING TIME 15 minutes SERVES 4

4 SKINLESS CHICKEN BREASTS,
   THINLY SLICED ACROSS THE GRAIN
VIRGIN OLIVE OIL
175G (6OZ) PROSCIUTTO SLICES, SLICED ACROSS
150ML (5FL OZ/⅔ CUP) MEDIUM-BODIED DRY
   WHITE WINE

150ML (5FL OZ/⅔ CUP) CHICKEN STOCK
150ML (5FL OZ/⅔ CUP) DOUBLE CREAM
350G (12OZ) CAMPANELLI
1½–2 TBSP LEMON JUICE
3 TBSP SHREDDED BASIL
SALT AND FRESHLY GROUND BLACK PEPPER

1   Stir-fry the chicken in 2 batches in a little oil until just cooked through; do not overcrowd the pan or overcook. Remove with a slotted spoon.
2   Fry the prosciutto in the oil for 2–3 minutes. Remove. Pour the wine and stock into the pan and boil until reduced by half. Add the cream and simmer until syrupy.
3   Meanwhile, cook and drain the pasta according to the packet instructions.
4   Return the chicken and prosciutto to the pan, add the lemon juice, basil and seasoning. Warm through gently. Toss with the pasta, and serve.

216
fettuccine with peas, prosciutto & sage

PREPARATION TIME 10 minutes COOKING TIME 5 minutes SERVES 4

100ML (3½FL OZ/⅓ CUP) SINGLE CREAM
1 LARGE EGG YOLK
150G (5OZ) SHELLED FRESH, OR FROZEN PEAS
3–4 OUTER LETTUCE LEAVES, SHREDDED
1 GARLIC CLOVE, FINELY CHOPPED

VIRGIN OLIVE OIL
8–10 SMALL SAGE LEAVES, FINELY SHREDDED
3 SLICES OF PROSCIUTTO, SLICED INTO RIBBONS
500G (1LB 2OZ) FRESH FETTUCCINE
SALT AND FRESHLY GROUND BLACK PEPPER

1   Stir the cream into the egg yolk and set aside.
2   Boil the peas until just tender, adding the lettuce leaves immediately before the peas are ready. Drain.
3   While the peas are cooking, fry the garlic in about 2 tbsp oil for 1 minute.
    Add the sage and prosciutto and cook for a further minute.
4   Meanwhile, cook and drain the pasta. Toss immediately with the egg yolk mixture,
    the peas and lettuce and seasoning. Serve with the sage and prosciutto scattered over.

217
tagliatelle with peas, prosciutto & basil

PREPARATION TIME 10 minutes COOKING TIME 10 minutes SERVES 4

400G (14OZ) TAGLIATELLE
225G (8OZ) SHELLED SMALL FRESH PEAS
85G (3OZ) UNSALTED BUTTER
115G (4OZ) PROSCIUTTO, CUT ACROSS INTO STRIPS

2 TBSP SHREDDED BASIL
6 TBSP FRESHLY GRATED PARMESAN,
    PLUS EXTRA TO SERVE
SALT AND FRESHLY GROUND BLACK PEPPER

1   Cook and drain the pasta according to the packet instructions.
2   Meanwhile, boil the peas for about 5 minutes, until just tender. Drain and then fry gently in the butter
    with the prosciutto for 2–3 minutes, stirring frequently. Toss with the pasta, basil, cheese and seasoning.
    Serve with extra Parmesan.

218
pappardelle with lamb & rosemary

PREPARATION TIME 10 minutes, COOKING TIME 15 minutes SERVES 4

250G (9OZ) BONELESS LAMB STEAKS,
    CUT ACROSS INTO 2.5CM (1IN) WIDE STRIPS
OLIVE OIL
2 GARLIC CLOVES, CRUSHED
250G (9OZ) CHESTNUT MUSHROOMS, SLICED
1 TSP FINELY CHOPPED ROSEMARY

115ML (4FL OZ/½ CUP) MEDIUM-BODIED
    DRY WHITE WINE
6 TBSP DOUBLE CREAM
SALT AND FRESHLY GROUND BLACK PEPPER
400G (14OZ) PAPPARDELLE
FINELY GRATED LEMON ZEST AND CHOPPED
    FLAT-LEAF PARSLEY, TO SERVE

1   Fry the lamb in a little oil in a large frying pan, stirring frequently, until sealed on the outside.
    Add the garlic, mushrooms and rosemary. Cook, stirring, until the mushrooms are tender.
    Pour in the wine and bubble until reduced by two-thirds. Stir in the cream. Season.
2   Meanwhile, cook and drain the pasta according to the packet instructions, reserving ½ cup
    of the cooking liquid. Toss with the lamb and mushroom sauce, adding enough reserved
    pasta liquid to moisten, if necessary. Sprinkle with lemon zest and parsley, and serve.

219
fusilli with turkey, mortadella & mozzarella

PREPARATION TIME 10 minutes COOKING TIME 50 minutes SERVES 4

I ONION, CHOPPED
I RED PEPPER, CHOPPED
350G (12oz) DICED TURKEY BREAST
115G (4oz) PIECE OF MORTADELLA, CHOPPED
4 TBSP MEDIUM-BODIED DRY WHITE WINE
2 GARLIC CLOVES, CRUSHED
400G CAN CHOPPED TOMATOES

85G (3oz) SUN-DRIED TOMATOES IN OIL,
    DRAINED (OIL RESERVED) AND SLICED
I TSP DRIED OREGANO
I TSP DRIED THYME
SALT AND FRESHLY GROUND BLACK PEPPER
300G (10oz) FUSILLI
225G (8oz) BUFFALO MOZZARELLA, SLICED
2 TBSP FRESHLY GRATED FONTINA

1   Fry the onion and red pepper in a little of the sun-dried tomato oil in a heavy-bottomed pan until soft.
2   Add the turkey and mortadella and fry, stirring frequently, until the turkey has changed colour. Pour in the wine, add the garlic, all the tomatoes and herbs, heat to just on simmering point and cook gently for about 15 minutes, stirring occasionally, until the turkey is just cooked; do not overcook. Season.
3   Preheat the oven to 190°C/375°F/gas 5.
4   Cook the fusilli for 1 minute less than usual. Drain and mix with the sauce. Spread half in a gratin dish. Cover with half the mozzarella, followed by the remaining pasta mixture. Top with the rest of the mozzarella and the fontina.
5   Bake in the preheated oven for 20–25 minutes until bubbling and the top is browned. Leave to stand for 5 minutes before serving.

220
lumache with chicken, aubergine & oregano

PREPARATION TIME 10 minutes COOKING TIME 25 minutes SERVES 4

I ONION, FINELY CHOPPED
OLIVE OIL
2 GARLIC CLOVES, FINELY CHOPPED
350G (12oz) CHICKEN BREASTS OR BONELESS LEGS
    OR THIGHS, CUT INTO 1CM (½IN) CUBES
I SMALLISH AUBERGINE, CUT INTO 1CM (½IN) CUBES
400G CAN CHERRY TOMATOES

2 TBSP SUN-DRIED TOMATO PASTE
12 PITTED KALAMATA OLIVES, HALVED
LEAVES FROM A SMALL BUNCH OF OREGANO,
    CHOPPED
350G (12oz) LUMACHE*
SALT AND FRESHLY GROUND BLACK PEPPER

1   Fry the onion in a little oil until soft and transparent. Add the garlic, fry for 1 minute, then stir in the chicken. Cook over a fairly high heat, stirring, until turning golden on the outside. Remove the mixture from the pan with a slotted spoon and set aside.
2   Add a little more oil to the pan and fry the aubergine until browned. Add the tomatoes and tomato paste and bring to the boil. Lower the heat, return the chicken mixture to the pan with the olives, oregano and seasoning. Cover and simmer very gently for about 15 minutes.
3   Meanwhile, cook and drain the pasta according to the packet instructions. Toss with the chicken sauce.

*   Conchiglie, farfalle, fusilli or sedani can also be used.

221
tagliatelle with chicken, courgettes & red pepper

PREPARATION TIME 10 minutes COOKING TIME 30 minutes SERVES 4

4 SKINLESS CHICKEN BREASTS, ABOUT 115–150G
    (4–5OZ) EACH
1 SMALL RED PEPPER, FINELY CHOPPED
2 TBSP CAPERS
2 TBSP FINELY CHOPPED MIXED FLAT-LEAF PARSLEY,
    THYME AND OREGANO
SALT AND FRESHLY GROUND BLACK PEPPER

2 TBSP VIRGIN OLIVE OIL
2 TBSP DRY WHITE VERMOUTH
2 SMALL COURGETTES, SLICED
400G (14OZ) TAGLIATELLE
1½ TBSP FINELY CHOPPED FLAT-LEAF PARSLEY
FRESHLY GRATED PARMESAN

1   Preheat the oven to 190°C/375°F/gas 5.
2   Lay the chicken breasts in a single layer on a piece of foil that is large enough to enclose them. Scatter over the red pepper, capers, herbs and seasoning. Fold up the sides of the foil and pour over the oil and vermouth. Twist the foil edges tightly together to seal, place on a baking sheet and bake in the preheated oven for 30 minutes until the chicken is cooked through.
3   Meanwhile, fry the courgettes in a little oil until soft and becoming flecked with brown.
4   About 10 minutes before the chicken is ready, cook and drain the tagliatelle according to the packet instructions.
5   Carefully remove the chicken from the foil (keep the cooking juices) and slice across the grain.
6   Toss the pasta with the chicken and reserved juices, the parsley and courgettes. Serve accompanied by freshly grated Parmesan.

222
macaroni, beef & beans

PREPARATION TIME 10 minutes COOKING TIME 30 minutes SERVES 4–6

I ONION, FINELY CHOPPED

I CARROT, FINELY CHOPPED

OLIVE OIL

3 GARLIC CLOVES, CHOPPED

250G (9oz) LEAN MINCED BEEF

I LITRE (1¾ PINTS/4 CUPS) BEEF STOCK

BOUQUET GARNI OF 2 SAGE LEAVES, SPRIG OF
    ROSEMARY AND 2 THYME SPRIGS

400G CAN CHOPPED PLUM TOMATOES

2–3 TBSP SUN-DRIED TOMATO PASTE

400G CAN BORLOTTI BEANS, DRAINED AND RINSED

225G (8oz) MACARONI

SALT AND FRESHLY GROUND BLACK PEPPER

FRESHLY GRATED PECORINO AND CHOPPED FLAT-LEAF
    PARSLEY, TO SERVE

I   Fry the onion and carrot in a little oil in a large pan until softened.
    Stir in the garlic and the beef and cook until lightly browned, stirring to break it up.
2   Pour in the stock, stirring, then add the bouquet garni, tomatoes, tomato paste and beans.
    Heat until just beginning to simmer, then stir in the macaroni and cook, uncovered,
    for 18–20 minutes until the macaroni is tender and the liquid reduced to make a soupy stew.
3   Discard the bouquet garni, season and serve sprinkled with pecorino and flat-leaf parsley.

223
ravioli with squash & prosciutto

PREPARATION TIME 45 minutes COOKING TIME I hour SERVES 4

2-EGG QUANTITY PASTA DOUGH (SEE PAGE 10)

SMALL KNOB OF UNSALTED BUTTER

LEAVES FROM A SMALL BUNCH OF MIXED HERBS,
    SUCH AS PARSLEY, BASIL, TARRAGON AND
    OREGANO, CHOPPED

FRESHLY GRATED PARMESAN, TO SERVE

FILLING

450G (1LB) PIECE OF BUTTERNUT SQUASH

VIRGIN OLIVE OIL

2 TBSP DOUBLE CREAM

I EGG YOLK

85G (3oz) PROSCIUTTO, FINELY CHOPPED

50G (2oz) PROVOLONE, GRATED

1½ TBSP SHREDDED BASIL

1½ TBSP FINELY CHOPPED FLAT-LEAF PARSLEY

SALT AND FRESHLY GROUND BLACK PEPPER

I   While the pasta dough is resting for 30 minutes, make the filling. Preheat the oven to
    190°C/375°F/gas 5. Brush the squash flesh with a little oil and bake in the preheated
    oven for about I hour until soft. Cool slightly and then scrape the flesh into a bowl,
    add the cream and mash with a potato masher or a fork. Mix in the egg yolk,
    prosciutto, provolone, herbs and seasoning.
2   Make the ravioli with the dough and filling (see page 11).
3   Cook the ravioli in simmering water, in batches, if necessary, for about 4 minutes per batch. Drain well.
4   Meanwhile, melt the butter with the herbs. Toss lightly with the ravioli. Serve with Parmesan.

224
gnocchi with chicken ragù

PREPARATION TIME 10 minutes COOKING TIME 25–30 minutes SERVES 4

I RED ONION, FINELY CHOPPED

2 GARLIC CLOVES, FINELY CHOPPED

VIRGIN OLIVE OIL

2 SKINLESS CHICKEN BREAST FILLETS,
  CUT INTO BITE-SIZED PIECES

I RED PEPPER, PEELED AND SLICED (SEE PAGE 67)

I YELLOW PEPPER, PEELED AND SLICED
  (SEE PAGE 67)

LEAVES FROM 3 SPRIGS OF THYME

400G CAN CHOPPED PLUM TOMATOES

85ML (3FL OZ/¼ CUP) RED WINE

HANDFUL OF PITTED GREEN AND BLACK OLIVES

I TBSP CAPERS

SALT AND FRESHLY GROUND BLACK PEPPER

400G (14OZ) GNOCCHI

CHOPPED FLAT-LEAF PARSLEY, TO SERVE

1 Fry the onion and garlic in a little oil until soft and pale gold. Add the chicken,
peppers and thyme and fry quickly, stirring, until the chicken has changed colour.

2 Stir in the tomatoes and wine. Simmer gently for about 15 minutes until the chicken
is cooked through and the sauce slightly thickened. Add the olives and capers. Season.

3 Meanwhile, cook and drain the pasta according to the packet instructions.
Toss with the sauce and sprinkle with plenty of parsley.

MEAT & POULTRY

135

225
elicoidali with artichokes, peppers, courgettes & prosciutto

PREPARATION TIME 10 minutes COOKING TIME 45 minutes SERVES 4–6

400G CAN ARTICHOKES, DRAINED

I PLUMP RED PEPPER, THICKLY SLICED

4 WELL-FLAVOURED PLUM TOMATOES, QUARTERED

I COURGETTE, HALVED LENGTHWAYS AND SLICED

3 GARLIC CLOVES, THINLY SLICED

SPRIG OF ROSEMARY

3 THYME SPRIGS

SALT AND FRESHLY GROUND BLACK PEPPER

VIRGIN OLIVE OIL

6 SLICES OF PROSCIUTTO,
  CUT ACROSS INTO STRIPS

2 TBSP PINE NUTS

350G (12OZ) ELICOIDALI*

FRESHLY GRATED PECORINO, TO SERVE

1 Preheat the oven to 200°C/400°F/gas 6.

2 Put all the vegetables and herb sprigs into a large roasting tin. Sprinkle seasoning over and trickle with
oil. Stir to ensure the vegetables are evenly coated. Roast in the preheated oven for about 45 minutes
until the vegetables have softened and are lightly browned, stirring a couple of times. Add the prosciutto
and pine nuts after 20–25 minutes.

3 Meanwhile, cook and drain the pasta according to the packet instructions.

4 Discard the herb sprigs from the roasting tin. Toss the remaining ingredients,
including the cooking juices in the pan, with the pasta. Serve with pecorino.

* Rigatoni or penne can also be used.

226
bucatini with pancetta, tomatoes, olives & herbs

PREPARATION TIME 10 minutes COOKING TIME 10 minutes SERVES 4

85G (3oz) PANCETTA, CUT ACROSS INTO STRIPS
OLIVE OIL
2 GARLIC CLOVES, FINELY CHOPPED
400G CAN CHOPPED PLUM TOMATOES
2 TBSP MIXED CHOPPED OREGANO,
  THYME, PARSLEY AND SAGE

12 KALAMATA OLIVES, SLICED OFF THE STONES
SALT AND FRESHLY GROUND BLACK PEPPER
400G (14oz) BUCATINI
FRESHLY GRATED PARMESAN, TO SERVE

1   Fry the pancetta in a little oil until just golden. Add the garlic and fry for 1–2 minutes. Stir in the tomatoes, herbs and olives. Simmer gently for about 15 minutes until thickened. Season.
2   Meanwhile, cook and drain the pasta according to the packet instructions. Toss with the sauce and serve with Parmesan.

227
conchiglie with pancetta, peas & ricotta

PREPARATION TIME 10 minutes COOKING TIME 10 minutes SERVES 4

400G (14oz) CONCHIGLIE
115G (4oz) PANCETTA, CUT ACROSS INTO STRIPS
VIRGIN OLIVE OIL
175G (6oz) FROZEN PEAS

150G (5oz) RICOTTA, CRUMBLED
35G (1¼oz) PARMESAN, FRESHLY GRATED
FRESHLY GROUND BLACK PEPPER

1   Cook and drain the pasta according to the packet instructions.
2   Meanwhile, fry the pancetta in a little olive oil until lightly browned and the fat runs, but do not allow it to become crisp. Add the peas and cook for 1–2 minutes, stirring. Toss with the pasta, ricotta, Parmesan and black pepper.

228
tonnarelli with radicchio, rosemary & prosciutto

PREPARATION TIME 10 minutes COOKING TIME 10 minutes SERVES 4

350G (12oz) TONNARELLI
2 GARLIC CLOVES, CHOPPED
LEAVES FROM A SMALL SPRIG OF ROSEMARY,
  FINELY CHOPPED
EXTRA-VIRGIN OLIVE OIL

6 SLICES OF PROSCIUTTO, SLICED
1 LARGE HEAD OF RADICCHIO, SHREDDED
50G (2oz) PARMESAN, FRESHLY GRATED
SALT AND FRESHLY GROUND BLACK PEPPER

1 Cook and drain the pasta according to the packet instructions, reserving ½ cup of the cooking water.
2 Meanwhile, fry the garlic and rosemary in a little oil for 1 minute. Add half the prosciutto and half the radicchio and fry briskly until beginning to wilt. Toss with the pasta, remaining prosciutto and radicchio, the Parmesan and seasoning. Add enough of the reserved cooking water to moisten and serve.

229
lumache with pancetta & artichokes

PREPARATION TIME 10 minutes COOKING TIME 10 minutes SERVES 4

400G (14oz) LUMACHE
185G (6½oz) PANCETTA, CUT ACROSS INTO STRIPS
2 GARLIC CLOVES, FINELY CHOPPED
280G JAR OF GRILLED ARTICHOKES IN OIL, DRAINED
  AND OIL RESERVED, HALVED

2½ TBSP FLAT-LEAF PARSLEY, FINELY CHOPPED
FRESHLY GRATED PARMESAN, TO SERVE

1 Cook and drain the pasta according to the packet instructions.
2 Meanwhile, fry the pancetta in 2 tbsp of the reserved oil until browned. Stir in the garlic for 1 minute, then add the artichokes and parsley. Cover and heat gently, shaking the pan occasionally, until warmed through. Toss with the pasta. Serve with the Parmesan.

230
penne with mushrooms & frazzled prosciutto

PREPARATION TIME 10 minutes COOKING TIME 10 minutes SERVES 4

175G (6oz) THINLY SLICED PROSCIUTTO
OLIVE OIL
2 SHALLOTS, SLICED
2 GARLIC CLOVES, FINELY CHOPPED
225G (8oz) CEPS OR BROWN-CAP/CHESTNUT
  MUSHROOMS, SLICED

3 TBSP MIXED CHOPPED FLAT-LEAF PARSLEY
  AND TARRAGON
SALT AND FRESHLY GROUND BLACK PEPPER
400G (14oz) PENNE
3 TBSP CRÈME FRAÎCHE
FRESHLY GRATED PARMESAN, TO SERVE

1   Briefly fry the prosciutto slices in a little oil in a large frying pan over a high heat; cook in batches, if necessary, so the pan is not crowded. Remove and keep warm.
2   Cook the shallots and garlic in the pan until soft but not coloured. Add the mushrooms and herbs and cook until softened and the liquid has evaporated. Season.
3   Meanwhile, cook and drain the pasta according to the packet instructions, reserving ½ cup of the cooking water. Toss with the crème fraîche, mushroom mixture, and reserved cooking water to moisten, as necessary. Top with the prosciutto and serve with Parmesan.

231
fusilli lunghi chicken with avocado & green pesto sauce

PREPARATION TIME 10 minutes COOKING TIME 15 minutes SERVES 4–6

450G (1LB) FUSILLI LUNGHI*
2 SHALLOTS, FINELY CHOPPED
1 TBSP VIRGIN OLIVE OIL
450G (1LB) CHICKEN BREASTS, CUT ACROSS
  INTO STRIPS
115ML (4FL OZ/SCANT ½ CUP) CRÈME FRAÎCHE

175ML (6FL OZ/SCANT ¾ CUP) PESTO
  (SEE PAGE 18)
1 LARGE, OR 1½ AVOCADO(S),
  CUT INTO 1CM (½IN) PIECES
SALT AND FRESHLY GROUND BLACK PEPPER
FRESHLY GRATED PARMESAN, TO SERVE

1   Cook and drain the pasta according to the packet instructions.
2   Meanwhile, fry the shallots until transparent. Add the chicken and fry until golden on the outside and just cooked through, but do not overcook.
3   Stir in the crème fraîche, pesto and avocado and heat through. Season and toss with the pasta. Serve with the Parmesan.

*   Farfalle, conchiglie, lumache or cavatappi can also be used.

232
lasagne al forno

PREPARATION TIME 15 minutes* COOKING TIME 35 minutes* SERVES 4–6

10–12 LASAGNE SHEETS
1 QUANTITY RAGÙ (SEE PAGE 16)
250G (9oz/1 CUP) RICOTTA, CRUMBLED

250G (9oz) BUFFALO MOZZARELLA,
   THINLY SLICED OR GRATED
3 TBSP FRESHLY GRATED PARMESAN

1   Preheat the oven to 200°C/400°F/gas 6.
2   Cook, drain and rinse the lasagne, even if using the no-pre-cook type (see page 15).
    Spread on a tea towel to dry.
3   Arrange a layer of lasagne over the bottom of over a large shallow baking dish
    (about 30 x 20 x 7.5cm/ 12 x 8 x 3in). Spread with some of the ragù.
    Scatter over about one third of the ricotta and mozzarella, followed by a layer
    of some of the ragù. Reserve some of the ragù for the top and repeat the layering
    of lasagne, ricotta and mozzarella, then ragù, to make four layers of pasta and three
    of filling. Finish with a layer of ragù and sprinkle over the Parmesan.
4   Bake in the preheated oven for about 25 minutes until the top is crisp and golden
    and the lasagne heated throughout. Allow to stand for 5 minutes before serving.

*   Assumes the ragù is already made.

233
strozzapreti with cauliflower, pancetta & parsley

PREPARATION TIME 10 minutes COOKING TIME 15–20 minutes SERVES 4

425G (15oz) CAULIFLOWER, DIVIDED INTO FLORETS
400G (14oz) STROZZAPRETI*
115G (4oz) PANCETTA, CUT INTO THIN STRIPS
VIRGIN OLIVE OIL
2 PLUMP GARLIC CLOVES, CRUSHED

PINCH OF CHILLI FLAKES
SALT AND FRESHLY GROUND BLACK PEPPER
2 TBSP FINELY CHOPPED FLAT-LEAF PARSLEY
4 TBSP FRESHLY GRATED PARMESAN,
   PLUS EXTRA TO SERVE

1   Boil or steam the cauliflower until tender. Cut into 1cm (½in) pieces.
2   Meanwhile, cook and drain the pasta according to the packet instructions, reserving ½ cup of the water.
3   At the same time, fry the pancetta in a little oil until brown but not crisp; add the garlic and chilli
    to cook for the last 1–2 minutes. Stir in the cauliflower pieces, season and fry, stirring occasionally,
    until lightly browned. Add the parsley shortly before the cauliflower is ready.
4   Toss with the pasta and cheese, and moisten with a little of the reserved water, if necessary.
    Serve with freshly grated Parmesan.

*   Farfalle or fusilli can also be used.

234

penne rigate with spinach, prosciutto & crumbled goats' cheese

PREPARATION TIME 5 minutes COOKING TIME 10 minutes SERVES 4–5

450G (1LB) PENNE RIGATE
2 GARLIC CLOVES, CRUSHED
VIRGIN OLIVE OIL
70G (2½oz) PROSCIUTTO, CUT ACROSS INTO STRIPS

225G (8oz) BABY SPINACH
225G (8oz) GOATS' CHEESE, CRUMBLED
FRESHLY GROUND BLACK PEPPER

1   Cook and drain the pasta according to the packet instructions.
2   Meanwhile, fry the garlic in a little oil for 1 minute, then add the prosciutto and cook for a further 2 minutes before adding the spinach. Cook, stirring frequently, until just wilted. Season and toss with the pasta and goats' cheese so that most of the cheese melts; heat gently, if necessary. Serve with freshly ground black pepper.

235

orecchiette with peas, pancetta & sage

PREPARATION TIME 10 minutes COOKING TIME 10 minutes SERVES 4

400G (14oz) ORECCHIETTE
225G (8oz) FRESH PEAS
200G (7oz) PANCETTA, FINELY CHOPPED
1 ONION, FINELY CHOPPED
OLIVE OIL

1 GARLIC CLOVE, FINELY CHOPPED
10 SAGE LEAVES, VERY FINELY SLIVERED,
    PLUS EXTRA FOR GARNISH
3 TBSP FRESHLY GRATED PARMESAN,
    PLUS EXTRA TO SERVE

1   Cook and drain the pasta according to the packet instructions, adding the peas for the last 5 minutes. Drain, reserving a little of the cooking water.
2   Meanwhile, fry the pancetta and onion in a little oil over a low heat until the pancetta and onion are both golden and the onion is soft. Add the garlic and sage, fry for 2–3 minutes, then toss with the pasta, Parmesan and 2–3 tbsp of the cooking water. Serve scattered with the extra sage and Parmesan.

236

eliche with prosciutto, peppers & peas

PREPARATION TIME 10 minutes COOKING TIME 10 minutes SERVES 4

375G (13oz) ELICHE
85G (3oz) SHELLED YOUNG PEAS, OR FROZEN
    PEAS, THAWED
115G (4oz) PROSCIUTTO, FINELY CHOPPED
SMALL KNOB OF UNSALTED BUTTER
SALT AND FRESHLY GROUND BLACK PEPPER

175G (6oz/SCANT ¾ CUP) RICOTTA
2 LARGE, FLESHY RED PEPPERS, GRILLED, PEELED
    AND CHOPPED (SEE PAGE 67)
4 TBSP FRESHLY GRATED PARMESAN, PLUS EXTRA
    TO SERVE

1   Cook and drain the pasta according to the packet instructions, reserving ½ cup of the cooking water.
2   Meanwhile, cook fresh peas in boiling water for 3–4 minutes until just tender. Drain.
3   Fry the prosciutto briefly in the butter and then stir in the cooked fresh, or thawed frozen, peas and cook for 1 minute. Season, taking care with the salt.
4   Blend 1–2 tbsp of the reserved water into the ricotta. Toss with the pasta and vegetables and Parmesan.

237
fusilli lunghi with asparagus & parma ham

PREPARATION TIME 10 minutes COOKING TIME 15 minutes SERVES 4

350G (12oz) SLIM ASPARAGUS SPEARS

400G (14oz) FUSILLI LUNGHI

115G (4oz) PARMA HAM, CUT INTO STRIPS

2 TBSP CHOPPED FLAT-LEAF PARSLEY

SMALL KNOB OF UNSALTED BUTTER

SALT AND FRESHLY GROUND BLACK PEPPER

½ LEMON

ABOUT 5 TBSP FRESHLY GRATED PARMESAN

1 Bring a saucepan of water large enough for the pasta to the boil. Add the asparagus and cook for 3–4 minutes until almost tender. Remove with a slotted spoon and drain on paper towels.

2 Return the water to the boil, add the pasta, cook and then drain according to the packet instructions, reserving ½ cup of the cooking water.

3 Meanwhile, heat the asparagus, Parma ham and parsley in the butter, stirring gently occasionally until warmed through. Season and squeeze over some lemon juice. Toss with the pasta and freshly grated Parmesan, adding reserved cooking water, as necessary, to moisten.

238

tagliatelle with turkey, marsala & mushrooms

PREPARATION TIME 10 minutes COOKING TIME 15 minutes SERVES 4

4 TURKEY ESCALOPES, TOTAL WEIGHT
  ABOUT 450G (1LB)
50G (2OZ/SCANT ¼ CUP) UNSALTED BUTTER
115G (4OZ) CHESTNUT MUSHROOMS, SLICED
115ML (4FL OZ/SCANT ½ CUP) MARSALA

115ML (4FL OZ/SCANT ½ CUP) DOUBLE CREAM
SQUEEZE OF LEMON JUICE
SALT AND FRESHLY GROUND BLACK PEPPER
400G (14OZ) TAGLIATELLE
CHOPPED FLAT-LEAF PARSLEY, TO SERVE

1   Lay the turkey escalopes between 2 sheets of clingfilm. Using a heavy-based saucepan, beat them just to flatten but don't overdo it. Cut across the grain into 3 or 4 pieces each.
2   Heat half the butter in a large frying pan and fry the turkey, in batches so the pan is not crowded, for about 1 minute on each side. Remove and keep warm.
3   Add the remaining butter to the pan and cook the mushrooms, stirring, for about 2 minutes, until tender and their liquid has evaporated. Stir in the marsala to dislodge the sediment and boil until reduced by half. Add the cream and boil until thickened slightly. Season with lemon juice, salt and pepper.
4   Meanwhile, cook and drain the pasta according to the packet instructions.
5   Just before the pasta is ready, return the turkey to the pan and heat through gently. Toss with the pasta and serve sprinkled with parsley.

239

chifferi with lentils & pancetta

PREPARATION TIME 10 minutes COOKING TIME 30 minutes SERVES 4–6

250G (9OZ) UMBRIAN (OR PUY) LENTILS
½ ONION, HALVED THROUGH THE ROOT END
1 ROSEMARY SPRIG
1 SAGE SPRIG
500G (1LB 2OZ) CHIFFERI*
115G (4OZ) PANCETTA, CUT ACROSS INTO FINE STRIPS
3 GARLIC CLOVES, CHOPPED

VIRGIN OLIVE OIL
4 LARGE WELL-FLAVOURED TOMATOES, SEEDED
  AND CHOPPED
HANDFUL OF FLAT-LEAF PARSLEY, CHOPPED
EXTRA-VIRGIN OLIVE OIL, TO SERVE
FRESHLY GRATED PARMESAN, TO SERVE

1   Bring the lentils, onion and herbs to the boil in 3 litres (5 pints/12 cups) water, then simmer for 15–20 minutes until the lentils are tender. Return to the boil, add the pasta, stir and cook until al dente, stirring occasionally.
2   Meanwhile, fry the pancetta and garlic in a little oil until the pancetta is lightly browned. Add the tomatoes and parsley and fry for 3–4 minutes until the tomatoes have softened but not disintegrated completely.
3   Drain the pasta and lentils, reserving about ½ cup of the cooking water. Discard the onion and herbs. Toss the pasta and lentils with the tomato mixture, adding enough of the reserved water to moisten. Serve with extra-virgin olive oil trickled into each portion and with freshly grated Parmesan.

*   Pipe rigate or gnocchi can also be used.

240
lasagne alla bolognese

PREPARATION TIME 15 minutes* COOKING TIME 35 minutes* SERVES 4–6

10–12 LASAGNE SHEETS
1 QUANTITY RAGÙ (SEE PAGE 16)
3 TBSP FRESHLY GRATED PARMESAN

BÉCHAMEL SAUCE
750ML (26FL OZ/3 CUPS) MILK
75G (2½OZ/SCANT ¼ CUP) BUTTER
6 TBSP PLAIN FLOUR

1 Preheat the oven to 200°C/400°F/gas 6.
2 Cook, drain and rinse the lasagne, even if using the no-pre-cook type (see page 15).
   Spread on a tea towel to dry.
3 Make the béchamel sauce (see page 17).
4 Arrange a layer of lasagne over the bottom of over a large shallow baking dish
   (about 30 x 20 x 7.5cm/ 12 x 8 x 3in). Next, spread a thin layer of béchamel over the
   bottom of the dish, followed by lasagne, then ragù (reserving some for the top). Add another layer
   of béchamel, followed by a layer of lasagne. Repeat the layering to make 4 layers of pasta
   and 3 of filling. Finish with a layer of ragù and sprinkle over the Parmesan.
5 Bake in the preheated oven for about 25 minutes until the top is crisp and golden
   and the lasagne heated throughout. Allow to stand for 5 minutes before serving.

* Assumes the béchamel and ragù are already made.

241
cannelloni with sausages & broccoli

PREPARATION TIME 10 minutes COOKING TIME 40 minutes SERVES 4

175G (6OZ) LASAGNE SHEETS
225G (8OZ) BROCCOLI
575ML (1 PINT/2½ CUPS) MILK
ABOUT 50G (2OZ) FRESH BREADCRUMBS
GRATED ZEST AND JUICE OF 1 LEMON
450G (1LB) FRESH ITALIAN PORK SAUSAGES,
   SKINS REMOVED

SALT AND FRESHLY GROUND BLACK PEPPER
50G (2OZ/SCANT ¼ CUP) UNSALTED BUTTER
50G (2OZ/SCANT ½ CUP) PLAIN FLOUR
115G (4OZ) PROVOLONE, GRATED
4 TBSP FRESHLY GRATED PARMESAN

1 Preheat the oven to 200°C/400°F/gas 6.
2 Cook, drain and rinse the lasagne, even if using the no-pre-cook type (see page 15).
   Spread on a tea towel to dry.
3 Meanwhile, boil the broccoli until completely tender, chop coarsely, then purée with 3 tbsp
   of the milk. Combine with the breadcrumbs, lemon zest and juice and the sausagemeat. Season.
4 Make a simple white sauce (see page 17) with the butter, flour and remaining milk. Off the heat,
   stir in the provolone.
5 If the lasagne sheets are large, cut them in half across. Divide the sausage and broccoli mixture
   among the sheets and roll up. Place, seam side down, in a single layer in an oiled large
   shallow baking dish. Pour over the cheese sauce and sprinkle with the Parmesan.
6 Bake in the preheated oven for about 30 minutes until golden and bubbling.

242
chicken & prosciutto cannelloni on spinach & mushrooms

PREPARATION TIME 15 minutes COOKING TIME 50 minutes SERVES 6

350G (12oz) BONELESS CHICKEN

BOUQUET GARNI OF 1 BAY LEAF, 2 THYME SPRIGS,
  1 ROSEMARY SPRIG AND 4 PARSLEY SPRIGS

1 ONION, SLICED

225G (8oz) CANNELLONI TUBES

2 GARLIC CLOVES, FINELY CHOPPED

KNOB OF UNSALTED BUTTER

225G (8oz) CHESTNUT/BROWN-CAP
  MUSHROOMS, SLICED

675G (1½LB) SPINACH, CHOPPED

SALT AND FRESHLY GROUND BLACK PEPPER

25G (1oz/2 TBSP) PLAIN FLOUR

150ML (5FL OZ/SCANT ⅔ CUP) DOUBLE CREAM

150ML (5FL OZ/SCANT ⅔ CUP) MEDIUM-BODIED DRY
  WHITE WINE

175G (6oz) PROSCIUTTO

150G (5oz) PROVOLONE, GRATED

2 TBSP FRESHLY GRATED PARMESAN

1 Put the chicken, herbs and onion into a pan with 425ml (15fl oz/1⅞ cups) water. Cover and bring to a simmer. Lower the heat so the water barely moves and poach the chicken for about 15 minutes. Lift out the chicken. Strain and measure the stock; you will need 300ml (10fl oz/scant 1¼ cups). If necessary, boil it to reduce to the correct amount.

2 Meanwhile, cook and drain the cannelloni tubes (see page 15) and spread on a tea towel to dry.

3 Preheat the oven to 190°C/375°F/gas 5. Oil a shallow 28 x 23cm (11 x 9in) baking dish.

4 Cook the garlic in a little butter for 1 minute. Add the mushrooms and cook for a further 5 minutes until softened, stirring. Add the spinach and cook until wilted, stirring occasionally. Season and spread the spinach mixture in the baking dish.

5 Make a white sauce with a knob of butter, the flour, measured stock, cream and wine (see page 17).

6 Finely chop the chicken with the prosciutto. Season, using little salt but plenty of black pepper, and beat in 150ml (5fl oz/scant ⅔ cup) of the white sauce. Divide among the cannelloni tubes and place in a single layer on the spinach mixture. Add all but 2 tbsp of the provolone to the remaining sauce. Pour over the tubes and sprinkle with the remaining provolone and the Parmesan.

7 Bake in the preheated oven for 30–35 minutes until golden.

243
pork & spinach cannelloni

PREPARATION TIME 10 minutes COOKING TIME 35 minutes SERVES 4

250G (9oz) SPINACH

2 GARLIC CLOVES, FINELY CHOPPED

OLIVE OIL

400G (14oz) MINCED PORK

115G (4oz) PIECE OF MORTADELLA, FINELY CHOPPED

250G (9oz/1 CUP) RICOTTA, BEATEN UNTIL SMOOTH

25G (1oz) PINE NUTS, LIGHTLY TOASTED

SALT AND FRESHLY GROUND BLACK PEPPER

250G (9oz) FRESH LASAGNE SHEETS

1 QUANTITY CHEESE SAUCE (SEE PAGE 17)

3 TBSP FRESHLY GRATED PARMESAN

1 Preheat the oven to 180°C/350°F/gas 4.

2 Cook the spinach in a covered pan, shaking it occasionally. Drain well, pressing out surplus water. Chop.

3 Fry the garlic in a little oil for 1 minute in a large frying pan and then stir in the pork for 4–5 minutes. Stir in the mortadella, spinach, ricotta, pine nuts and seasoning. Remove from the heat.

4 Cook and drain the lasagne sheets (see page 15) and spread on a tea towel to dry.

5 Spread a small amount of the cheese sauce in the bottom of an oiled shallow baking dish.

6 Divide the filling among the lasagne sheets, spreading it along one edge, about 1cm (½in) in. Roll over to form tubes and place seam side down in the baking dish. Pour over the remaining sauce, sprinkle over the Parmesan and bake in the preheated oven for 20–25 minutes until bubbling and browned.

cannelloni with beef, roast shallots & garlic

PREPARATION TIME 5 minutes COOKING TIME 50 minutes SERVES 4

1 HEAD OF GARLIC, DIVIDED INTO CLOVES

5 SHALLOTS

VIRGIN OLIVE OIL

15G (½oz) DRIED MUSHROOMS

115ML (4FL OZ/SCANT ½ CUP) VEGETABLE STOCK, BOILING

500G (1LB 2OZ) LEAN MINCED BEEF

150ML (5FL OZ/SCANT ⅔ CUP) RED WINE

1½ TBSP THYME

ABOUT 8 LASAGNE SHEETS

2 TBSP SUN-DRIED TOMATO PASTE

300ML (10FL OZ/SCANT 1¼ CUPS) SINGLE CREAM

50G (2OZ) FONTINA, FRESHLY GRATED

1 Preheat the oven to 180°C/350°F/gas 4.
2 Put the garlic and shallots in a small roasting tin, trickle over some oil and stir so the shallots and garlic are evenly coated. Bake in the preheated oven for 25 minutes until soft. Leave the oven on, increasing the temperature to 200°C/400°F/gas 6.
3 When the garlic and shallots are cool enough to handle, pop the flesh from the skins of the garlic cloves, peel the shallots and then mash them together
4 Meanwhile, soak the mushrooms in the boiling stock for 20 minutes. Drain (strain and reserve the stock) and chop finely.
5 Cook the meat a little oil in a frying pan, stirring to break up the meat until it has browned. Add the mushroom liquid, mushrooms, wine and thyme and cook gently until most of the liquid has evaporated, but it should not be too dry. Stir in the mashed garlic and shallots.
6 Cook the lasagne, even if using the no-pre-cook type (see page 15), and lay the separate sheets flat on a tea towel. Spoon the meat mixture along one long edge, roll up to enclose the filling and cut each tube in half.
7 Using a greased, shallow baking dish, layer half the tubes, seam side down, half the sauce and half the cheese. Repeat the layering.
8 Stir the sun-dried tomato paste into the cream, pour over the cannelloni, cover with foil and bake in the preheated oven for 10 minutes, then bake uncovered for a further 10–15 minutes until lightly browned.

braised lamb shanks with pasta

PREPARATION TIME 10 minutes COOKING TIME 1½ hours SERVES 6

6 SMALL LAMB SHANKS

OLIVE OIL

1 LARGE ONION, HALVED AND THINLY SLICED

3 GARLIC CLOVES, FINELY CHOPPED

2 SMALL CARROTS, SLICED

2 CELERY STICKS, SLICED

25G (1OZ) DRIED PORCINI MUSHROOMS, FINELY SNIPPED

8 SUN-DRIED TOMATOES, SLICED

400G CAN CHERRY TOMATOES

570ML (1 PINT/2½ CUPS) RED WINE

570ML (1 PINT/2½ CUPS) VEGETABLE STOCK

BOUQUET GARNI OF 1 BAY LEAF AND SEVERAL THYME SPRIGS

115G (4OZ) ELBOW MACARONI

1 Preheat the oven to 170°C/325°F/gas 3.
2 In batches, fry the lamb shanks in olive oil in a large flameproof casserole dish until lightly browned. Set aside.
3 Add the onion, garlic, carrot and celery to the casserole, adding more oil if necessary, and fry until soft and golden. Add the dried mushrooms, sun-dried tomatoes, cherry tomatoes, wine, stock and herbs. Simmer for 10 minutes, then put the shanks on top, cover with a tight-fitting lid and cook in the preheated oven for about 1¼ hours until the lamb is very tender and falling off the bone.
4 Remove the lamb from the casserole, cover and keep warm. Bring the casserole to the boil, add the pasta and simmer until al dente. Serve with the lamb.

246
baked rigatoni alla bolognese

PREPARATION TIME 5 minutes* COOKING TIME 30 minutes SERVES 4–6

450G (1LB) RIGATONI
6 TBSP FRESHLY GRATED PARMESAN
1 QUANTITY RAGÙ (SEE PAGE 16), WARMED
VIRGIN OLIVE OIL

BÉCHAMEL SAUCE
450ML (16FL OZ) MILK
50G (2OZ) UNSALTED BUTTER
50G (2OZ) PLAIN FLOUR
FLAVOURINGS (SEE PAGE 17)

1 Preheat the oven to 200°C/400°F/gas 6.
2 Cook the rigatoni for 2 minutes less than usual, and then drain well.
3 Meanwhile, make the béchamel sauce (see page 17).
4 Toss the pasta with 4 tbsp of the cheese, then the ragù and béchamel sauce. When well mixed, spread evenly in a gratin dish, sprinkle over the remaining Parmesan and trickle over a little oil.
5 Bake in the preheated oven for 15–20 minutes until the top is brown. Allow to stand for 5 minutes before serving.

* Assumes the ragù is already made.

247
pennette with chicken livers & marsala

PREPARATION TIME 10 minutes COOKING TIME 10 minutes SERVES 4

400G (14oz) PENNETTE
2 GARLIC CLOVES, FINELY CHOPPED
4 TSP FINELY CHOPPED SMALL SAGE LEAVES
2 TBSP OLIVE OIL
40G (1½oz/2½ TBSP) UNSALTED BUTTER

350G (12oz) CHICKEN LIVERS,
  CUT INTO SMALL PIECES
4 TBSP MARSALA
4 TBSP MEDIUM-BODIED DRY WHITE WINE
SALT AND FRESHLY GROUND BLACK PEPPER
FRESHLY GRATED PARMESAN, TO SERVE

1   Cook and drain the pasta according to the packet instructions, reserving about ½ cup of the water.
2   Meanwhile, fry the garlic and sage in a little oil and the butter for 2 minutes. Add the chicken livers
    and fry briskly, stirring, for 1–2 minutes until the outside has changed colour.
3   Pour in the marsala and wine and continue to cook briskly to thicken slightly. Season and toss with
    the pasta, sprinkle with freshly grated Parmesan and add enough of the reserved cooking water,
    if necessary, to moisten. Serve with extra Parmesan.

248
tagliatelle with pancetta,
rocket & gorgonzola

PREPARATION TIME 10 minutes COOKING TIME 10 minutes SERVES 4

400G (14oz) TAGLIATELLE
175G (6oz) PANCETTA, CHOPPED
VIRGIN OLIVE OIL
2 GARLIC CLOVES, FINELY CHOPPED
4 TBSP DOUBLE CREAM

SALT AND FRESHLY GROUND BLACK PEPPER
175G (6oz) GORGONZOLA, QUITE FINELY CHOPPED
100G (3½oz) ROCKET
25G (1oz) WALNUT HALVES, CHOPPED

1   Cook and drain the tagliatelle according to the packet instructions, reserving ½ cup of the cooking water.
2   Meanwhile, brown the pancetta in a little oil. Add the garlic, fry for 1 minute, then add the cream. Warm
    through without boiling before seasoning and tossing with the pasta, cheese and rocket. Add enough of
    the reserved cooking water, if necessary, to moisten. Serve with the walnuts scattered over.

249
bucatini with pancetta, tomatoes & chillies

PREPARATION TIME 10 minutes COOKING TIME 30 minutes SERVES 4

1 ONION, FINELY CHOPPED
115G (4oz) PANCETTA, CUT INTO STRIPS
VIRGIN OLIVE OIL
1 GARLIC CLOVE, FINELY CHOPPED
PINCH OF CHILLI FLAKES, TO TASTE
5 TBSP MEDIUM-BODIED DRY WHITE WINE

2 X 400G CANS CHOPPED PLUM TOMATOES
SALT AND FRESHLY GROUND BLACK PEPPER
400G (14oz) BUCATINI
3 TBSP FRESHLY GRATED PARMESAN, PLUS EXTRA
  TO SERVE

1   Fry the onion and pancetta in a little oil until the pancetta is brown but not crisp, and the onion is soft
    and turning golden. Add the garlic and chilli towards the end of the cooking. Pour in the wine and
    bubble until evaporated by about three-quarters. Add the tomatoes and simmer until thickened. Season.
2   Meanwhile, cook and drain the pasta according to the packet instructions. Toss with the sauce and cheese
    and serve with additional cheese.

cannelloni with spinach & prosciutto filling

PREPARATION TIME 15 minutes COOKING TIME 35 minutes SERVES 4

675G (1½LB) SPINACH
6 LASAGNE SHEETS, ABOUT 18 X 7.5CM (7 X 3IN)
115G (4oz) FONTINA, GRATED
12 THIN SLICES PROSCIUTTO
3 TBSP FRESHLY GRATED PARMESAN
1 QUANTITY GRILLED TOMATO SAUCE (SEE
    PAGE 18), WARMED

WHITE SAUCE
50G (2oz/SCANT ¼ CUP) UNSALTED BUTTER
50G (2oz/SCANT ½ CUP) PLAIN FLOUR
300ML (10FL oz/SCANT 1¼ CUPS) MILK

1   Preheat the oven to 200°C/400°F/gas 6.
2   Cook the spinach in a covered pan over a medium heat until wilted.
    Drain well, squeeze out surplus moisture and chop finely.
3   Cook, drain and rinse the lasagne, even if using the no-pre-cook type (see page 15).
    Halve each sheet across and spread on a tea towel to dry.
4   Meanwhile, make the simple white sauce (see page 17) with the butter, flour and milk.
    Stir in the fontina and spinach.
5   Lay a slice of prosciutto on each lasagne sheet, top with the spinach sauce and roll up.
    Place, seam side down and just touching, in a single layer in an oiled large shallow baking dish.
    Pour over the white sauce, sprinkle with the Parmesan and bake in the preheated oven for about
    30 minutes until heated through. Serve with the grilled tomato sauce.

turkey meatballs al forno

PREPARATION TIME 10 minutes COOKING TIME 1 hour SERVES 6

350G (12oz) ZITI*
1.4KG (3LB) WELL-FLAVOURED TOMATOES,
    SEEDED AND CHOPPED
3 GARLIC CLOVES, FINELY CHOPPED
LEAVES FROM A BUNCH OF BASIL, SHREDDED
SALT AND FRESHLY GROUND BLACK PEPPER
500G (1LB 2oz) MINCED TURKEY

LEAVES FROM 4 FLAT-LEAF PARSLEY SPRIGS,
    FINELY CHOPPED
115G (4oz) FRESHLY GRATED PARMESAN
1 EGG, BEATEN
JUICE OF ½ LEMON
OLIVE OIL, FOR FRYING

1   Cook and drain the pasta according to the packet instructions, giving it 2 minutes less than usual.
2   Meanwhile, simmer the tomatoes and two-thirds of the garlic in a pan for 10–15 minutes until most
    of the liquid has evaporated (don't let it become too thick). Add the basil and purée the sauce. Season.
3   While the sauce is cooking, combine the minced turkey, parsley, one-quarter of the Parmesan, the egg,
    lemon juice, remaining garlic and seasoning, preferably using your hands. With wet hands,
    form the mixture into balls approximately 2cm (¾in) in diameter.
4   Preheat the oven to 190°C/375°F/gas 5.
5   Fry the meatballs in batches in a little oil in a large frying pan, for 2–4 minutes
    until brown on the outside but still pink in the centre. Drain on kitchen paper.
6   Gently stir the pasta into the sauce and spoon one-third of the mixture into a deep baking dish,
    such as a soufflé dish. Add a layer of half the turkey balls and sprinkle with one third of the remaining
    Parmesan. Top with another third of the pasta mixture, then the remaining meatballs and half the
    rest of the Parmesan. Finish with the last of the pasta and sprinkle over the last of the Parmesan.
7   Bake in the preheated oven for 30–40 minutes until heated through, then allow to stand for
    5 minutes before serving.

*   Rigatoni can also be used.

MEAT & POULTRY

sausage & aubergine lasagne

PREPARATION TIME 20 minutes COOKING TIME 50 minutes SERVES 6

250G (9oz) **LASAGNE SHEETS**
250G (9oz) **SPICY FRESH ITALIAN SAUSAGES**
375G (13oz) **AUBERGINES, CUT INTO 5MM (¼IN) SLICES**
OLIVE OIL
SALT AND FRESHLY GROUND BLACK PEPPER
85G (3oz) **PARMESAN, GRATED**
175G (6oz) **BUFFALO MOZZARELLA, SLICED**
375G (13oz) **WELL-FLAVOURED TOMATOES, SLICED**

WHITE SAUCE
750ML (26FL oz/3¼ CUPS) **MILK**
70G (2½oz/¼ CUP) **BUTTER**
35G (1¼oz) **PLAIN FLOUR**
1 BAY LEAF, TORN ACROSS

1   Preheat the oven to 180°C/350°F/gas 4.
2   Cook, drain and rinse the lasagne, even if using the no-pre-cook type (see page 15).
    Spread on a tea towel to dry.
3   Meanwhile, grill the sausages until evenly browned. Drain on kitchen paper and then slice thinly.
4   Lay the aubergine slices in a single layer on a large baking sheet (you may need to use 2 sheets),
    brush lightly with oil and season. Grill until tender and brown on both sides.
5   While the aubergines are cooking, make the white sauce (see page 17), adding the bay leaf to the milk.
    Discard the bay leaf when the sauce is ready, then add three-quarters of the Parmesan.
6   Spread a thin layer of the sauce over the bottom of a large shallow baking dish. Cover with a layer of
    lasagne sheets and arrange half the aubergine and sausage slices on top. Add a further layer of sauce,
    one of lasagne and then half the mozzarella. Cover with half the tomatoes, another layer of lasagne
    sheets, the remaining aubergines and sausages, more sauce, lasagne and the rest of the mozzarella
    and tomatoes. Finish with a generous layer of cheese sauce. Sprinkle over the remaining Parmesan.
7   Bake in the preheated oven for about 30 minutes until bubbling and brown.

MEAT & POULTRY

149

253
gnocchi with borlotti beans & pancetta

PREPARATION TIME 10 minutes COOKING TIME 15 minutes SERVES 4

I ONION, CHOPPED

2 GARLIC CLOVES, CHOPPED

VIRGIN OLIVE OIL

100G (3½oz) PANCETTA, CHOPPED

350G (12oz) CANNED CHOPPED PLUM TOMATOES

175G (6oz) COOKED OR CANNED BORLOTTI BEANS

3 TBSP DOUBLE CREAM

3 TBSP CHOPPED FRESH BASIL

SALT AND FRESHLY GROUND BLACK PEPPER

400G (14oz) GNOCCHI

EXTRA-VIRGIN OLIVE OIL AND FRESHLY GRATED
   PARMESAN, TO SERVE

1   Fry the onion and garlic in a little oil in a heavy pan until softened. Add the pancetta and cook until beginning to colour. Stir in the tomatoes and beans, bubble for 5 minutes, then add the cream. Cook gently until heated through. Mash the beans coarsely, or use a hand blender. Stir in the basil and seasoning.
2   Meanwhile, cook and drain the gnocchi according to the packet instructions, reserving a little of the cooking water.
3   Add sufficient of the cooking water to loosen the sauce, if necessary, then toss with the pasta. Serve with extra-virgin olive oil and Parmesan.

254
tortellini with spinach, ricotta & prosciutto

PREPARATION TIME 50–60 minutes COOKING TIME 10–15 minutes SERVES 4

2-EGG QUANTITY PASTA DOUGH (SEE PAGE 10)

50G (2oz) PROSCIUTTO, CUT INTO STRIPS

450G (1LB) SPINACH

200G (7oz/¾ CUP) RICOTTA

I EGG YOLK

SALT AND FRESHLY GROUND BLACK PEPPER

KNOB OF UNSALTED BUTTER

2 GARLIC CLOVES, HALVED

PARMESAN SHAVINGS, TO SERVE

1   While the dough is resting, fry the prosciutto for a couple of minutes.
2   Meanwhile, cook the spinach in a covered pan over a medium heat, until wilted and soft. Drain well and press out surplus moisture. Chop finely. Combine with the prosciutto, ricotta, egg yolk and seasoning.
3   Make tortellini with the pasta and filling (see page 11).
4   Heat the butter in a small pan with the garlic over a medium heat for 3–4 minutes, until the garlic just turns golden. Discard the garlic. Keep the butter warm over a very low heat.
5   Cook the tortellini, in batches if necessary, in simmering water for 3–4 minutes until puffy. Remove with a slotted spoon, drain well and pour over the butter. Serve with Parmesan shavings scattered over.

255
mushroom & salami al forno

PREPARATION TIME 5 minutes COOKING TIME 35 minutes SERVES 4

I ONION, HALVED AND THINLY SLICED
I LEEK, THINLY SLICED
3 GARLIC CLOVES, THINLY SLICED
OLIVE OIL, FOR FRYING
150G (5oz) SALAMI, DICED
225G (8oz) RIGATONI

350G (12oz) CHESTNUT MUSHROOMS, SLICED
2 TBSP CHOPPED FLAT-LEAF PARSLEY
200ML (7FL OZ/¾ CUP) DOUBLE CREAM
SALT AND FRESHLY GROUND BLACK PEPPER
3 TBSP BREADCRUMBS
2 TBSP FRESHLY GRATED PARMESAN

1   Preheat the oven to 200°C/400°F/gas 6.
2   Fry the onion, leek and garlic in olive oil in a frying pan until soft and turning golden. Stir in the salami and cook for 2 minutes.
3   Meanwhile, cook and drain the pasta according to the packet instructions, allowing 1 minute less than usual. Remove the vegetables and salami from the pan with a slotted spoon and add to the pasta.
4   Fry half the mushrooms in the pan over a high heat for 2 minutes. Scoop out and add to the pasta. Repeat with the remaining mushrooms, adding the cream as well to the pasta. Season and toss everything together so the cream coats the other ingredients. Transfer to a baking dish, sprinkle over the breadcrumbs and Parmesan mixed together, and bake in the preheated oven for 20 minutes.

256
tagliatelle with chicken, lemon & basil

PREPARATION TIME 10 minutes COOKING TIME 15 minutes SERVES 4

350G (12oz) TAGLIATELLE
450G (1LB) SKINLESS CHICKEN BREASTS, THINLY
   SLICED ACROSS THE GRAIN
VIRGIN OLIVE OIL
150G (5oz) FROZEN BROAD BEANS, THAWED

JUICE OF I LARGE, JUICY LEMON
3 TBSP CRÈME FRAÎCHE
SALT AND FRESHLY GROUND BLACK PEPPER
LEAVES FROM A SMALL HANDFUL BASIL, SHREDDED
FRESHLY GRATED PARMESAN, TO SERVE

1   Cook and drain the pasta according to the packet instructions, reserving about ½ cup of the cooking water.
2   Meanwhile, fry the chicken in a little oil in a large frying pan until cooked through and golden.
3   Add the broad beans, cook for 2 minutes, then stir in the lemon juice and crème fraîche. Warm through gently. Season and toss with the pasta and basil, and enough of the reserved cooking water, if necessary, to moisten. Serve with grated Parmesan.

vegetable &
vegetarian dishes

Pasta was originally a staple part of the diet of the less well-off. Many people grew their own vegetables so these made the obvious choice for combining with pasta. In some recipes vegetables are given minimal preparation and quickly sliced or chopped, and cooked briefly to maintain their flavours, textures and nutritive value. On other occasions, they can be cooked slowly to mellow and meld the flavours into a rich-tasting sauce; for example, the slow cooking of the onions in Gemelli with Melting Onion Sauce reduces them to a smooth, sweet sauce. For lovers of lasagne there are popular combinations such as spinach and cheese or, for a lighter dish, a vegetable lasagne where the white sauce is replaced by goats' cheese, cream and eggs.

CHAPTER
4

257

torchietti with courgettes, lemon & pine nuts

PREPARATION TIME 10 minutes COOKING TIME 10 minutes SERVES 4

2 PLUMP GARLIC CLOVES, THINLY SLICED
VIRGIN OLIVE OIL
550G (1¼LB) SMALL COURGETTES, PARED
    LENGTHWAYS INTO STRIPS (SEE PAGE 212)
GRATED ZEST AND JUICE OF 1 LARGE LEMON
85ML (3FL OZ/SCANT ⅓ CUP) DOUBLE CREAM

SALT AND FRESHLY GROUND BLACK PEPPER
350G (12oz) TORCHIETTI
2 TBSP FINELY CHOPPED FLAT-LEAF PARSLEY
5 TBSP PINE NUTS, LIGHTLY TOASTED
FRESHLY GRATED PARMESAN, TO SERVE

1   Warm the garlic in 4 tbsp oil for 5 minutes; do not allow to become too hot. Discard the garlic.
2   Fry the courgettes briskly in the garlic-infused oil in batches, until golden. Return all the courgettes to
    the pan with the lemon zest and juice and the cream. Bubble for 2–3 minutes until thickened slightly,
    then season.
3   Meanwhile, cook and drain the pasta according to the packet instructions. Toss with the courgette sauce,
    parsley and pine nuts. Serve sprinkled with Parmesan.

trofie with broccoli sauce

PREPARATION TIME 5 minutes COOKING TIME 20 minutes SERVES 3—4

675G (1½LB) BROCCOLI FLORETS
SALT
2 GARLIC CLOVES, FINELY CHOPPED
VIRGIN OLIVE OIL
225G (8OZ) TROFIE*

115ML (4FL OZ/SCANT ½ CUP) DOUBLE CREAM
3 TBSP LEMON JUICE
2 TBSP FRESHLY GRATED PARMESAN, PLUS EXTRA
   TO SERVE

1   Boil the broccoli in salted water until very tender. Drain, reserving ½ cup of the cooking water.
    Refresh the broccoli under running cold water. Drain and chop quite finely.
2   Fry the garlic in a little oil for 1 minute, then add the broccoli and cook, stirring, for about
    3 minutes, until dry.
3   Meanwhile, cook and drain the pasta according to the packet instructions.
4   Stir the cream and lemon juice into the broccoli and simmer gently for 3—4 minutes. Add enough
    of the broccoli water to give the consistency of single cream. Stir in the Parmesan. Toss with the
    pasta and serve with additional Parmesan.

*   Cavatappi or fusilli lunghi can also be used.

VEGETABLE & VEGETARIAN DISHES

155

eliche with broccoli, breadcrumbs, sultanas & pine nuts

PREPARATION TIME 10 minutes COOKING TIME 10 minutes SERVES 4

50G (2OZ) SULTANAS (OPTIONAL)
300G (10OZ) ELICHE
175G (6OZ) BROCCOLI, CUT INTO FLORETS, STEMS
   QUITE FINELY CHOPPED
1 TBSP SUN-DRIED TOMATO PASTE
85G (3OZ) FRESH BREADCRUMBS

115ML (4FL OZ/SCANT ½ CUP) VIRGIN OLIVE OIL
2 GARLIC CLOVES, FINELY CHOPPED
3 TBSP PINE NUTS
3 TBSP CHOPPED FLAT-LEAF PARSLEY
SALT AND FRESHLY GROUND BLACK PEPPER

1   Soak the sultanas, if using, in a little boiling water for 5 minutes.
2   Cook the pasta according to the packet instructions, adding the broccoli 4—5 minutes before the end.
    Drain, reserving 1 tbsp of the cooking water and mixing it with the tomato paste.
3   Fry the breadcrumbs in the oil in a frying pan until starting to become crisp. Add the garlic and pine
    nuts and fry, stirring, until the pine nuts begin to colour. Stir in the parsley, then toss with the
    pasta and broccoli, the tomato liquid, drained sultanas, if using, and seasoning.

260
riccioli with broccoli, parmesan & pine nuts

PREPARATION TIME 5 minutes COOKING TIME 10 minutes SERVES 4

400G (14oz) RICCIOLI
450G (1LB) BROCCOLI FLORETS
4 TBSP VIRGIN OLIVE OIL
2 GARLIC CLOVES, FINELY CHOPPED

JUICE OF 1 LEMON
SALT AND FRESHLY GROUND BLACK PEPPER
2–3 TBSP PINE NUTS, LIGHTLY TOASTED
FRESHLY GRATED PARMESAN, TO SERVE

1   Cook the pasta according to the packet instructions, adding the broccoli for the last 4 minutes of the cooking. Drain the pasta and broccoli.
2   Meanwhile, combine the oil, garlic, lemon juice and seasoning. Toss with the pasta, broccoli and pine nuts. Serve with plenty of Parmesan.

261
orecchiette with peas & feta

PREPARATION TIME 5 minutes COOKING TIME 10 minutes SERVES 4

400G (14oz) ORECCHIETTE*
I ONION, FINELY CHOPPED
SMALL KNOB OF UNSALTED BUTTER
300ML (10FL oz/1¼ CUPS) HOT VEGETABLE STOCK

175G (6oz) FRESH PEAS
115G (4oz) FETA, CRUMBLED
1–2 TBSP CHOPPED FRESH DILL
FRESHLY GROUND BLACK PEPPER

1   Cook and drain the orecchiette according to the packet instructions.
2   Meanwhile, fry the onion in the butter until translucent and soft but not coloured. Add half the stock.
    Boil until almost evaporated. Pour in the remaining stock and add the peas. Boil until the peas
    are tender; there should still be some liquid left. Toss with the pasta, feta, dill and seasoning
    (salt may not be necessary because of the saltiness of the cheese).

*   Conchiglie can also be used.

262
chifferi with peas & parmesan

PREPARATION TIME 5 minutes COOKING TIME 10 minutes SERVES 4

400G (14oz) CHIFFERI*
225G (8oz) FROZEN PETITS POIS
115G (4oz) UNSALTED BUTTER, DICED

85G (3oz) PARMESAN, FRESHLY GRATED
SALT AND FRESHLY GROUND BLACK PEPPER

1   Cook and drain the pasta according to the packet instructions, adding the peas for the final 2 minutes.
2   Toss with the butter and most of the Parmesan. Season, using plenty of black pepper,
    and serve with the remaining Parmesan.

*   Gnocchi and cavatelli can also be used.

263
cavatappi with minted lettuce & peas

PREPARATION TIME 10 minutes COOKING TIME 10 minutes SERVES 4

I ONION, FINELY CHOPPED
40G (1½oz/2 TBSP) UNSALTED BUTTER
175G (6oz) LITTLE GEM LETTUCE
150ML (5FL oz/SCANT ⅔ CUP) MEDIUM-BODIED DRY
    WHITE WINE

225G (8oz) FROZEN PETITS POIS
SALT AND FRESHLY GROUND BLACK PEPPER
400G (14oz) CAVATAPPI
2 TBSP CHOPPED MINT
4 TBSP CRÈME FRAÎCHE

1   Fry the onion in the butter in a large frying pan, preferably non-stick, until softened.
2   Meanwhile, cut off the end of the cores of the Little Gem lettuce, but don't remove all the core.
    Slice each head lengthways into 6–8 wedges; the remaining core will hold the leaves together.
3   Pour the wine into the pan, boil until most of it has evaporated, then add the lettuce. Cook, stirring,
    until wilted and tinged with brown. Stir in the peas to warm through just before the end. Season.
4   Meanwhile, cook and drain the pasta according to the packet instructions, reserving ½ cup of the cooking
    water. Toss with the lettuce and peas, and add the mint. Stir in the reserved cooking water,
    if necessary, to moisten. Serve each portion topped with a spoonful of crème fraîche.

pappardelle with roast squash & grilled goats' cheese

PREPARATION TIME 10 minutes COOKING TIME 30 minutes SERVES 4

1 SMALL BUTTERNUT SQUASH, PEELED, SEEDED
   AND CUT INTO 2. 5cm (1in) CHUNKS
SEVERAL THYME SPRIGS
2 GARLIC CLOVES, CRUSHED
3 tbsp VIRGIN OLIVE OIL
300g (10oz) PAPPARDELLE*

4 SLICES OF GOATS' CHEESE LOG
4 tbsp FINELY CHOPPED FLAT-LEAF PARSLEY
FINELY GRATED ZEST OF ½ LEMON
SALT AND FRESHLY GROUND BLACK PEPPER
EXTRA-VIRGIN OLIVE OIL AND FRESHLY GRATED
   PARMESAN, TO SERVE

1 Preheat the oven to 200°C/400°F/gas 6.
2 Put the squash into a large roasting tin, add the thyme, garlic and oil. Stir together to coat the squash,
   then roast in the preheated oven for 25–30 minutes until the squash is tender and tinged with brown.
   Discard the thyme.
3 Meanwhile, cook the pasta according to the packet instructions, reserving ½ cup of the cooking water.
4 Lay the goats' cheese on a piece of lightly oiled foil and grill for 3–4 minutes until lightly browned
   and softened.
5 Toss the pasta with the squash and any pan juices, the parsley, lemon zest and seasoning, adding
   enough reserved cooking water to moisten. Serve with the oil and Parmesan and top each
   portion with goats' cheese.

* Cavatappi and eliche can also be used.

conchiglie with broad beans, nuts & lemon sauce

PREPARATION TIME 10 minutes COOKING TIME 10 minutes SERVES 4

85G (3oz) LIGHTLY TOASTED HAZELNUTS,
  COARSELY CHOPPED
4 GARLIC CLOVES, VERY THINLY SLICED
50G (2oz) UNSALTED BUTTER, DICED
COARSELY GRATED ZEST AND JUICE OF 1½–2 LEMONS
250G (9oz) CONCHIGLIE

175G (6oz) PODDED FRESH, OR THAWED FROZEN,
  BABY BROAD BEANS
4 TBSP SHREDDED BASIL
2 TBSP CHOPPED FLAT-LEAF PARSLEY
2 TBSP SINGLE CREAM
SALT AND FRESHLY GROUND BLACK PEPPER
FRESHLY GRATED PARMESAN, TO SERVE (OPTIONAL)

1 Cook the hazelnuts and garlic in the butter for 30–60 seconds, then add the lemon zest and remove from the heat.
2 Cook and drain the conchiglie according to the packet instructions, adding the beans about 4 minutes before the end of the cooking for fresh beans, 2 minutes for frozen ones.
3 Toss the pasta and beans with the butter mixture. Cover for 1 minute, then toss in the herbs, lemon juice, cream and seasoning. Serve with freshly grated Parmesan, if liked.

VEGETABLE & VEGETARIAN DISHES

159

orecchiette with broccoli, sun-dried tomatoes & thyme

PREPARATION TIME 10 minutes COOKING TIME 10 minutes SERVES 4

400G (14oz) ORECCHIETTE
300G (10oz) BROCCOLI FLORETS
3 GARLIC CLOVES, BRUISED BUT LEFT WHOLE
PINCH OF CHILLI FLAKES
1 TBSP FRESH THYME
5 TBSP VIRGIN OLIVE OIL OR OIL FROM
  THE TOMATOES

10 PIECES OF SUN-DRIED TOMATOES IN OIL,
  DRAINED AND SLICED
4 TBSP CHOPPED FLAT-LEAF PARSLEY
1 TSP FINELY GRATED LEMON ZEST
40G (1½oz) PARMESAN, FRESHLY GRATED,
  PLUS EXTRA TO SERVE
FRESHLY GROUND BLACK PEPPER

1 Cook and drain the pasta according to the packet instructions, adding the broccoli for the final 3–4 minutes of the cooking time.
2 Meanwhile, fry the garlic, chilli and thyme in the oil over a low heat for 5 minutes, so the oil is infused with garlic. Discard the garlic, and add the sun-dried tomatoes. Toss with the pasta, parsley, lemon zest, Parmesan and black pepper. Serve with more Parmesan.

267
trofie with goats' cheese & lemon

PREPARATION TIME 5 minutes COOKING TIME 10 minutes SERVES 2

200G (7oz) TROFIE*

150G (5oz) SOFT GOATS' CHEESE LOG,
 THICKLY SLICED

2 GARLIC CLOVES, THINLY SLICED

SMALL KNOB OF UNSALTED BUTTER

2 TBSP EXTRA-VIRGIN OLIVE OIL

FINELY GRATED ZEST OF 1 LEMON

2 TBSP LEMON JUICE

50G (2oz) ROCKET

FRESHLY GROUND BLACK PEPPER

1   Cook and drain the trofie according to the packet instructions, reserving ½ cup of the cooking water.
2   Meanwhile, place the goats' cheese on a lightly oiled piece of foil, place under a preheated grill and heat
    for 4–5 minutes until pale golden and starting to melt.
3   At the same time, fry the garlic in the butter and oil for 30 seconds. Add the lemon zest and juice.
    Toss with the pasta, rocket, black pepper and a little of the reserved cooking water, if necessary,
    to moisten. Serve each portion topped with goats' cheese.

*   Fusilli and farfalle can also be used.

268
fettuccine with asparagus, peas & lemon

PREPARATION TIME 5 minutes COOKING TIME 10 minutes SERVES 4

450G (1LB) SLIM ASPARAGUS, HALVED CROSSWAYS

375G (13oz) FETTUCCINE*

175G (6oz) FRESH PEAS

GRATED ZEST AND JUICE OF 1 LEMON

2 TBSP OLIVE OIL

4 TBSP SINGLE CREAM

4 TBSP FRESHLY GRATED PARMESAN

2–3 TBSP SHREDDED MINT, TO TASTE

SALT AND FRESHLY GROUND BLACK PEPPER

1   Cook the asparagus on a hot ridged grill pan until evenly flecked with brown.
2   Meanwhile, cook and drain the pasta according to the packet instructions,
    adding the peas for the last 3–4 minutes, depending on size.
3   At the same time, fry the lemon zest in the oil for about 3 minutes.
    Add the lemon juice and warm through.
4   Toss the fettuccine and peas with the lemon mixture, the cream,
    basil, asparagus, cheese, mint and seasoning.

*   Tagliatelle can also be used.

lasagnette with mixed mushrooms & herbs

PREPARATION TIME 10 minutes COOKING TIME 15 minutes SERVES 4

550G (1¼LB) ANY COMBINATION OF MIXED
  MUSHROOMS, SUCH AS CEPS, OYSTER, SHIITAKE,
  CHESTNUT, ENOKI AND ANY WILD MUSHROOMS
  THAT ARE AVAILABLE, SLICED, HALVED OR
  QUARTERED AS APPROPRIATE*
3 SHALLOTS, FINELY CHOPPED
VIRGIN OLIVE OIL
3 GARLIC CLOVES, THINLY SLICED

300ML (10FL OZ/SCANT 1¼ CUPS) MEDIUM-BODIED DRY
  WHITE WINE
4 TBSP MIXED CHOPPED FLAT-LEAF PARSLEY
  AND SMALL SAGE LEAVES
SALT AND FRESHLY GROUND BLACK PEPPER
400G (14OZ) LASAGNETTE
SHAVED PARMESAN, TO SERVE

1   If using oyster or enoki mushrooms, keep them separate to fry for the shortest time.
2   Fry the shallots, and mushrooms in batches in a little oil in a large frying pan until lightly coloured.
    Add the garlic with the last batch. Remove all the mushrooms from the pan and set aside.
    Stir in the wine and boil until reduced by about half. Return the mushrooms to the pan,
    add the herbs and seasoning and warm through gently.
3   Meanwhile, cook and drain the pasta according to the packet instructions. Return to the
    pan and lightly toss in the mushroom sauce. Serve with Parmesan shavings.

*   For additional flavour, pour 150ml (5fl oz/⅔ cup) boiling water over 15g (½oz) dried wild
    mushrooms, leave to soak for 20 minutes before straining off and reserving the liquid.
    Chop the dried mushrooms finely and add them and the liquid with the wine.

VEGETABLE & VEGETARIAN DISHES

161

270
penne with mediterranean vegetables

PREPARATION TIME 10 minutes COOKING TIME 30 minutes SERVES 4

I AUBERGINE, CUT INTO IcM (½IN) CUBES
VIRGIN OLIVE OIL
225G (8oz) SUMMER SQUASH, SUCH AS PATTY PAN,
    QUARTERED
I RED PEPPER, THINLY SLICED
I RED ONION, THINLY SLICED
4 LARGE WELL-FLAVOURED PLUM TOMATOES,
    CHOPPED

2 GARLIC CLOVES, CHOPPED
I ½ TBSP CHOPPED OREGANO
SALT AND FRESHLY GROUND BLACK PEPPER
400G (14oz) PENNE
FRESHLY GRATED PARMESAN, TO SERVE

1   Stir-fry the aubergine in a little oil in a large wok or deep sauté pan until browned.
    Remove with a slotted spoon and drain on kitchen paper.
2   Then stir-fry the squash until lightly softened. Using a slotted spoon, transfer to kitchen paper.
    Repeat with the peppers, cooking until limp. Quickly fry the onion until lightly browned.
    Return the cooked vegetables to the wok, stir in the tomatoes, garlic, oregano and
    seasoning and cook for 15 minutes, stirring occasionally, until tender.
3   Meanwhile, cook and drain the pasta according to the packet instructions.
4   Toss the vegetables with the pasta. Serve with the Parmesan.

162

271
fusilli lunghi with grilled mediterranean vegetables

PREPARATION TIME 15 minutes COOKING TIME 20 minutes SERVES 4

I FENNEL BULB, CUT LENGTHWAYS INTO WEDGES
I SMALL AUBERGINE, SLICED
2 COURGETTES, CUT INTO THIN LENGTHWAYS STRIPS
    (SEE PAGE 212)
I LARGE, FLESHY RED PEPPER, CUT INTO STRIPS
5 WELL-FLAVOURED PLUM TOMATOES,
    HALVED LENGTHWAYS

4 GARLIC CLOVES
3 TBSP EXTRA-VIRGIN OLIVE OIL
I TBSP THYME LEAVES
I TSP LEMON ZEST
BALSAMIC VINEGAR, FOR SPRINKLING
400G (14oz) FUSILLI LUNGHI
PESTO (SEE PAGE 18), TO SERVE

1   Boil the fennel for 2 minutes. Drain well.
2   Put all the vegetables and the garlic in an ovenproof bowl. Combine the oil, thyme and lemon zest, then
    stir into the vegetables to coat evenly. Cook under a preheated grill for 15–20 minutes until tender and
    flecked with brown, stirring as necessary to ensure even cooking. Sprinkle with a little balsamic vinegar.
3   Meanwhile, cook and drain the pasta according to packet instructions. Toss with the vegetables and
    any juices in the grill pan, and serve with the pesto.

272

penne rigate with cheeses, celery & almonds

PREPARATION TIME 10 minutes COOKING TIME 15 minutes SERVES 4

50G (2oz) ALMONDS
VIRGIN OLIVE OIL
5 SMALL CELERY STICKS, THINLY SLICED
150ML (5FL OZ/SCANT ⅔ CUP) SINGLE CREAM
200G (7oz) PENNE RIGATE*

115G (4oz) FRESH GOATS' CHEESE LOG,
   CUT ACROSS INTO 4 SLICES
115G (4oz/SCANT ½ CUP) RICOTTA, CRUMBLED
115G (4oz) GORGONZOLA, CRUMBLED
SALT AND FRESHLY GROUND BLACK PEPPER
HANDFUL OF ROCKET LEAVES, TO SERVE

1   Lightly brown the almonds in 2 tbsp oil. Scoop out with a slotted spoon and drain on paper towels. Add the celery to the oil and fry until softened but not browned. Pour in the cream and heat gently to warm through.
2   Meanwhile, cook and drain the pasta according to the packet instructions.
3   At the same time, place the goats' cheese on a sheet of foil under a preheated grill until golden.
4   Toss the pasta with the celery, cream, ricotta, Gorgonzola, almonds and seasoning. Scatter rocket over each serving, top with a slice of goats' cheese and grind over plenty of black pepper.

*   Sedani can also be used.

273

taglioni with summer vegetables & fresh herb sauce

PREPARATION TIME 15 minutes, plus standing time COOKING TIME 15 minutes SERVES 4

25G (1oz) MIXED CHOPPED HERBS, SUCH AS CHIVES,
   BASIL, THYME, PARSLEY AND OREGANO
EXTRA-VIRGIN OLIVE OIL
675G (1½LB) MIXED VEGETABLES SUCH AS QUARTERED
   PATTY PAN SQUASH, MANGE TOUT, BABY BROAD
   BEANS, BROCCOLI FLORETS, CAULIFLOWER FLORETS

2 SHALLOTS, FINELY CHOPPED
400G (14oz) TAGLIONI
5 TBSP RICOTTA
SALT AND FRESHLY GROUND BLACK PEPPER
FRESHLY GRATED PARMESAN,
   TO SERVE

1   Combine the herbs and 2 tbsp oil and leave for a few hours.
2   Blanch the vegetables (but not the shallots) separately in enough boiling salted water for the pasta, for 1–3 minutes, according to type, until just tender. Drain well. Return the water to the boil.
3   Soften the shallots in 85ml (3fl oz/scant ⅓ cup) oil, then add the blanched vegetables and heat through, stirring, but do not brown.
4   Meanwhile, cook the taglioni in the vegetable water according to the packet instructions. Drain, reserving a little of the cooking water. Toss with the vegetables, ricotta, herb sauce and seasoning. Add enough reserved water, if necessary, to moisten. Serve with plenty of Parmesan.

bucatini with roast tomatoes

PREPARATION TIME 10 minutes COOKING TIME 1 hour SERVES 4

6 WELL-FLAVOURED PLUM TOMATOES, HALVED
LENGTHWAYS
2 PLUMP GARLIC CLOVES, THINLY SLICED
1 SPRIG OF ROSEMARY, BROKEN INTO PIECES
1 TBSP THYME LEAVES
SALT AND FRESHLY GROUND BLACK PEPPER

5 TBSP EXTRA-VIRGIN OLIVE OIL
400G (14oz) BUCATINI*
3 TBSP FRESHLY GRATED PARMESAN,
PLUS EXTRA TO SERVE
2 TBSP FRESHLY GRATED PECORINO

1 Preheat the oven to 350°C/180°F/gas 4.
2 Place the tomatoes, cut side up, in a single layer on a baking sheet, tucking the garlic and rosemary
   between the pieces. Sprinkle with the thyme and seasoning and trickle over a little oil. Roast in the
   preheated oven for about 1 hour, until the tomatoes have shrunk slightly and begun to brown.
   Reserve the juices in the tin but discard the rosemary. Chop the tomatoes, if liked.
3 Meanwhile, cook and drain the pasta according to the packet instructions.
4 Toss the pasta with the tomatoes, cooking juices and cheeses. Serve sprinkled with additional Parmesan.

* Tagliatelle, spaghetti, pappardelle or linguine can also be used.

VEGETABLE & VEGETARIAN DISHES

cavatappi with spring vegetables & herbs

PREPARATION TIME 5 minutes COOKING TIME 20 minutes SERVES 4

150G (5oz) FRENCH BEANS
250G (9oz) SLIM ASPARAGUS
1 GARLIC CLOVE, CRUSHED
150G (5oz) BABY LEEKS, QUARTERED LENGTHWAYS
WITH ROOT ENDS LEFT ATTACHED
200G (7oz) SMALL COURGETTES, SLICED
VIRGIN OLIVE OIL

350G (12oz) CAVATAPPI*
JUICE OF 1 LARGE LEMON
SMALL HANDFUL CHOPPED MIXED HERBS, SUCH AS
PARSLEY, THYME, OREGANO AND TARRAGON
2 TBSP EXTRA-VIRGIN OLIVE OIL
SALT AND FRESHLY GROUND BLACK PEPPER
FRESHLY GRATED PARMESAN, TO SERVE

1 Cook the beans and asparagus in salted boiling water for 3–4 minutes until just tender.
   Drain, rinse in cold water and drain well. Cut the asparagus into 4cm (1½in) lengths.
2 Cook the garlic, leeks and courgettes in a little virgin olive oil in a large frying pan until
   the courgettes and leeks are just tender. Stir in the asparagus and beans to warm through.
3 Meanwhile, cook and drain the pasta according to the packet instructions.
4 Toss the vegetables with the pasta, lemon juice, herbs, a little extra-virgin oil and seasoning.
   Serve with grated Parmesan.

* Fusilli can also be used.

tagliatelle alla primavera

PREPARATION TIME 10 minutes COOKING TIME 15 minutes SERVES 4

225G (8oz) SLIM BABY CARROTS
175G (6oz) SLIM ASPARAGUS SPEARS
115G (4oz) BROCCOLI FLORETS
115G (4oz) SUGAR-SNAP PEAS
2 COURGETTES, DICED
SMALL KNOB OF UNSALTED BUTTER
225ML (8FL OZ/SCANT 1 CUP) DOUBLE CREAM

1 BUNCH OF SPRING ONIONS,
   CUT INTO 4CM (1½IN) LENGTHS
3–4 TBSP FRESHLY GRATED PARMESAN
SALT AND FRESHLY GROUND BLACK PEPPER
400G (14oz) TAGLIATELLE
2 TBSP MIXED THYME, CHOPPED CHIVES
   AND FLAT-LEAF PARSLEY

1   Cook the carrots, asparagus and broccoli in boiling salted water for 3–4 minutes until
    just tender, adding the sugar-snap peas about 2 minutes before the end of the cooking.
    Drain, refresh under running cold water and drain thoroughly.
2   Cook the courgettes in the butter until soft but not coloured.
    Stir in the carrots for a couple of minutes.
3   Add the cream and spring onions to the courgettes and carrots and bubble,
    stirring frequently, until lightly reduced by about one-third. Add the asparagus, sugar-snaps,
    broccoli, Parmesan and seasoning; warm through.
4   Meanwhile, cook and drain the pasta according to the packet instructions.
    Toss with the vegetable sauce. Serve sprinkled with the herbs.

165

linguine with new potatoes, beans & pesto

PREPARATION TIME 5 minutes COOKING TIME 15 minutes SERVES 4

4–5 SMALL NEW POTATOES, UNPEELED

400G (14oz) LINGUINE

115G (4oz) FRENCH BEANS

1 QUANTITY PESTO (SEE PAGE 18), OR TO TASTE

FRESHLY GROUND BLACK PEPPER

1   Boil the potatoes in a pan of water that is large enough for the pasta, until tender. Remove the potatoes, drain well and slice. Bring the water back to the boil.

2   Cook the pasta in the pan according to the packet instructions, adding the beans 4–5 minutes before the end. Add the potato slices for the final minute.

3   Drain the pasta, beans and potatoes, reserving a few spoons of the cooking water. Toss with pesto to taste and black pepper, adding enough of the reserved water to moisten. Serve immediately.

278
penne with artichokes, tomatoes & olives

PREPARATION TIME 5 minutes COOKING TIME 10 minutes SERVES 4

400G (14oz) PENNE

1 RED ONION, THINLY SLICED

14 ROASTED ARTICHOKES IN OIL, DRAINED
    AND CHOPPED, OIL RESERVED

2 GARLIC CLOVES, CHOPPED

8 HALVES OF SUN-BLUSH TOMATOES, CHOPPED

10 PITTED BLACK OLIVES, CHOPPED

40G (1½oz) PECORINO, FRESHLY GRATED, PLUS EXTRA
    TO SERVE

100G (3½oz) ROCKET

SALT AND FRESHLY GROUND BLACK PEPPER

1   Cook and drain the pasta according to the packet instructions.
2   Meanwhile, fry the red onion in 1 tbsp of the artichoke oil until softened and beginning to brown.
    Add the garlic towards the end of the cooking.
3   Stir in the tomatoes, artichokes and olives. Heat through. Toss with the pasta, cheese,
    rocket and seasoning. Serve with additional pecorino.

279
fusilli lunghi with spinach & gorgonzola

PREPARATION TIME 5 minutes COOKING TIME 10 minutes SERVES 4

400G (14oz) FUSILLI LUNGHI

150G (5oz) GORGONZOLA, DICED

85ML (3FL oz/SCANT ⅓ CUP) MILK

SMALL KNOB OF UNSALTED BUTTER

450G (1LB) SPINACH

FRESHLY GROUND BLACK PEPPER

LIGHTLY TOASTED PINE NUTS, TO SERVE

1   Cook and drain the fusilli lunghi according to the packet instructions.
2   Meanwhile, gently melt the Gorgonzola in a pan with the milk and butter.
3   Cook the spinach in a dry saucepan for 2–3 minutes, stirring occasionally, until wilted.
    Drain well in a sieve, pressing out surplus liquid.
4   Toss the spinach, cheese sauce and plenty of black pepper with the pasta. Serve sprinkled with pine nuts.

280

tagliatelle with green beans & herbs

PREPARATION TIME 10 minutes COOKING TIME 15 minutes SERVES 4

350G (12oz) MIXED SLIM RUNNER BEANS (THINLY
  SLICED LENGTHWAYS), FRENCH BEANS (HALVED
  ACROSS) AND FRESH PEAS
400G (14oz) TAGLIATELLE
1 GARLIC CLOVE, CRUSHED
OLIVE OIL
150G (5oz) SOFT, MILD GOATS' CHEESE, CHOPPED
SMALL BUNCH OF FLAT-LEAF PARSLEY,
  FINELY CHOPPED

LEAVES FROM A SMALL BUNCH OF YOUNG MINT,
  FINELY CHOPPED
100ML (3½FL oz/SCANT ½ CUP) CRÈME FRAÎCHE
SALT AND FRESHLY GROUND BLACK PEPPER
2 TBSP LIGHTLY TOASTED PINE NUTS
SHAVED PECORINO, TO SERVE

1   Bring the pan of water for the pasta to the boil, add the beans and peas and cook for 3–4 minutes
    until almost tender. Remove with a slotted spoon. Add the pasta to the pan and cook according to
    the packet instructions.
2   Meanwhile, fry the garlic in a little oil in a frying pan for about 2 minutes. Add the goats' cheese,
    herbs and crème fraîche. Warm through and add the beans. Season.
3   Drain the pasta and toss with the sauce. Serve scattered with the pine nuts and pecorino.

281

tagliatelle, asparagus, broad bean & courgette salad

PREPARATION TIME 10 minutes COOKING TIME 10 minutes SERVES 4

225G (8oz) ASPARAGUS, CUT INTO 2.5CM (1IN)
  LENGTHS
50G (2oz) SHELLED BABY BROAD BEANS
115G (4oz) BABY COURGETTES, THICKLY SLICED
500G (1LB 2oz) FRESH TAGLIATELLE (SEE PAGE 9)
12 SUN-BLUSH TOMATOES
FRESHLY GRATED PARMESAN, TO SERVE

DRESSING
2 TBSP VIRGIN OLIVE OIL
JUICE OF 1 LARGE LEMON
2 SPRING ONIONS, FINELY CHOPPED
2 TBSP COARSELY CHOPPED TARRAGON
SALT AND FRESHLY GROUND BLACK PEPPER

1   Bring a pan of water large enough for cooking the pasta to the boil. Boil the asparagus for 2 minutes.
    Remove with a slotted spoon. Repeat with the broad beans, cooking them for 2–3 minutes,
    and then the courgette slices, cooking them for 1 minute. Set aside.
2   Meanwhile, make the dressing by whisking the ingredients together with seasoning.
3   Cook and drain the tagliatelle (see page 13), reserving ½ cup of the cooking water. Toss with the
    vegetables, sun-blush tomatoes and dressing, and about 4 tbsp of the reserved cooking water,
    to moisten. Serve with plenty of freshly grated Parmesan.

282

warm pasta, mushroom
& grilled vegetable salad

PREPARATION TIME 10 minutes COOKING TIME 25 minutes SERVES 4–6

I GARLIC CLOVE, SLICED

4 TBSP OLIVE OIL

I AUBERGINE, CUT LENGTHWAYS
  INTO I CM (½IN) STRIPS

225G (8OZ) MIXED OYSTER AND SHIITAKE
  MUSHROOMS, SLICED

115G (4OZ) SUN-DRIED TOMATOES IN OIL

I SMALL RED PEPPER, GRILLED,
  PEELED AND SLICED (SEE PAGE 67)

I SMALL YELLOW PEPPER, GRILLED,
  PEELED AND SLICED (SEE PAGE 67)

I RED CHILLI, SEEDED AND THINLY SLICED

225G (8OZ) ROAST ARTICHOKES IN OIL,
  DRAINED AND HALVED

115G (4OZ) PITTED OIL-CURED BLACK OLIVES

2 TBSP BALSAMIC VINEGAR

SALT AND FRESHLY GROUND BLACK PEPPER

450G (ILB) RIGATONI

1   Warm the garlic in the oil in a small saucepan over a very low heat for 15 minutes; do not allow it to get too hot or the garlic will fry. Scoop out the garlic.
2   Brush the aubergine slices generously with the garlic oil and cook under a preheated, very hot grill for about 8 minutes until soft and charred on both sides.
3   Meanwhile, cook the mushrooms with the sun-dried tomatoes and their oil over a high heat for about 3 minutes, stirring frequently. Transfer to a large bowl and add the peppers, chilli, aubergines, artichokes, olives, balsamic vinegar and seasoning. Cover to keep warm.
4   Cook and drain the pasta according to the packet instructions. Toss with the vegetable mixture and serve.

283

tonnarelli with roast peppers,
aubergines, fennel & olives

PREPARATION TIME 10 minutes COOKING TIME 20–25 minutes SERVES 4

2 RED PEPPERS, CUT INTO BITE-SIZED PIECES

I SMALL AUBERGINE, CUT INTO BITE-SIZED PIECES

I SMALL FENNEL BULB, CUT INTO BITE-SIZED PIECES

5 WELL-FLAVOURED RIPE PLUM TOMATOES,
  QUARTERED

6 GARLIC CLOVES

PINCH OF CRUSHED CHILLI FLAKES

VIRGIN OLIVE OIL

SALT AND FRESHLY GROUND BLACK PEPPER

400G (14OZ) TONNARELLI*

115G (4OZ) PITTED GREEN OLIVES

115G (4OZ/SCANT ½ CUP) RICOTTA

SMALL HANDFUL OF BASIL LEAVES, SHREDDED

FRESHLY GRATED PARMESAN, TO SERVE

1   Preheat the oven to 200°C/400°F/gas 6.
2   Put the peppers, aubergine, fennel, tomatoes, garlic and chilli flakes in roasting tin. Trickle over some oil, season and stir to combine the ingredients. Spread in an even layer. Bake in the preheated oven for 20–25 minutes until softened and lightly charred.
3   Meanwhile, cook and drain the pasta according to the packet instructions. Toss with 2 tbsp oil, the cooked vegetables, olives, ricotta and basil. Serve with freshly grated Parmesan.

*   Penne, ditali or cavatappi can also be used.

strozzapreti with cauliflower, saffron & tomatoes

PREPARATION TIME 10 minutes, plus 10 minutes soaking COOKING TIME 15 minutes SERVES 4

PINCH OF SAFFRON THREADS, CRUSHED

1 SMALL CAULIFLOWER, DIVIDED INTO FLORETS

350G (12oz) STROZZAPRETI

1 SMALL ONION, FINELY CHOPPED

VIRGIN OLIVE OIL

2 GARLIC CLOVES, FINELY CHOPPED

5 WELL-FLAVOURED TOMATOES, PEELED, IF LIKED, SEEDED AND CHOPPED

40G (1½oz) PARMESAN, FRESHLY GRATED, PLUS EXTRA TO SERVE

1 Pour a little boiling water over the saffron and leave to soak for about 10 minutes.

2 Meanwhile, cook the cauliflower in boiling salted water until almost tender, and then drain. Cook the pasta according to the packet instructions, and then drain.

3 While the cauliflower is cooking, fry the onion in a little oil until soft and transparent, adding the garlic towards the end of the cooking time. Add the tomatoes, drained cauliflower and saffron water and cook, stirring frequently, for 2–3 minutes.

4 Stir the pasta and Parmesan into the cauliflower mixture for about 30 seconds, then serve with extra Parmesan.

* Conchiglie, farfalle or gnocchi can also be used.

285
pasta provençal

PREPARATION TIME 10 minutes COOKING TIME 20 minutes SERVES 4

3 TBSP EXTRA-VIRGIN OLIVE OIL

1½–2 TBSP BALSAMIC VINEGAR

I SMALL GARLIC CLOVE, FINELY CHOPPED

I TBSP CHOPPED CAPERS

25G (1oz) PARMESAN, FRESHLY GRATED

SALT AND FRESHLY GROUND BLACK PEPPER

I LARGE RED PEPPER, HALVED

I COURGETTE, THINLY SLICED

3 WELL-FLAVOURED PLUM TOMATOES, QUARTERED

I AUBERGINE, THINLY SLICED

200G (7oz) ELICHE*

2 TBSP SHREDDED BASIL

1   Make a dressing by whisking the oil with the vinegar, garlic, capers and Parmesan. Season.
2   Grill the pepper halves for 8–12 minutes until charred and blistered. Discard the charred patches and slice the peppers. At the same time, grill the courgette slices for about 3–4 minutes per side until soft and flecked with brown. When there is space on the grill, cook the tomatoes for about 5 minutes until lightly charred.
3   Meanwhile, cook the aubergine slices on a hot ridged grill pan for about 3–4 minutes per side until soft and marked with char lines. Cut into strips and toss with the other vegetables.
4   While the vegetables are cooking, cook and drain the pasta according to the packet instructions. Toss with the vegetables, basil and dressing.

*   Fusilli and cavatappi can also be used.

286
tagliatelle with red peppers & mozzarella

PREPARATION TIME 10 minutes COOKING TIME 15 minutes SERVES 4

250G (9oz) TAGLIATELLE

6 MIXED GRILLED RED AND YELLOW PEPPER HALVES
  IN OIL, DRAINED AND SLICED*

3 TBSP EXTRA-VIRGIN OLIVE OIL

JUICE OF ½ LEMON

LEAVES FROM A SMALL BUNCH OF FLAT-LEAF
  PARSLEY, CHOPPED

SALT AND FRESHLY GROUND BLACK PEPPER

150G (5oz) BUFFALO MOZZARELLA, CUBED

20 PITTED OIL-CURED BLACK OLIVES, HALVED

I TBSP SALT-PACKED CAPERS, RINSED
  AND DRIED

1   Cook and drain the tagliatelle according to the packet instructions.
2   Meanwhile, place the pepper strips under a hot grill until sizzling.
3   While the peppers are cooking, whisk the oil with the lemon juice, then add the parsley and the peppers when they are ready. Season.
4   Toss the pasta with the cheese, then add the dressing, olives and capers. Serve straight away, so the cheese is just melting.

*   If these are not available, use bottled red peppers instead. Rinse them and toss in oil before putting under the grill.

287

penne with creamy tomato & basil sauce

PREPARATION TIME 5 minutes COOKING TIME 10 minutes SERVES 4

1 ONION, FINELY CHOPPED
2 GARLIC CLOVES, CRUSHED
VIRGIN OLIVE OIL
2 X 400G CANS CHOPPED PLUM TOMATOES
115ML (4FL OZ/SCANT ½ CUP) DOUBLE CREAM

SALT AND FRESHLY GROUND BLACK PEPPER
SMALL HANDFUL OF BASIL LEAVES, SHREDDED
400G (14OZ) PENNE
FRESHLY GRATED PARMESAN,
  TO SERVE

1 Fry the onion and garlic in a little oil in a heavy pan until softened. Pour in the tomatoes and simmer gently, stirring occasionally until thick and darkened to a deeper red. Purée in a blender, return to the pan and add the cream. Heat though without allowing to boil. Season and add the basil.
2 Meanwhile, cook and drain the pasta according to the packet instructions.
Toss with the sauce and serve with Parmesan.

288

pappardelle with mushrooms & leeks

PREPARATION TIME 10 minutes COOKING TIME 10 minutes SERVES 4

300G (10OZ) SHIITAKE MUSHROOMS, SLICED
5 BABY LEEKS, SLICED
VIRGIN OLIVE OIL
3 GARLIC CLOVES, CRUSHED
SALT AND FRESHLY GROUND BLACK PEPPER
300G (10OZ) FRESH PAPPARDELLE

LEAVES FROM A SMALL BUNCH OF FLAT-LEAF
  PARSLEY, FINELY CHOPPED
FINELY GRATED ZEST OF ½ LEMON
4 TBSP FRESHLY GRATED PARMESAN,
  PLUS EXTRA TO SERVE

1 Fry the shiitake and leeks in oil in a large frying pan until golden, adding the garlic towards the end. Season.
2 Cook and drain the pasta according to the packet instructions, reserving ½ cup of the water. Toss the pasta with the vegetables, parsley, lemon zest, cheese and about 5–6 tbsp of the reserved water, to moisten. Serve with additional Parmesan.

289
tagliatelle with asparagus & parmesan

PREPARATION TIME 5 minutes COOKING TIME 15 minutes SERVES 4

350G (12oz) ASPARAGUS, CUT INTO
  5CM (2IN) LENGTHS
300G (10oz) TAGLIATELLE
1 GARLIC CLOVE, FINELY CHOPPED

50G (2oz/SCANT ¼ CUP) UNSALTED BUTTER
1 TBSP LEMON JUICE
SALT AND FRESHLY GROUND BLACK PEPPER
FRESHLY GRATED PARMESAN, TO SERVE

1 Bring enough water to the boil for cooking the pasta. Add the asparagus, cook for 2 minutes and remove with a slotted spoon. Add the pasta to the water, cook and drain according to the packet instructions, reserving ½ cup of the cooking water.
2 Meanwhile, fry the asparagus with the garlic in the butter for about 3 minutes over a medium heat so that it does not brown. Add the lemon juice and seasoning. Toss with the pasta, adding a little of the cooking water, if necessary, to moisten. Serve with freshly grated Parmesan.

290
tagliatelle with tomatoes, mozzarella & herbs

PREPARATION TIME 10 minutes COOKING TIME 10 minutes SERVES 4

550G (1¼LB) RIPE PLUM TOMATOES, SEEDED AND
  QUITE FINELY CHOPPED
225G (8oz) BUFFALO MOZZARELLA, DICED
LEAVES FROM A BUNCH OF MIXED HERBS, SUCH AS
  BASIL, PARSLEY, MARJORAM AND THYME, CHOPPED

SALT AND FRESHLY GROUND BLACK PEPPER
6 TBSP EXTRA-VIRGIN OLIVE OIL
400G (14oz) TAGLIATELLE

1 Combine the tomatoes, cheese, herbs and seasoning.
2 Heat the oil in a small saucepan until it is very hot, and then stir into the tomato mixture. Set aside.
3 Cook and drain the pasta according to the packet instructions. Toss thoroughly with the tomato mixture, then cover and leave for about 2 minutes so the mozzarella starts to melt.

291

pappardelle with roast mushrooms

PREPARATION TIME 5 minutes COOKING TIME 15 minutes SERVES 4

675G (1½LB) MIXED MUSHROOMS, SUCH AS SHIITAKE
AND OYSTER, BROKEN INTO HALVES OR QUARTERS
AS NECESSARY
3½ TBSP VIRGIN OLIVE OIL
JUICE OF 1 LEMON

SALT AND FRESHLY GROUND BLACK PEPPER
SMALL KNOB OF UNSALTED BUTTER
450G (1LB) FRESH PAPPARDELLE (SEE PAGE 10)*
2 TBSP CHOPPED FLAT-LEAF PARSLEY
FRESHLY GRATED PARMESAN, TO SERVE

1 Preheat the oven to 180°C/350°F/gas 4.
2 Put the mushrooms in a roasting tin. Trickle over the oil and lemon juice. Add seasoning and stir the
   mushrooms to coat. Dot with the butter and roast in the preheated oven for 15 minutes.
3 Meanwhile, cook and drain the pasta (see page 13). Toss with the mushrooms, the cooking juices,
   and the parsley and serve with freshly grated Parmesan.

* Dried pappardelle can also be used.

292

casareccia with broccoli & gorgonzola

PREPARATION TIME 5 minutes COOKING TIME 10 minutes SERVES 4

350G (12OZ) CASARECCIA*
300G (14OZ) BROCCOLI FLORETS
150ML (5FL OZ/SCANT ⅔ CUP) MEDIUM-BODIED DRY
   WHITE WINE
175G (6OZ) GORGONZOLA, CHOPPED

FRESHLY GROUND BLACK PEPPER
50G (2OZ) WALNUT HALVES,
   LIGHTLY TOASTED AND CHOPPED
FRESHLY GRATED PARMESAN,
   TO SERVE

1 Cook and drain the pasta according to the packet instructions, adding the broccoli for the final
   3–4 minutes of the cooking time.
2 Meanwhile, in a separate pan, boil the wine rapidly until reduced by half. Remove from the heat
   and stir in the Gorgonzola so that it is just beginning to melt. Season with black pepper
   and toss with the pasta, broccoli and walnuts. Serve with Parmesan.

* Other pasta shapes such as gnocchi, conchiglie, pipe rigate or radiatori can also be used.

293
farfalle with peas, mint & ricotta

PREPARATION TIME 5 minutes COOKING TIME 10 minutes SERVES 4

300g (10oz) FARFALLE

450G (1LB) FRESH OR FROZEN PEAS

250G (9oz) RICOTTA

SMALL LEAVES FROM A SMALL BUNCH OF MINT

SALT AND FRESHLY GROUND BLACK PEPPER

PARMESAN SHAVINGS, TO SERVE

1 Cook and drain the pasta according to the packet instructions.
2 Meanwhile, cook fresh peas in boiling water for 4–5 minutes, frozen peas for 2 minutes
   and then drain, reserving 2 tbsp of the cooking water.
3 Purée one-third of the peas with the ricotta, reserved water, and mint leaves. Transfer
   to a small non stick saucepan, season and warm through gently, stirring frequently.
4 Add the remaining peas to the pasta just before it is ready, to warm through.
   Drain and toss with the sauce. Serve topped with Parmesan shavings.

294

black pepper tagliatelle
with three-cheese sauce

PREPARATION TIME 5 minutes COOKING TIME 5 minutes SERVES 4

400G (14oz) FRESH BLACK PEPPER TAGLIATELLE
  (SEE PAGE 10), OR PLAIN FRESH TAGLIATELLE
115ML (4FL OZ/½ CUP) DOUBLE CREAM
85G (3oz/SCANT ⅓ CUP) RICOTTA
85G (3oz) GORGONZOLA, FINELY CHOPPED

40G (1½oz) PARMESAN, FRESHLY GRATED
SALT AND FRESHLY GROUND BLACK PEPPER
50G (2oz) WALNUT HALVES,
  LIGHTLY TOASTED AND CHOPPED

1   Gently heat the cream, ricotta, Gorgonzola and Parmesan in a pan, stirring occasionally until
    the Gorgonzola has almost melted. Season; if using plain tagliatelle, use plenty of black pepper.
2   Meanwhile, cook and drain the pasta according to the instructions. Toss with the sauce and walnuts.

295

pasta, leeks & cheese al forno

PREPARATION TIME 10 minutes COOKING TIME 45 minutes SERVES 4

275G (9oz) PASTA SUCH AS CHIFFERI, FUSILLI
  OR MACARONI
2 SMALL LEEKS, HALVED LENGTHWAYS,
  THINLY SLICED
2 GARLIC CLOVES, FINELY CHOPPED
SMALL KNOB OF UNSALTED BUTTER

3 EGGS, BEATEN
200G (7oz/SCANT ⅞ CUP) RICOTTA
225ML (8FL OZ/SCANT 1 CUP) MILK
SALT AND FRESHLY GROUND BLACK PEPPER
175G (6oz) FONTINA, GRATED

1   Preheat the oven to 190°C/375°F/gas 5.
2   Cook and drain the pasta according to the packet instructions, giving it 2 minutes less than usual.
3   While the pasta is cooking, fry the leek and garlic in the butter until softened.
4   Meanwhile, stir the eggs into the ricotta, then stir in the milk until smooth. Season. Mix with the pasta,
    cheese and leek mixture. Pour into a large buttered baking dish. Bake in the preheated oven for about
    35 minutes until just set and golden on top.

296
pappardelle with roast cherry tomatoes, basil & ricotta

PREPARATION TIME 10 minutes COOKING TIME 10 minutes SERVES 4

675G (1½LB) RIPE, WELL-FLAVOURED CHERRY
  TOMATOES, HALVED
2 PLUMP GARLIC CLOVES, FINELY CHOPPED
½ TSP DRIED OREGANO
SALT AND FRESHLY GROUND BLACK PEPPER

5 TBSP VIRGIN OLIVE OIL
400G (14oz) PAPPARDELLE
150G (5oz) RICOTTA, CRUMBLED
HANDFUL OF BASIL LEAVES, SHREDDED

1   Preheat the oven to 200°C/400°F/gas 6.
2   Put the tomatoes in a roasting tray. Sprinkle over the garlic, oregano and seasoning. Trickle over the oil and roast in the preheated oven for about 20–25 minutes until they are beginning to collapse.
3   Meanwhile, cook and drain the pasta according to the packet instructions. Toss with the ricotta, tomatoes and their cooking juices and basil.

297
tagliatelle with broad beans & goats' cheese

PREPARATION TIME 5 minutes COOKING TIME 10 minutes SERVES 4

400G (14oz) TAGLIATELLE*
450G (1LB) SHELLED BABY BROAD BEANS
3 TBSP OLIVE OIL
300G (10oz) SOFT, RINDLESS GOATS' CHEESE

SMALL LEAVES FROM A SMALL BUNCH OF
  MINT, CHOPPED
SALT AND FRESHLY GROUND BLACK PEPPER
FRESHLY GRATED PARMESAN, TO SERVE

1   Cook and drain the pasta according to the packet instructions, adding the broad beans about 4 minutes before the end of cooking, reserving ½ cup of the cooking water.
2   Meanwhile, stir the oil into the goats' cheese, then add the mint and seasoning. Toss with the pasta, adding a little of the cooking water, if necessary, to moisten, and serve with freshly grated Parmesan.

*   Pasta shapes such as conchiglie or gnocchi can also be used.

298

cavatappi with artichokes, mushrooms & peas

PREPARATION TIME 10 minutes COOKING TIME 10 minutes SERVES 4

300G (10oz) CAVATAPPI

450G (1LB) FRESH PEAS, PODDED

175–225G (6–8oz) BROWN-CAP/CHESTNUT
   MUSHROOMS, QUARTERED

1 GARLIC CLOVE, CHOPPED

OLIVE OIL

1 BUNCH OF SPRING ONIONS, COARSELY CHOPPED

6–8 GRILLED ARTICHOKES IN OIL,
   DRAINED AND HALVED OR QUARTERED

PINCH OF THYME LEAVES

1 TBSP CHOPPED FLAT-LEAF PARSLEY

SALT AND FRESHLY GROUND BLACK PEPPER

1 TBSP CHOPPED BASIL

FRESHLY GRATED PARMESAN, TO SERVE

1   Cook and drain the pasta according to the packet instructions.

2   Meanwhile, boil the peas in a smaller pan of water until just tender. Drain, reserving 2–3 tbsp of the cooking water.

3   At the same time, fry the mushrooms and garlic in a little oil, stirring occasionally, for 3–4 minutes until the mushrooms are tender. Stir in the spring onions, artichokes, thyme, parsley, peas, reserved cooking water to moisten and seasoning. Cover and heat together for a couple of minutes. Add the basil and toss with the pasta. Serve with freshly grated Parmesan.

299

linguine, tomatoes, peppers & black olives en papillote

PREPARATION TIME 10 minutes COOKING TIME 20 minutes SERVES 4

525ML (18FL oz/SCANT 2¼ CUPS) PASSATA

2 GARLIC CLOVES, FINELY CHOPPED

225G (8oz) LINGUINE

3 PLUM TOMATOES, SEEDED AND SLIVERED

1 SMALL RED PEPPER, THINLY SLICED

20 PITTED OIL-CURED BLACK OLIVES, QUARTERED

LEAVES FROM A SMALL BUNCH OF BASIL, SHREDDED

1 TBSP CHOPPED FLAT-LEAF PARSLEY

SALT AND FRESHLY GROUND BLACK PEPPER

FRESHLY GRATED PARMESAN, TO SERVE

1   Preheat the oven to 190°C/375°F/gas 5. Cut 4 pieces of greaseproof paper measuring 30cm (12in) square and lightly oil.

2   Simmer the passata with the garlic until slightly reduced.

3   Meanwhile, cook the linguine according to the packet instructions but for 1 minute less than usual, then drain. Toss with the tomato sauce, the slivered tomatoes, red pepper, olives, herbs and seasoning.

4   Place one-quarter in the centre of each of the 4 oiled pieces of greaseproof paper. Fold the paper loosely over the mixture and twist the edges together firmly to seal well. Place in a shallow roasting tin and bake in the preheated oven for 15 minutes. Serve with freshly grated Parmesan.

300
tortiglioni with aubergine & tomato

PREPARATION TIME 10 minutes plus an optional 30 minutes standing COOKING TIME 35 minutes SERVES 4

2 SMALL AUBERGINES, COARSELY CHOPPED
SALT AND FRESHLY GROUND BLACK PEPPER
1 ONION, THICKLY SLICED LENGTHWAYS
VIRGIN OLIVE OIL
3 GARLIC CLOVES, FINELY CHOPPED
400G CAN CHOPPED PLUM TOMATOES
50G (2oz) SUN-DRIED TOMATOES IN OIL,
   DRAINED AND CHOPPED

150ML (5FL OZ/SCANT ⅔ CUP) RED OR MEDIUM-BODIED
   DRY WHITE WINE
50G (2oz) PITTED KALAMATA OLIVES
2 TBSP OREGANO
350G (12oz) TORTIGLIONI
115G (4oz) FONTINA, GRATED
40G (1½oz) PARMESAN,
   FRESHLY GRATED

1   If you wish, in order that the aubergine absorbs less oil, sprinkle it with salt and leave
    in a colander placed on a plate, to drain for 30 minutes. Rinse well and dry thoroughly.
2   Fry the onion in a little oil in a large frying pan and fry until softened. Add the garlic, fry for
    30 seconds, then add the aubergine and cook for 3 minutes, stirring frequently. Add the tomatoes,
    sun-dried tomatoes and wine. Cover and simmer gently for about 15 minutes until the aubergine
    is tender. Add the olives, oregano and seasoning.
3   Meanwhile, cook and drain the pasta according to the packet instructions. Toss with the aubergine sauce.
4   Transfer to a gratin dish, sprinkle over the cheeses and put under a preheated grill until the cheese
    is melted and golden. Alternatively, bake in a preheated oven at 200°C/400°F/gas 6 for 20 minutes.

301
riccioli with broccoli,
taleggio & almonds

PREPARATION TIME 5 minutes COOKING TIME 10 minutes SERVES 4

350G (13oz) RICCIOLI*
1 LEEK, THINLY SLICED
1 GARLIC CLOVE, FINELY CHOPPED
OLIVE OIL
300G (10oz) BROCCOLI FLORETS

175ML (6FL OZ/SCANT ¾ CUP) MEDIUM-BODIED DRY
   WHITE WINE
50G (2oz) TALEGGIO, GRATED
2–3 TBSP FLAKED ALMONDS, LIGHTLY TOASTED
SALT AND FRESHLY GROUND BLACK PEPPER
FRESHLY GRATED PARMESAN, TO SERVE

1   Cook and drain the pasta according to the packet instructions.
2   Meanwhile, fry the leek and garlic in a little oil for 2–3 minutes until translucent. Add the broccoli and
    cook for a further 1 minute before pouring in the wine. Simmer until the broccoli is tender and the wine
    almost evaporated, stirring carefully occasionally; there should be enough wine left to moisten the sauce.
3   Remove the pan from the heat, add the Taleggio, and then toss with the pasta, almonds and seasoning.
    Serve with Parmesan.

*   Orecchiette, gnocchi and conchiglie can also be used.

302

green & white tagliatelle
with ricotta, tomatoes & basil

PREPARATION TIME 5 minutes plus 30 minutes standing COOKING TIME 5 minutes SERVES 4

550G (1¼LB) RIPE, WELL-FLAVOURED TOMATOES,
 PREFERABLY PLUM, CHOPPED
I GARLIC CLOVE, FINELY CHOPPED
3 TBSP EXTRA-VIRGIN OLIVE OIL
SALT AND FRESHLY GROUND BLACK PEPPER

375G (13oz) FRESH GREEN AND WHITE TAGLIATELLE
 (PAGLIA E FIENO)
150G (5oz/SCANT ⅔ CUP) RICOTTA, CRUMBLED
SMALL HANDFUL OF BASIL LEAVES, SHREDDED

1 Combine the tomatoes with the garlic, oil and seasoning. Leave to stand for at least 30 minutes.
2 Cook and drain the pasta. Toss with the ricotta, basil and tomatoes. Serve warm or at room temperature.

303

penne with aubergines, olives & basil

PREPARATION TIME 10 minutes COOKING TIME 15 minutes SERVES 4

2 AUBERGINES, ABOUT 450G (1LB) IN TOTAL, CHOPPED
4 GARLIC CLOVES, THINLY SLICED
5 TBSP VIRGIN OLIVE OIL
2 TBSP SUN-DRIED TOMATO PASTE
I TSP DRIED OREGANO

12 PITTED BLACK OLIVES, SLICED
SALT AND FRESHLY GROUND BLACK PEPPER
ABOUT 2 TSP BALSAMIC VINEGAR
400G (14oz) PENNE
HANDFUL OF BASIL LEAVES, SHREDDED

1 Fry the aubergine and garlic in the oil in a large frying pan until browned. Stir in the tomato paste and
   4 tbsp hot water. Add the oregano and olives and cook gently until the aubergines are tender, stirring
   occasionally. Add more water if they become too dry. Season and sprinkle with balsamic vinegar to taste.
2 Meanwhile, cook and drain the pasta according to the packet instructions, reserving ½ cup of the cooking
   water. Toss with the aubergine sauce and basil, adding reserved cooking water if necessary to moisten.

304

strozzapreti with peppers & mushrooms

PREPARATION TIME 10 minutes COOKING TIME 15 minutes SERVES 4

4 GARLIC CLOVES, FINELY CHOPPED
I ROSEMARY SPRIG
2 SAGE SPRIGS
5 TBSP VIRGIN OLIVE OIL
500G (1LB 2oz) CHESTNUT OR BROWN-CAP
 MUSHROOMS, SLICED

2 RED PEPPERS, SLICED
SALT AND FRESHLY GROUND BLACK PEPPER
400G (14oz) STROZZAPRETI
40G (1½oz) PARMESAN,
 FRESHLY GRATED

1 Fry the garlic and herb sprigs in the oil for about 2 minutes, until the garlic is beginning
   to brown. Scoop out with a slotted spoon, and discard the garlic and herbs.
2 Add the mushrooms to the pan and fry briskly until their moisture has evaporated.
   Add the peppers and cook over a medium-high heat until tender. Season.
3 Meanwhile, cook and drain the pasta according to the packet instructions.
   Toss with the vegetables and Parmesan, and serve.

305
penne rigate with spicy tomato sauce

PREPARATION TIME 5 minutes COOKING TIME 20 minutes SERVES 4

I ONION, THINLY SLICED
5 TBSP VIRGIN OLIVE OIL
3 GARLIC CLOVES, SLICED
I TSP CRUSHED CHILLI FLAKES
2 X 400G CANS CHOPPED PLUM TOMATOES

SALT AND FRESHLY GROUND BLACK PEPPER
400G (14oz) PENNE RIGATE
2 TBSP SHREDDED BASIL LEAVES
2 TBSP FRESHLY GRATED PARMESAN

1 Fry the onion in the oil until soft and golden, adding the garlic and chilli for the last 2 minutes.
   Pour in the tomatoes and simmer for about 15 minutes until thickened, stirring frequently. Season.
2 Meanwhile, cook and drain the pasta according to the packet instructions.
   Toss with the sauce, basil and Parmesan.

306
ditali with tomatoes,
garlic & grilled peppers

PREPARATION TIME 10 minutes COOKING TIME 25 minutes SERVES 4

2 PLUMP GARLIC CLOVES, FINELY CHOPPED
PINCH OF CHILLI FLAKES
VIRGIN OLIVE OIL
500G (1LB 2oz) WELL-FLAVOURED TOMATOES,
   PEELED, SEEDED AND CHOPPED

2 PLUMP RED PEPPERS, GRILLED,
   PEELED AND FINELY CHOPPED
400G (14oz) DITALI
FRESHLY GRATED PARMESAN,
   TO SERVE (OPTIONAL)

1 Fry the garlic and chillies in some olive oil for 1 minute. Add the tomatoes and cook for
   about 20 minutes, stirring occasionally, until thickened. Stir in the peppers and cook
   gently for a further 5 minutes or so; do not allow the sauce to become too thick.
2 Meanwhile, cook and drain the pasta according to the packet instructions.
   Toss with the sauce, and serve with freshly grated Parmesan, if liked.

307
penne with broad beans,
parsley & pecorino

PREPARATION TIME 10 minutes COOKING TIME 10 minutes SERVES 4

400G (14oz) PENNE
350G (12oz) FRESH OR FROZEN BROAD BEANS,
   THAWED
2 GARLIC CLOVES, FINELY CHOPPED

VIRGIN OLIVE OIL
2 TBSP CHOPPED FLAT-LEAF PARSLEY
4 TBSP FRESHLY GRATED PECORINO,
   PLUS EXTRA TO SERVE

1 Cook and drain the pasta according to the packet instructions, adding the broad beans for the last
   3–4 minutes.
2 Meanwhile, fry the garlic in some olive oil for 1 minute. Stir in the pasta and broad beans
   to coat with the oil, then toss with the parsley and pecorino. Serve with extra pecorino.

308
pennette with broccoli, pine nuts & chilli

PREPARATION TIME 5 minutes COOKING TIME 10 minutes SERVES 4

250G (9oz) BROCCOLI FLORETS
400G (14oz) PENNETTE
PINCH OF CHILLI FLAKES
1 GARLIC CLOVE, FINELY CHOPPED

4 TBSP PINE NUTS
OLIVE OIL
SALT
FRESHLY GRATED PARMESAN, TO SERVE

1   Bring enough water to the boil for cooking the pasta. Add the broccoli, cook for about 3–4 minutes until just tender, and remove with a slotted spoon. Add the pasta to the water, cook and drain according to the packet instructions, reserving ½ cup of the cooking water.
2   Meanwhile, fry the chilli flakes, garlic and pine nuts in a little oil for 2 minutes; do not allow the nuts and garlic to burn. Add the broccoli and heat through, stirring frequently. Season with salt.
3   Toss with the pasta, adding a little of the cooking water, if necessary, to moisten, and serve with freshly grated Parmesan.

182

309
fusilli with courgettes, tomatoes & basil

PREPARATION TIME 10 minutes COOKING TIME 10 minutes SERVES 4

350G (12oz) FUSILLI
2 SLIM COURGETTES, SLICED INTO DISCS
VIRGIN OLIVE OIL
1 PLUMP GARLIC CLOVE, CRUSHED
2 WELL-FLAVOURED TOMATOES, SEEDED AND
   CHOPPED

1 TBSP CHOPPED FLAT-LEAF PARSLEY
JUICE OF ½ LEMON
SALT AND FRESHLY GROUND BLACK PEPPER
115G (4oz) BUFFALO MOZZARELLA, CHOPPED
1½ TBSP SHREDDED BASIL

1   Cook the pasta according to the packet instructions, and drain lightly.
2   Meanwhile, fry the courgettes in a little oil for 3–4 minutes until almost tender. Add the garlic and cook for 1–2 minutes. Stir in the tomatoes, parsley, lemon juice, 2 tbsp olive oil and seasoning just to warm through; do not cook.
3   Add the mozzarella and basil and toss with the pasta; cover and leave for 1–2 minutes, over a very low heat, if necessary, so the mozzarella begins to melt.

agnolotti with grilled vegetable dressing

PREPARATION TIME 10 minutes plus 1 hour standing COOKING TIME 20 minutes SERVES 4

½ RED PEPPER, HALVED

½ YELLOW PEPPER, HALVED

1 COURGETTE, HALVED LENGTHWAYS

6 GARLIC CLOVES, UNPEELED

SALT AND FRESHLY GROUND BLACK PEPPER

115ML (4FL OZ/SCANT ½ CUP) MIXED VIRGIN OLIVE OIL
AND OIL FROM THE TOMATOES

2 TBSP WHITE WINE VINEGAR

2 SUN-DRIED TOMATOES IN OIL, DRAINED
(OIL RESERVED) AND FINELY CHOPPED

1 TBSP PINE NUTS, LIGHTLY TOASTED

1 QUANTITY CHEESE AND HERB AGNOLOTTI
(SEE PAGE 195)*

1   Put the peppers, courgette and garlic on a non-stick baking tray. Spray with oil, stirring the vegetables
    so they are evenly coated. Sprinkle with seasoning. Grill until lightly charred and becoming tender,
    stirring occasionally.

2   Meanwhile, whisk the oil with the vinegar until emulsified.

3   Peel the garlic and mash the flesh with a pinch of salt. Whisk into the dressing, and add the sun-dried
    tomatoes and pine nuts.

4   Discard charred patches from the other vegetables and chop them finely. Combine the vegetables
    and dressing.

5   Cook the agnolotti, in batches if necessary, in gently simmering water for about 4 minutes,
    and drain. Put into a large shallow dish and spoon over the roast vegetable dressing.
    Leave for 1 hour before serving.

*   The dressing can also be served with other stuffed pastas such as tortellini, ravioli or raviolini.

183

311
farfalle with mushrooms,
sun-dried tomatoes & spinach

PREPARATION TIME 10 minutes COOKING TIME 15 minutes SERVES 4

I ONION, FINELY CHOPPED

VIRGIN OLIVE OIL

2 GARLIC CLOVES, CHOPPED

250G (9oz) BROWN-CAP/CHESTNUT MUSHROOMS,
   THINLY SLICED

175ML (6FL oz/SCANT ¾ CUP) MEDIUM-BODIED DRY
   WHITE WINE

175G (6oz) SMALL SPINACH LEAVES

85G (3oz) SUN-DRIED TOMATOES IN OIL,
   DRAINED AND SLICED

SALT AND FRESHLY GROUND BLACK PEPPER

350G (12oz) FARFALLE

CHOPPED FLAT-LEAF PARSLEY, LIGHTLY TOASTED PINE
   NUTS AND FRESHLY GRATED PARMESAN, TO SERVE

1   Fry the onion in a little olive oil in a large frying pan, until soft and pale golden. Add the garlic
    and mushrooms and fry briskly for 2 minutes. Pour in the wine, bubble to reduce slightly,
    then add the spinach and tomatoes. Cook until the spinach has wilted. Season.
2   Meanwhile, cook and drain the pasta according to the packet instructions. Toss with the mushroom
    mixture. Scatter over parsley and pine nuts, toss lightly and serve with Parmesan.

312
spinach & ricotta ravioli

PREPARATION TIME 45 minutes COOKING TIME 15 minutes SERVES 4

2-EGG QUANTITY OF PASTA DOUGH
   (SEE PAGE 10)

FILLING

2 GARLIC CLOVES, CRUSHED

15G (½oz/3 TSP) UNSALTED BUTTER

200G (7oz) BABY SPINACH LEAVES

150G (5oz) RICOTTA, BEATEN UNTIL SMOOTH

85G (3oz) PARMESAN, FINELY GRATED,
   PLUS EXTRA TO SERVE

SALT AND FRESHLY GROUND BLACK PEPPER

GRILLED TOMATO SAUCE (SEE PAGE 18)

1   Make the pasta dough (see page 9).
2   For the ravioli filling, fry the garlic in the butter for I minute. Add the spinach and cook, stirring,
    for 2–3 minutes until wilted. Allow to cool and then mix in the ricotta, Parmesan and seasoning.
    Make the ravioli (see page 11).
3   Cook the ravioli in batches in gently boiling water for 4–5 minutes per batch.
4   Meanwhile, warm the sauce.
5   Drain the ravioli and serve with the sauce, accompanied by Parmesan.

marille with roast vegetables & fontina

PREPARATION TIME 15 minutes COOKING TIME 35 minutes SERVES 4

I AUBERGINE, CUT INTO BITE-SIZED PIECES

4 SMALL COURGETTES, CUT INTO BITE-SIZED PIECES

3 MIXED RED AND YELLOW PEPPERS,
   CUT INTO BITE-SIZED PIECES

6 GARLIC CLOVES

4 TBSP EXTRA-VIRGIN OLIVE OIL

LEAVES FROM 4–5 THYME SPRIGS

SALT AND FRESHLY GROUND BLACK PEPPER

4 WELL-FLAVOURED PLUM TOMATOES,
   HALVED LENGTHWAYS

175G (6oz) MARILLE

150G (5oz) FONTINA, THINLY SLICED

BALSAMIC VINEGAR AND A SMALL HANDFUL
   OF BASIL LEAVES, SHREDDED, TO SERVE

1 Preheat the oven to 220°C/425°F/gas 7.
2 Put the aubergine, courgettes, peppers and garlic in a large roasting tin. Pour over the oil, sprinkle with thyme and seasoning and mix together well. Roast in the preheated oven for about 35 minutes until tender and well browned. Add the tomatoes for the final 20 minutes.
3 About 15 minutes before the vegetables are ready, cook and drain the pasta according to the packet instructions. Toss with the vegetables and fontina, sprinkle with balsamic vinegar and basil and serve.

orecchiette with mushrooms & tomato

PREPARATION TIME 10 minutes plus 15 minutes soaking COOKING TIME 15 minutes SERVES 4

15G (½oz) DRIED MUSHROOMS

400G (14oz) ORECCHIETTE

I SMALL ONION, FINELY CHOPPED

2 GARLIC CLOVES, FINELY CHOPPED

VIRGIN OLIVE OIL

I TBSP FINELY CHOPPED FLAT-LEAF PARSLEY

350G (12oz) CHESTNUT/BROWN-CAP
   MUSHROOMS, SLICED

230G CAN PLUM TOMATOES, DRAINED AND CHOPPED

SALT AND FRESHLY GROUND BLACK PEPPER

FRESHLY GRATED PARMESAN, TO SERVE

1 Soak the mushrooms in just enough boiling water to cover, for 15 minutes. Drain, reserving the water. Finely chop the mushrooms.
2 Cook and drain the pasta according to the packet instructions.
3 Meanwhile, fry the onion and garlic in a little oil in a large frying pan until beginning to colour. Add the dried mushrooms and reserved water and boil until almost evaporated. Add the parsley and fresh mushrooms and fry briskly, stirring, until their liquid has evaporated. Add the tomatoes and heat through briefly. Season. Toss with the pasta, and serve with plenty of Parmesan.

315
fusilli with leeks, garlic & parmesan

PREPARATION TIME 10 minutes COOKING TIME 15 minutes SERVES 4

400G (14oz) FUSILLI
5 GARLIC CLOVES, THINLY SLICED
5 TBSP EXTRA-VIRGIN OLIVE OIL
3 LEEKS, HALVED LENGTHWAYS AND VERY THINLY

SLICED ACROSS
SALT AND FRESHLY GROUND BLACK PEPPER
8 TBSP FRESHLY GRATED PARMESAN,
   PLUS EXTRA TO SERVE

1   Cook and drain the pasta according to the packet instructions, reserving ½ cup of the cooking water.
2   Meanwhile, cook the garlic in the oil in a large frying pan for about 2 minutes until turning golden.
    Add the leeks and cook, stirring, for about 3 minutes until wilted. Cover and cook for about
    10 minutes until tender, stirring occasionally. Season.
3   Toss the pasta with the Parmesan and the leek mixture, adding reserved cooking water,
    if necessary, to moisten. Serve with additional Parmesan.

316
tagliatelle with spinach, lemon & parmesan

PREPARATION TIME 10 minutes COOKING TIME 10 minutes SERVES 4

350G (12oz) TAGLIATELLE
600G (1LB 5oz) BABY SPINACH LEAVES
6 TBSP DOUBLE CREAM

115G (4oz) PARMESAN, FRESHLY GRATED,
   PLUS EXTRA, TO SERVE
SALT AND FRESHLY GROUND BLACK PEPPER
JUICE OF 1 LEMON, OR TO TASTE

1   Cook and drain the pasta according to the packet instructions.
2   Meanwhile, cook the spinach in large pan without any water, stirring until wilted and the liquid has
    evaporated. Toss with the pasta, cream, Parmesan and seasoning and lemon juice, to taste.

317
tagliatelle with peas, asparagus & saffron sauce

PREPARATION TIME 5 minutes plus 15 minutes soaking COOKING TIME 15 minutes SERVES 4

PINCH OF SAFFRON THREADS, CRUSHED
350G (12oz) SLIM ASPARAGUS SPEARS
150G (5oz) FRESH OR FROZEN PEAS
400G (14oz) TAGLIATELLE

KNOB OF UNSALTED BUTTER
225ML (8FL OZ/SCANT 1 CUP) DOUBLE CREAM
6 TBSP FRESHLY GRATED PARMESAN
SALT AND FRESHLY GROUND BLACK PEPPER

1   Soak the saffron in 3 tbsp boiling water for 15 minutes.
2   Meanwhile, cut the tips off the asparagus and reserve. Cook the stems and peas in a large pan of
    boiling water for 2 minutes, add the asparagus tips and cook for a further 1 minute. Drain, reserving
    the cooking water.
3   Cook the pasta in the reserved water according to the packet instructions and drain.
4   While the pasta is cooking, melt the butter, add the asparagus and peas and stir for 1–2 minutes before
    adding the saffron liquid and cream. Heat gently until simmering and then stir in half the cheese
    and seasoning. Toss with the pasta and serve with the remaining Parmesan sprinkled over.

tagliatelle with spinach & ricotta

PREPARATION TIME 5 minutes COOKING TIME 10 minutes SERVES 4

400G (14oz) TAGLIATELLE
450G (1LB) BABY SPINACH LEAVES
SALT AND FRESHLY GROUND BLACK PEPPER

225G (7oz) RICOTTA, CRUMBLED
50G (2oz) PARMESAN, FRESHLY GRATED,
PLUS EXTRA TO SERVE

1   Cook and drain the pasta according to the packet instructions, reserving ½ cup of the cooking water.
2   Meanwhile, cook the spinach without any water in a large saucepan, stirring occasionally until
    it wilts. Season.
3   Toss the pasta with the ricotta and Parmesan and then the spinach. Serve with extra Parmesan.

quick pasta with chickpeas & spinach

PREPARATION TIME 5 minutes COOKING TIME 10 minutes SERVES 4

2 X 400G CANS CHICKPEAS, DRAINED AND RINSED
1 QUANTITY WINTER TOMATO SAUCE (SEE PAGE 19)
500G (1LB 2oz) FRESH PASTA

225G (8oz) SPINACH
PARMESAN SHAVINGS, AND VIRGIN OLIVE OIL
(OPTIONAL), TO SERVE

1   Heat the chickpeas in the tomato sauce until the sauce is just boiling.
2   Meanwhile, cook the pasta in the boiling water according to the packet instructions. Drain, reserving about
    4 tbsp of the cooking water.
3   Toss the spinach with the pasta until it wilts, and then combine with the chickpea mixture and reserved
    water. Serve topped with Parmesan shavings, and a trickle of virgin olive oil, if liked.

riccioli with peppers & cherry tomatoes

PREPARATION TIME 10 minutes COOKING TIME 15 minutes SERVES 4

1 ONION, CHOPPED
VIRGIN OLIVE OIL
2 GARLIC CLOVES, CHOPPED
2 RED PEPPERS, THINLY SLICED LENGTHWAYS
2 YELLOW PEPPERS, THINLY SLICED LENGTHWAYS

225G (8oz) CHERRY TOMATOES, HALVED
SALT AND FRESHLY GROUND BLACK PEPPER
LEAVES FROM A SMALL BUNCH OF BASIL, SHREDDED
400G (14oz) RICCIOLI*
FRESHLY GRATED PARMESAN, TO SERVE

1   Fry the onion in a little oil until soft and golden. Add the garlic and fry for 1 minute. Stir in the peppers
    and cook, stirring frequently, until they begin to soften. Add the tomatoes and cook for about
    5 minutes until they are softened but retain their shape. Season and add the basil.
2   Meanwhile, cook and drain the pasta according to the packet instructions, reserving ½ cup of the
    cooking water.
3   Toss the pasta with the sauce, adding a little of the cooking water, if necessary, to moisten,
    and serve with freshly grated Parmesan.

*   Cavatappi or fusilli can also be used.

321
gnocchi with lentil sauce

PREPARATION TIME 10 minutes COOKING TIME 25 minutes SERVES 4

250G (9oz) UMBRIAN (OR PUY) LENTILS
½ ONION, HALVED THROUGH THE ROOT END
I ROSEMARY SPRIG
I SAGE SPRIG
400G (14oz) GNOCCHI*
4 WELL-FLAVOURED TOMATOES,
  SEEDED AND CHOPPED

3 GARLIC CLOVES, CHOPPED
HANDFUL OF FLAT-LEAF PARSLEY, CHOPPED
VIRGIN OLIVE OIL
EXTRA-VIRGIN OLIVE OIL (OPTIONAL),
  AND FRESHLY GRATED PECORINO, TO SERVE

1 Bring the lentils, onion and herbs to the boil in 3 litres (5 pints/12 cups) water, then simmer for 15–20 minutes until the lentils are tender. Return to the boil, add the pasta, stir and cook until al dente, stirring occasionally.

2 Meanwhile, fry the tomatoes, garlic and parsley in a little oil for 3–4 minutes until the tomatoes have softened but not disintegrated completely.

3 Drain the pasta and lentils, reserving about ½ cup of the cooking water. Discard the onion and herbs. Toss the pasta and lentils with the tomato mixture. If not serving with the olive oil, add enough of the reserved water to moisten. Serve with extra-virgin olive oil trickled into each portion, if liked, and pecorino.

* Chifferi or pipe rigate can also be used.

322
cavatappi with roast aubergines, peppers & basil

PREPARATION TIME 10 minutes COOKING TIME 35 minutes SERVES 4

2 AUBERGINES, WEIGHING 450–675G (1–1½LB) TOTAL
2 PLUMP RED PEPPERS
5 GARLIC CLOVES IN THEIR SKINS
6 TBSP EXTRA-VIRGIN OLIVE OIL
20 PITTED NIÇOISE OR GAETA OLIVES, CHOPPED
400G (14oz) CAVATAPPI

SALT AND FRESHLY GROUND BLACK PEPPER
BALSAMIC VINEGAR, TO TASTE
SMALL HANDFUL OF BASIL LEAVES, SHREDDED
FRESHLY GRATED PROVOLONE OR PARMESAN,
  TO SERVE

1 Preheat the oven to 200°C/400°F/gas 6.

2 Prick the aubergines in several places and cook in the preheated oven for 20–30 minutes, turning once, until softened, wrinkled and lightly charred. At the same time, cook the peppers in the oven for 15–20 minutes until lightly charred and soft, and the garlic until softened.

3 Peel the peppers and cut into slices. Pop the garlic cloves from their skins into a bowl and mash with the oil. Transfer to a frying pan.

4 When the aubergines are cool enough to handle, peel off the skin and chop the flesh. Add to the frying pan, with the red peppers and olives. Season with salt, pepper and balsamic vinegar, and warm gently.

5 Meanwhile, cook and drain the pasta according to the packet instructions. Toss with the vegetables and basil. Serve with freshly grated provolone or Parmesan.

323
gemelli with melting onion sauce

PREPARATION TIME 10 minutes COOKING TIME 40 minutes SERVES 4

675G (1½LB) LARGE ONIONS, VERY THINLY SLICED

3 GARLIC CLOVES, FINELY SLICED

I BAY LEAF

SMALL SPRIG OF ROSEMARY

3 TBSP OLIVE OIL

SALT AND FRESHLY GROUND BLACK PEPPER

115ML (4FL OZ/½ CUP) MEDIUM-BODIED DRY
WHITE WINE

2–3 TBSP CHOPPED FLAT-LEAF PARSLEY

400G (14OZ) GEMELLI*

150G (5OZ) PECORINO, GRATED

1   Put the onions, garlic, bay leaf and rosemary into a large heavy frying pan with the oil and sprinkle with salt. Cook gently for 10 minutes, then cover the onions closely with a circle of greaseproof paper and cook over a low heat until the onions turn a rich golden brown.

2   Stir in the wine and cook briskly, stirring, until the wine has evaporated. Discard the bay leaf and rosemary. Add black pepper and the parsley.

3   Meanwhile, cook and drain the pasta according to the packet instructions. Toss with the onions and most of the pecorino. Serve with the remaining pecorino sprinkled over.

*   Strozzapreti or penne rigate can also be used.

324
panzarotti

PREPARATION TIME 40 minutes plus 1 hour resting for the dough COOKING TIME 10–15 minutes SERVES 4

PASTA DOUGH
225G (8oz/scant 2 cups) **PLAIN FLOUR**
2 **EGGS**
2 TBSP **VIRGIN OLIVE OIL**

50G (2oz) **BUFFALO MOZZARELLA, FINELY GRATED**
70G (2½oz/scant ⅓ cup) **RICOTTA**
25G (1oz) **PARMESAN, FRESHLY GRATED,**
    PLUS EXTRA TO SERVE
50G (2oz) **DOLCELATTE, CHOPPED**
SALT AND FRESHLY GROUND BLACK PEPPER
SMALL HANDFUL OF MIXED FLAT-LEAF
    PARSLEY AND CHIVES, FINELY CHOPPED
OLIVE OIL, FOR DEEP FRYING

1 Make the dough (see page 10), wrap and leave to rest for 30 minutes.
2 Meanwhile, using a fork, mash the 4 cheeses with the seasoning, taking care with the salt but using plenty of black pepper. Work in the herbs.
3 Make 5cm (2in) raviolini (see page 12) with the dough and filling. Leave to rest 30 minutes in a cool place but preferably not the fridge.
4 Heat a deep pan of oil to 180°C/350°F* for frying the panzarotti. Add the panzarotti in batches, frying them for 2–3 minutes per batch until golden; do not overcrowd the pan. Drain on kitchen paper and sprinkle with grated Parmesan.

* If you don't have a suitable thermometer,
drop a cube of bread into the oil;
if it turns golden in 1 minute,
the oil is ready.

190

325
spinach & lentil lasagne

PREPARATION TIME 10 minutes COOKING TIME 45 minutes SERVES 6

300G (10oz) GREEN LENTILS
1 ONION, FINELY CHOPPED
1 SMALL CARROT, FINELY CHOPPED
2 GARLIC CLOVES, THINLY SLICED
450G (1LB) SPINACH, CHOPPED
2–3 TBSP RED PESTO (SEE PAGE 19)

SALT AND FRESHLY GROUND BLACK PEPPER
2 X 400G CANS CHOPPED PLUM TOMATOES
300ML (10FL oz/SCANT 1¼ CUPS) PASSATA
175G (6oz) LASAGNE SHEETS
50G (2oz) PECORINO, FRESHLY GRATED

1   Cook the lentils, onion, carrot and garlic just covered with water for about 20 minutes until tender and almost dry; if necessary, strain off surplus liquid. Add the spinach and cook, stirring frequently until it has wilted. Stir in the red pesto and seasoning.
2   Meanwhile, simmer the tomatoes and passata for about 10 minutes until slightly reduced.
3   While the tomatoes are cooking, cook and drain the lasagne, even if using the no-pre-cook type (see page 15) and spread on a clean tea towel to dry.
4   Preheat the oven to 200°C/400°F/gas 6.
5   Spread a little of the tomato sauce over the bottom of an oiled large shallow baking dish. Cover with a layer of lasagne, then some of the lentil sauce, followed by a layer of tomato. Continue layering, ending with spinach sauce. Scatter over the cheese.
6   Bake in the preheated oven for about 25 minutes until bubbling and golden. Leave to stand for 5 minutes before serving.

326
spinach & cheese lasagne

PREPARATION TIME 15 minutes COOKING TIME 45 minutes SERVES 4–6

12 SHEETS FRESH LASAGNE
900G (2LB) SPINACH
SMALL KNOB OF UNSALTED BUTTER
225G (8oz/SCANT 1 CUP) RICOTTA
175G (6oz) GORGONZOLA, CRUMBLED
SALT AND FRESHLY GROUND BLACK PEPPER
4 TBSP PINE NUTS, LIGHTLY TOASTED
50G (2oz) PARMESAN, FRESHLY GRATED
200G (7oz) BUFFALO MOZZARELLA, GRATED

BÉCHAMEL SAUCE
50G (2oz/SCANT ¼ CUP) UNSALTED BUTTER
40G (1½oz/4 TBSP) PLAIN FLOUR
725ML (1¼ PINTS/8 CUPS) MILK

1   Cook and drain the lasagne (see page 15) and spread on a tea towel to drain.
2   Meanwhile, make the béchamel sauce (see page 17).
3   Preheat the oven to 180°C/350°F/gas 4.
4   While the béchamel is simmering, cook the spinach in a large pan, stirring frequently until wilted and soft. Drain, chop coarsely and then squeeze out as much water as possible. Combine with the butter, ricotta, Gorgonzola and seasoning.
5   Barely cover the base of an oiled shallow baking dish with béchamel sauce. Cover with 3 of the lasagne sheets, then one-quarter of the spinach mixture and scatter over one-quarter of the pine nuts. Pour over a quarter of the remaining béchamel and sprinkle one-quarter of the Parmesan on top. Repeat the layers, adding one-third of the mozzarella with the pine nuts until the ingredients are used, ending with mozzarella and Parmesan.
6   Bake in the preheated oven for 30–35 minutes until bubbling and golden. Leave to stand for 5 minutes before serving.

ricotta, parmesan & squash ravioli

PREPARATION TIME 45 minutes COOKING TIME 1¼ hours SERVES 4

2-EGG QUANTITY PASTA DOUGH (SEE PAGE 10).
50g (2oz) UNSALTED BUTTER
FINELY GRATED ZEST OF 1 LEMON
40G (1½oz) PINE NUTS, LIGHTLY TOASTED
PARMESAN, TO SERVE

FILLING
450G (1LB) PIECE OF BUTTERNUT SQUASH
VIRGIN OLIVE OIL
150G (5oz/SCANT ⅔ CUP) RICOTTA, BEATEN
  UNTIL SMOOTH
85G (3oz) PARMESAN, FINELY GRATED
SALT AND FRESHLY GROUND BLACK PEPPER

1   Make the pasta dough (see page 10).
2   While the dough is resting, make the filling. Preheat the oven to 190°C/375°F/gas 5. Brush the squash
    flesh with a little oil and bake in the preheated oven for about 1 hour until soft. Cool slightly and then
    scrape into a bowl, add the ricotta and mash with a potato masher or fork. Mix in the Parmesan and
    seasoning. Make the ravioli (see page 11).
3   Melt the butter over a very low heat, add the lemon zest and set aside to infuse while cooking the pasta.
4   Cook the ravioli in gently boiling water, in batches, if necessary, for about 4 minutes per batch. Drain well.
    Scatter the pine nuts over the ravioli and pour over the lemon butter. Serve with grated Parmesan.

pappardelle with roast fennel & dolcelatte

PREPARATION TIME 5 minutes COOKING TIME 35 minutes SERVES 4

2 FENNEL BULBS, THINLY SLICED, FEATHERY TOPS
  RESERVED
VIRGIN OLIVE OIL
SALT AND FRESHLY GROUND BLACK PEPPER
300ML (10FL OZ/SCANT 1¼ CUPS) MEDIUM-BODIED DRY
  WHITE WINE

350G (12oz) PAPPARDELLE
225G (8oz) DOLCELATTE, CRUMBLED
4 TBSP WALNUTS, LIGHTLY TOASTED
  AND COARSELY CHOPPED

1   Preheat the oven to 200°C/425°F/gas 7.
2   Put the fennel slices in a heavy-duty roasting tin, trickle over a little oil, season then stir the fennel
    to ensure it is evenly coated with oil. Spread in a single layer. Roast in the preheated oven for about
    25–30 minutes until lightly charred; stir occasionally.
3   Remove the fennel from the tin and keep warm. Stir the wine into the tin and boil on the hob until
    reduced by half.
4   Meanwhile, cook and drain the pasta according to the packet instructions. Toss with the reduced wine,
    cheese, fennel and seasoning. Scatter over the walnuts and reserved feathery tops.

329

tonnarelli with radicchio & taleggio

PREPARATION TIME 10 minutes COOKING TIME 25 minutes SERVES 4

I RED ONION, HALVED LENGTHWAYS
   AND THINLY SLICED
VIRGIN OLIVE OIL
I GARLIC CLOVE, FINELY CHOPPED
4 LARGE HEADS OF RADICCHIO, SHREDDED
115ML (4FL OZ/SCANT ½ CUP) MEDIUM-BODIED DRY
   WHITE WINE

5 TBSP VEGETABLE STOCK OR WATER
100G (3½oz) TALEGGIO, CHOPPED
SALT AND FRESHLY GROUND BLACK PEPPER
375G (13oz) TONNARELLI*
FRESHLY GRATED PARMESAN,
   TO SERVE

1 Fry the red onion in a little oil in a large frying pan until softened. Add the garlic, fry for 1 minute,
   then stir in the radicchio and fry, stirring occasionally, until turning brown.
2 Pour in the wine and stock, bring to the boil and then simmer, uncovered, until the liquid has evaporated
   and the radicchio is almost tender; leave some parts with bite. The liquid should have almost evaporated.
   Add the Taleggio and seasoning and warm very gently until the cheese is just melting.
3 Meanwhile, cook and drain the pasta according to the packet instructions.
   Toss with the radicchio sauce. Serve with freshly grated Parmesan.

* Spaghetti can also be used.

330

penne rigate with aubergines & ricotta

PREPARATION TIME 10 minutes COOKING TIME 15 minutes SERVES 4

2 SMALL AUBERGINES, THICKLY SLICED
EXTRA-VIRGIN OLIVE OIL, PLUS EXTRA FOR GRILLING
SALT AND FRESHLY GROUND BLACK PEPPER
I SMALL ONION, FINELY CHOPPED
3 GARLIC CLOVES, THINLY SLICED
I RED CHILLI, SEEDED AND FINELY CHOPPED

400G CAN CHOPPED PLUM TOMATOES
3 TBSP CHOPPED FLAT-LEAF PARSLEY
12 PITTED BLACK OLIVES, HALVED
400G (14oz) PENNE RIGATE
175G (6oz/SCANT ¾ CUP) RICOTTA, CRUMBLED
SHREDDED BASIL LEAVES, TO SERVE

1 Spread the aubergine slices in a single layer on a large baking sheet, brush both sides with oil and
   sprinkle with seasoning. Cook under a preheated hot grill for 3–6 minutes per side until browned
   and softened. When cool enough to handle, cut into strips.
2 Meanwhile, fry the onion in a little oil in a frying pan until softened. Add the garlic and chilli and fry
   for 1 minute. Stir in the tomatoes and parsley and simmer for 10–15 minutes until thickened.
   Add the olives and seasoning.
3 Meanwhile, cook and drain the pasta according to the packet instructions. Toss with half the aubergine
   strips, half the ricotta, and the tomato sauce. Serve with the remaining aubergine strips on top
   and scatter over the remaining ricotta and the basil.

ziti with red peppers & basil

PREPARATION TIME 10 minutes COOKING TIME 20 minutes SERVES 4

3 GARLIC CLOVES, HALVED LENGTHWAYS
3 TBSP VIRGIN OLIVE OIL
4 LARGE, PLUMP RED PEPPERS,
   QUARTERED LENGTHWAYS
SALT AND FRESHLY GROUND BLACK PEPPER

BALSAMIC VINEGAR
400G (14oz) ZITI
SMALL HANDFUL OF BASIL LEAVES, SHREDDED
6 TBSP PARMESAN, FRESHLY GRATED,
   PLUS EXTRA TO SERVE

1   Heat the garlic in the oil over a very low heat for 10 minutes until the oil is infused. Discard the garlic.
2   Meanwhile, slice the pepper quarters lengthways into 1cm (½in) wide strips, then cut across the strips, into halves.
3   Cook the peppers in the garlic-infused oil over quite a high heat until they are tender yet still retain their shape; do not allow them to become mushy. Season with salt, plenty of freshly ground black pepper and balsamic vinegar.
4   Meanwhile, cook and drain the pasta according to the packet instructions.
   Toss with the peppers and the pan juices, the basil and Parmesan.

*   Penne rigate can also be used.

194

332

artichoke & mushroom lasagne

PREPARATION TIME 15 minutes COOKING TIME 50 minutes SERVES 4–6

5 SHALLOTS, FINELY CHOPPED
VIRGIN OLIVE OIL
3 GARLIC CLOVES, FINELY CHOPPED
750G (1LB 10oz) MIXED MUSHROOMS SUCH AS
   SHIITAKE, OYSTER, BROWN-CAP/CHESTNUT, HALVED,
   QUARTERED OR SLICED ACCORDING TO SIZE
1¾ TBSP LEMON JUICE
LEAVES FROM A BUNCH OF
   FLAT-LEAF PARSLEY, CHOPPED
SALT AND FRESHLY GROUND BLACK PEPPER

200G (7oz) FRESH LASAGNE VERDE SHEETS
250G (9oz/1 CUP) RICOTTA
250G (9oz) DRAINED ROAST ARTICHOKES
   IN OIL, HALVED
50G (2oz) PARMESAN, FRESHLY GRATED

BÉCHAMEL SAUCE
45G (3 TBSP) BUTTER
4½ TBSP PLAIN FLOUR
750ML (1¼ PINTS/3 CUPS) MILK

1   Fry the shallots in a little oil in a large frying pan until soft and becoming golden, adding the garlic for the final 3 minutes or so. Add the mushrooms, the lemon juice and half of the parsley and fry, stirring occasionally, for 10–15 minutes until softened and browned. Add the remaining parsley and seasoning.
2   Meanwhile, make the béchamel sauce (see page 17). While the sauce is simmering, cook, drain and rinse the lasagne, even if using the no-pre-cook type (see page 15). Spread on a tea towel to dry.
3   Preheat the oven to 200°C/400°F/gas 6.
4   Spread a thin layer of béchamel sauce in the bottom of an oiled large shallow baking dish. Cover with a layer of lasagne, then one-quarter of the ricotta, followed by one-quarter of the mushroom mixture and half the artichokes. Sprinkle with some of the Parmesan. Continue layering, ending with a layer of béchamel and a good sprinkling of Parmesan.
5   Bake in the oven for about 30 minutes until golden and bubbling. Stand for 5 minutes before serving.

cheese & herb agnolotti

PREPARATION TIME 45 minutes COOKING TIME 15 minutes SERVES 4

2-EGG QUANTITY OF PASTA DOUGH
  (SEE PAGE 10)
I GARLIC CLOVE
OLIVE OIL
300G (10oz) RICOTTA
85G (3oz) PARMESAN, FRESHLY GRATED
I EGG YOLK

2 HANDFULS CHOPPED MIXED HERBS SUCH AS
  BASIL, FLAT-LEAF PARSLEY, THYME AND OREGANO
FRESHLY GROUND BLACK PEPPER
ABOUT 50G (2oz/scant ¼ cup) UNSALTED BUTTER
50G (2oz) PARMESAN, FRESHLY GRATED
GRILLED CHERRY TOMATOES ON THE VINE,
  TO SERVE (OPTIONAL)

1   While the pasta dough is resting, fry the garlic in a little oil for 1–2 minutes. Leave to cool,
    then combine with the ricotta, Parmesan, egg yolk, herbs and black pepper;
    salt might not be necessary because of the saltiness of the Parmesan.
2   Make the agnolotti (see page 10) with the pasta dough and herb filling.
3   Cook the agnolotti in batches in gently boiling water for 4–5 minutes per batch.
4   Meanwhile, melt the butter with the Parmesan, but do not allow to become too hot.
    Season with black pepper.
5   Drain the agnolotti and pour over the melted butter and Parmesan.
    Serve accompanied by the grilled tomatoes, if liked.

VEGETABLE & VEGETARIAN DISHES

195

spinach & mushroom lasagne

PREPARATION TIME 10 minutes COOKING TIME 1 hour SERVES 4

2 ONIONS, HALVED AND SLICED
2 BAY LEAVES
I TSP DRIED OREGANO
SALT AND FRESHLY GROUND BLACK PEPPER
VIRGIN OLIVE OIL
3 PLUMP GARLIC CLOVES, CHOPPED
400G (14oz) BROWN-CAP/CHESTNUT
  MUSHROOMS, SLICED

I TBSP SUN-DRIED TOMATO PASTE
2 X 400G CANS CHOPPED TOMATOES
175G (6oz) LASAGNE SHEETS
400G (14oz) FRESH SPINACH
I QUANTITY BÉCHAMEL SAUCE
  (SEE PAGE 17)
6 TBSP FRESHLY GRATED PARMESAN

1   Cook the onions with the bay leaves, oregano and seasoning in a little oil in a large frying pan, stirring
    occasionally, until the onions are very soft and lightly browned, adding the garlic about halfway through.
2   Add the mushrooms and cook, stirring occasionally, until the liquid has evaporated. Stir in the tomato
    paste and tomatoes, bring to the boil, then cook gently for 20 minutes until reduced to a thick sauce.
3   At the same time, cook, drain and rinse the lasagne, even if using the no-pre-cook type (see page 15).
    Spread on a tea towel to dry.
4   Meanwhile, cook the spinach in a large covered pan, shaking the pan 2 or 3 times for about
    3 minutes until the spinach has wilted and softened. Drain well and squeeze out excess moisture.
5   Preheat the oven to 190°C/375°F/gas 5.
6   Spread a thinnish layer of béchamel sauce over the bottom of an oiled shallow baking dish. Cover with
    a layer of lasagne followed by the mushroom mixture, then spinach. Repeat the layering until all lasagne
    and vegetables have been used, then end with a layer of béchamel sauce. Sprinkle over the Parmesan.
7   Bake in the preheated oven for about 25–30 minutes until bubbling and golden.

335
courgette & ricotta cannelloni

PREPARATION TIME 15 minutes* COOKING TIME 25 minutes SERVES 4

APPROXIMATELY 12 LASAGNE VERDE SHEETS
1 ONION, CHOPPED
OLIVE OIL FOR COOKING
4 COURGETTES, GRATED
2 GARLIC CLOVES, SQUASHED AND FINELY CHOPPED
ZEST OF 1 LEMON

250G (9oz/1 cup) RICOTTA
SALT AND FRESHLY GROUND BLACK PEPPER
1 QUANTITY FRESH TOMATO SAUCE (SEE PAGE 18) OR
  WINTER TOMATO SAUCE (SEE PAGE 19), WARMED
50G (2oz) PARMESAN, FRESHLY GRATED

1   Cook and drain the lasagne sheets (see page 15) and spread on a tea towel to dry.
2   Preheat the oven to 200°C/400°F/gas 6.
3   Fry the onion in a little oil until soft but not coloured. Stir in the courgettes and garlic and continue cooking, stirring frequently, until soft. Remove from the heat and add the lemon zest, half the ricotta and seasoning.
4   Spread the courgette mixture down the centre of each lasagne sheet. Roll into tubes.
5   Pour half the sauce into an oiled large, shallow baking dish. Place the tubes on top, seam-side down. Pour over the remaining sauce, dot with the remaining ricotta and sprinkle with the Parmesan.
6   Bake in the preheated oven for 15 minutes, until golden.

*   Assumes the sauce is already made.

336
squash & mushroom lasagne

PREPARATION TIME 15 minutes COOKING TIME 45 minutes SERVES 4–6

900G (2LB) BUTTERNUT SQUASH, HALVED, PEELED,
  SEEDED AND THINLY SLICED ACROSS
VIRGIN OLIVE OIL
SALT AND FRESHLY GROUND BLACK PEPPER
1½ TBSP PESTO (SEE PAGE 18)
6 LASAGNE SHEETS
600G (1LB 5oz) MIXED MUSHROOMS, SUCH AS
  BROWN-CAP/CHESTNUT, SHIITAKE AND
  OYSTER, SLICED

3 GARLIC CLOVES, FINELY CHOPPED
115ML (4FL oz/Scant ½ cup) HALF-FAT CRÈME FRAÎCHE
600G (1LB 5oz) SPINACH
25G (1oz) PARMESAN, FRESHLY GRATED
50G (2oz) FONTINA, GRATED

1   Preheat the oven to 230°C/450°F/gas 8.
2   Put the squash into a roasting tin, trickle over about 2 tbsp oil, turn the pieces to coat with oil, season and bake in the preheated oven for about 20 minutes until tender and lightly browned around the edges. Cool slightly and then mix with the pesto. Lower the oven temperature to 190°C/375°F/gas 5.
3   Meanwhile, cook, drain and rinse the lasagne, even if using the no-pre-cook type (see page 15). Spread on a tea towel to dry.
4   While the lasagne sheets are cooking, fry the mushrooms in a little oil until tender and their juices are beginning to flow, adding half the garlic 1 minute before the end. Add 1 tbsp of crème fraîche and simmer for 2 minutes. Season and set aside.
5   Cook the spinach in a large saucepan, stirring occasionally, until wilted. Drain and squeeze out excess liquid. Stir in the Parmesan, remaining garlic and 4 tbsp of crème fraîche. Season.
6   Reserve a little of each vegetable. Layer the lasagne and remaining vegetables in a large oiled dish, starting with spinach and ending with lasagne. Cover with the reserved vegetables and spread over the remaining crème fraîche. Season with pepper and sprinkle over the fontina. Bake for 25 minutes until golden.

337
roast vegetable lasagne

PREPARATION TIME 15 minutes plus 1 hour draining COOKING TIME 55 minutes SERVES 6

1 SMALL AUBERGINE, CUT INTO 2. 5CM (1IN) CUBES
2 COURGETTES, CUT INTO 2. 5CM (1IN) CUBES
SALT AND FRESHLY GROUND BLACK PEPPER
1 RED PEPPER, CUT INTO 2. 5CM (1IN) SQUARES
1 FENNEL BULB, QUITE FINELY CHOPPED
4 PLUMP GARLIC CLOVES, CUT INTO THIN SLIVERS
VIRGIN OLIVE OIL
50G (2OZ) PITTED OIL-CURED BLACK OLIVES, HALVED
3 TBSP BASIL, COARSELY SHREDDED

50G (2OZ) PARMESAN, FRESHLY GRATED
APPROXIMATELY 10 SHEETS LASAGNE
40G/1½ OZ EACH TALEGGIO AND MOZZARELLA,
  GRATED AND MIXED

BÉCHAMEL SAUCE
35G (1¼OZ/2½ TBSP) PLAIN FLOUR
40G (1½OZ/2½ TBSP) UNSALTED BUTTER
570ML (1 PINT/SCANT 2½ CUPS) MILK

1 Put the aubergine and courgettes in a large colander, sprinkle over some salt, stir to mix, then leave to drain for about 1 hour. Rinse well and dry thoroughly.
2 Preheat the oven to 240°C/475°F/gas 9.
3 Put all the vegetables and the garlic in a roasting tin, trickle over a little oil and stir to coat the vegetables. Bake on the top shelf of the preheated oven for 30 minutes until browned at the edges, stirring occasionally. Remove from the oven (turn the oven down to 190°C/375°F/gas 5) and mix the olives, basil and seasoning with the cooked vegetables.
4 Meanwhile, cook, drain and rinse the lasagne, even if using the no-pre-cook type (see page 15). Spread on a tea towel to dry.
5 While the lasagne is cooking, make the béchamel sauce (see page 17). Stir 3 tbsp of the Parmesan into the sauce and spread one-quarter over the bottom of a greased large, shallow baking dish. Cover with one third of the vegetables. Scatter over one-third of the mozzarella and Taleggio, followed by a single layer of lasagne sheets. Repeat the layering and finish with the remaining cheese sauce. Sprinkle over the remaining Parmesan. Bake in the oven for 20–25 minutes until the top is golden.

vegetable lasagne with goats' cheese topping

PREPARATION TIME 10 minutes plus 30 minutes standing COOKING TIME 35 minutes SERVES 6

2 AUBERGINES, CUT INTO 1cm (½in) CUBES

2 ONIONS, THINLY SLICED

VIRGIN OLIVE OIL

4 GARLIC CLOVES, FINELY CHOPPED

5 PLUM TOMATOES, CUT INTO 1cm (½in) PIECES

4 TBSP RED WINE

ABOUT 2 TBSP SUN-DRIED TOMATO PASTE

1 TBSP DRIED OREGANO

2 RED AND 2 YELLOW PEPPERS

APPROXIMATELY 10 LASAGNE VERDE SHEETS

TOPPING

2 EGGS, BEATEN

150ML (5FL OZ/SCANT ⅔ CUP) SINGLE CREAM

350G (12OZ) SOFT GOATS' CHEESE

SALT AND FRESHLY GROUND BLACK PEPPER

3 TBSP FRESH BREADCRUMBS

4 TBSP FRESHLY GRATED PECORINO

1   Sprinkle the aubergine with salt in a colander and leave to drain for 30 minutes. Rinse and dry thoroughly.

2   Fry the onions in a little oil until soft and lightly coloured. Stir in the garlic and aubergine, cook for 2–3 minutes then add the tomatoes, wine, tomato paste and oregano. Cover and simmer for 15–20 minutes. Stir occasionally to prevent sticking.

3   Meanwhile, grill the peppers, then peel and slice them (see page 67). Cook, drain and rinse the lasagne, even if using the no-pre-cook type (see page 15). Spread on a tea towel to dry.

4   Make the topping by stirring the eggs and cream into the goats' cheese until smooth. Season.

5   Preheat the oven to 190°C/375°F/gas 5.

6   Add the peppers and seasoning to the aubergine mixture and spread about one-third in an oiled large, shallow baking dish. Cover with a layer of lasagne, trimming to fit the dish as necessary. Repeat the layering twice. Pour over the topping to cover evenly. Sprinkle with the breadcrumbs and pecorino.

7   Bake in the preheated oven for about 30 minutes until the top is lightly browned. Leave to stand for 5 minutes before serving.

tagliatelle with slow-cooked fennel & garlic

PREPARATION TIME 10 minutes COOKING TIME 40 minutes SERVES 4

1 FENNEL BULB, THINLY SLICED, FEATHERY TOPS
  RESERVED

1 ONION, THINLY SLICED

4 GARLIC CLOVES, THINLY SLICED

PINCH OF CHILLI FLAKES

50G (2OZ/SCANT ¼ CUP) UNSALTED BUTTER

1 TSP CASTER SUGAR

SALT AND FRESHLY GROUND BLACK PEPPER

115ML (4FL OZ/SCANT ½ CUP) MEDIUM-BODIED DRY
  WHITE WINE

150ML (5FL OZ/SCANT ⅔ CUP) DOUBLE CREAM

400G (14OZ) TAGLIATELLE

4 TBSP FRESHLY GRATED PARMESAN, PLUS EXTRA
  TO SERVE

CHOPPED FENNEL HERB, TO SERVE (OPTIONAL)

1   Cook the fennel, onion, garlic and chilli in the butter, sugar and seasoning in a heavy frying pan covered with a large disc of greaseproof paper over a low heat, stirring occasionally, for 25–30 minutes until very soft. Stir in 1–2 tbsp hot water if the vegetables become too dry.

2   Stir in the wine, increase the heat and simmer, uncovered, until it has almost evaporated.
    Add the cream and simmer until the sauce has thickened, but do not allow it to become too thick.

3   Meanwhile, cook and drain the tagliatelle according to the packet instructions. Toss with the Parmesan and fennel sauce and sprinkle over the reserved fennel tops, or chopped fennel herb.
    Serve with additional Parmesan.

340
sedani with roast vegetables
& olives al forno

PREPARATION TIME 15 minutes plus optional 1 hour draining COOKING TIME 50 minutes SERVES 4

2 COURGETTES, CUT INTO BITE-SIZED CHUNKS
1 SMALL AUBERGINE, CUT INTO BITE-SIZED CHUNKS
SALT
1 HEAD OF CHICORY, CUT INTO BITE-SIZED PIECES
1 RED ONION, CUT INTO WEDGES
1 RED PEPPER, CUT INTO BITE-SIZED CHUNKS
3 GARLIC CLOVES, CHOPPED
1 SPRIG OF ROSEMARY

2 SPRIGS OF THYME
VIRGIN OLIVE OIL
4 RIPE WELL-FLAVOURED TOMATOES, QUARTERED
175G (6oz) SEDANI*
50G (2oz) PITTED BLACK OLIVES
1 QUANTITY CHEESE SAUCE (SEE PAGE 17)
85G (3oz) BUFFALO MOZZARELLA, THINLY SLICED
1½ TBSP FRESHLY GRATED PARMESAN

1   Layer the courgettes and aubergines in a colander, sprinkling salt over each layer. Leave to drain for
    1 hour. Rinse well and dry thoroughly**.
2   Preheat the oven to 220°C/425°F/gas 7.
3   Put the courgettes and aubergine in a large roasting tin with the chicory, onion, pepper, garlic and
    herbs. Trickle over a little oil, stir together to coat the vegetables and spread them out. Roast in the top
    of the preheated oven for about 30 minutes until tender and charred in patches. Add the tomatoes after
    15 minutes. Discard the herbs and lower the oven temperature to 200°C/400°F/gas 6.
4   Just before the vegetables are ready, cook the pasta according to the packet instructions but for 1 minute
    less than usual, then drain. Combine with the vegetables, olives and cheese sauce. Layer in a large,
    shallow baking dish with the mozzarella, finishing with mozzarella. Sprinkle over the Parmesan.
5   Bake for about 10 minutes until the top is golden.

*   Penne or rigatoni can also be used.
** This step can be omitted, if you wish.

341
macaroni, fennel, pine nut
& cheese al forno

PREPARATION TIME 15 minutes COOKING TIME 30 minutes SERVES 4

350G (12oz) FENNEL, HALVED LENGTHWAYS, THEN
    THINLY SLICED
1 ONION, THINLY SLICED
VIRGIN OLIVE OIL
2 GARLIC CLOVES, CHOPPED

225G (8oz) MACARONI
50G (2oz) PINE NUTS, LIGHTLY TOASTED
350G (12oz) RICOTTA, CRUMBLED
SALT AND FRESHLY GROUND BLACK PEPPER
175G (6oz) BUFFALO MOZZARELLA, THINLY SLICED

1   Preheat the oven to 180°C/350°F/gas 4.
2   Boil the fennel for 5 minutes until tender. Drain well, reserving the cooking water. Coarsely chop
    the fennel.
3   Meanwhile, fry the onion in a little oil until soft. Stir in the garlic and chopped fennel and cook for about
    4 minutes until the vegetables are lightly flecked with brown. Remove from the heat and leave to cool.
4   Meanwhile, cook the macaroni in the fennel water plus additional water according to the packet
    instructions but for 1 minute less than usual, then drain well. Spread half in a buttered large, shallow
    baking dish.
5   Add the pine nuts, ricotta and seasoning to the fennel sauce. Spread half over the macaroni.
    Repeat the layers. Lay the mozzarella over the top and bake in the preheated oven for
    15–20 minutes until the mozzarella is golden and melted.

342
broad bean & basil cannelloni

PREPARATION TIME 20 minutes COOKING TIME 40 minutes SERVES 4

12 CANNELLONI TUBES

350G (12oz) SHELLED FRESH BROAD BEANS,
  OR FROZEN BABY BROAD BEANS

225G (8oz/SCANT 1 CUP) RICOTTA

1 GARLIC CLOVE, CRUSHED

2–3 TBSP BASIL, FINELY CHOPPED

FRESHLY GROUND BLACK PEPPER

½ QUANTITY TOMATO AND BASIL SAUCE (SEE
  PAGE 18)

50G (2oz) MOZZARELLA, GRATED

2 TBSP FRESHLY GRATED PARMESAN

CHEESE SAUCE

40G (1½oz/3 TBSP) UNSALTED BUTTER

2½ TBSP PLAIN FLOUR

450ML (15FL OZ/1⅞ CUPS) MILK

50G (2oz) PARMESAN,
  FRESHLY GRATED

1   Cook and drain the cannelloni tubes (see page 15).
2   Meanwhile, make the simple cheese sauce (see page 17).
3   Preheat the oven to 200°C/400°F/gas 6.
4   Boil the broad beans in salted water until tender. Drain and rinse in cold water. Put into a food
    processor with the ricotta, garlic and basil. Pulse until mixed to a nubbly texture. Season with black
    pepper. Spoon into a large piping bag (or thick plastic food bag with a corner snipped off) and pipe
    into the cannelloni tubes.
5   Spread the tomato sauce over the base of a large, shallow baking dish and lay the tubes in the dish.
    Cover completely with the cheese sauce and sprinkle over the mozzarella and Parmesan.
6   Bake in the preheated oven for 30–35 minutes until bubbling and golden.

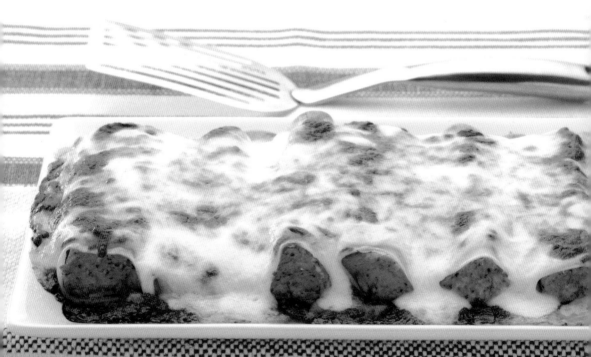

343

elicoidali with roast vegetables & pesto

PREPARATION TIME 15 minutes COOKING TIME 30—40 minutes SERVES 4

2 LEEKS WITH THE ROOT ENDS LEFT ON,
  QUARTERED LENGTHWAYS
2 COURGETTES, CUT INTO LARGE CHUNKS
2 RED PEPPERS, QUARTERED
1 AUBERGINE, CUT INTO LARGE CHUNKS
1 HEAD OF GARLIC, SEPARATED INTO CLOVES,
  1 FINELY CHOPPED

VIRGIN OLIVE OIL
4 WELL-FLAVOURED PLUM TOMATOES,
  HALVED
350G (12oz) ELICOIDALI
3 TBSP PESTO (SEE PAGE 18)
RICOTTA, TO SERVE (OPTIONAL)

1   Preheat the oven to 200°C/400°F/gas 6.
2   Put all the vegetables, except the tomatoes, into a large roasting tin with the whole garlic cloves.
    Trickle over some oil, stir together to coat the vegetables and spread them out. Roast in the top
    of the preheated oven for 30—40 minutes until tender and charred in patches. Stir and add the
    tomatoes after 15 minutes.
3   Just before the vegetables are ready, cook and drain the pasta according to the packet instructions.
4   When the vegetables are cooked, use scissors to cut the vegetables into small pieces and combine
    with the chopped garlic.
5   Toss the pasta with the pesto and vegetables Stir in a spoonful or two of the juices remaining
    in the roasting tin. Serve topped with a spoonful of ricotta, if liked.

344

marille with spinach, aubergines & peppers al forno

PREPARATION TIME 15 minutes COOKING TIME 1¼ hours SERVES 4

1 AUBERGINE, CUT INTO BITE-SIZED PIECES
225G (8oz) BUTTERNUT OR ONION SQUASH, CUT INTO
  BITE-SIZED PIECES
1 RED PEPPER AND 1 YELLOW PEPPER, CUT INTO
  BITE-SIZED PIECES
2 GARLIC CLOVES, THINLY SLICED
VIRGIN OLIVE OIL
SALT AND FRESHLY GROUND BLACK PEPPER
115G (4oz) MARILLE
225G (8oz) FROZEN SPINACH, THAWED AND
  SQUEEZED DRY, OR 450G (1LB) FRESH SPINACH

BÉCHAMEL SAUCE
25G (1oz/1½ TBSP) UNSALTED BUTTER
25G (1oz/2 TBSP) PLAIN FLOUR
425ML (15FL oz/1⅞ CUP) MILK
2 TBSP WHOLEGRAIN MUSTARD
115G (4oz) PARMESAN, FRESHLY GRATED
70G (2½oz) SOFT CHEESE WITH GARLIC AND HERBS

1   Preheat the oven to 220°C/425°F/gas 7.
2   Put the aubergine, squash, peppers and garlic in a roasting tin, trickle over the oil and sprinkle with
    seasoning. Stir, then spread in an even layer. Roast in the preheated oven for 35—40 minutes until
    tender and lightly charred. Lower the oven temperature to 200°C/400°F/gas 6.
3   About 15 minutes before the vegetables are ready, cook and drain the pasta according to the packet
    instructions but for 1½ minutes less than usual.
4   Meanwhile, make the sauce (see page 17) and stir in the mustard, half the Parmesan, and the soft cheese.
5   Combine the pasta with the vegetables and cooking juices, the spinach and sauce. Transfer to a gratin
    dish, sprinkle over the remaining cheese and bake for 25—30 minutes until golden.

345
baked peppers & aubergine
with three cheeses

PREPARATION TIME 10 minutes* COOKING TIME 40 minutes* SERVES 4

2 RED PEPPERS, CUT INTO 1CM (½IN) PIECES
1 AUBERGINE, CUT INTO 1CM (½IN) PIECES
3 GARLIC CLOVES, CHOPPED
VIRGIN OLIVE OIL
SALT AND FRESHLY GROUND BLACK PEPPER
400G (14OZ) RIGATONI

1 QUANTITY WINTER TOMATO SAUCE
   (SEE PAGE 19), WARMED
SMALL HANDFUL OF BASIL LEAVES, SHREDDED
115G (4OZ) BUFFALO MOZZARELLA, GRATED
115G (4OZ/SCANT ½ CUP) RICOTTA, CRUMBLED
50G (2OZ) PARMESAN, FRESHLY GRATED
FRESHLY GRATED PECORINO, TO SERVE

1   Preheat the oven to 200°C/400°F/gas 6.
2   Put the vegetables and garlic in a roasting tin. Trickle over some olive oil, season and stir the vegetables
    to ensure they are evenly coated. Spread in an even layer. Roast in the preheated oven for
    20–25 minutes until soft and lightly charred. Leave the oven on.
3   Meanwhile, cook and drain the pasta according to the packet instructions,
    but giving it 1 minute less cooking time than usual.
4   Toss the pasta with the tomato sauce, the vegetables and cooking juices, and the basil.
    Spread half in a large, shallow baking dish. Cover with the mozzarella, ricotta and half the
    Parmesan. Top with the remaining pasta mixture and sprinkle over the remaining Parmesan.
5   Bake in the oven at 200°C/400°F/gas 6 for about 15 minutes until bubbling
    and the top is golden. Leave to stand for 5 minutes before serving.

*   Assumes the sauce is already made.

202

346
mushroom & aubergine pasticcio

PREPARATION TIME 10 minutes COOKING TIME 1 hour SERVES 6

1 ONION, HALVED AND THINLY SLICED
OLIVE OIL
175G (6OZ) BROWN-CAP/CHESTNUT MUSHROOMS,
   THICKLY SLICED
2 GARLIC CLOVES, CRUSHED
1 LARGISH AUBERGINE, CHOPPED
1 ROSEMARY SPRIG AND 3 THYME SPRIGS, TIED
   TOGETHER
2–3 TSP SUN-DRIED TOMATO PASTE

400G CAN CHERRY TOMATOES
SALT AND FRESHLY GROUND BLACK PEPPER
275G (9OZ) CAVATAPPI, FUSILLI OR CURVED MACARONI
1 TBSP RED PESTO (SEE PAGE 19)
2 EGGS, BEATEN
225G (8OZ) RICOTTA
175ML (6FL OZ/SCANT ¾ CUP) SINGLE CREAM
4 TBSP FRESHLY GRATED PARMESAN

1   Fry the onion in a little oil in a heavy-based pan until tender and lightly browned. Add the mushrooms
    and fry until lightly coloured. Remove to a plate and set aside. Stir in the garlic, aubergine and herbs
    and cook for 2–3 minutes until lightly coloured.
2   Dissolve the tomato paste in 4 tbsp water. Return the mushrooms to the pan, stir in the dissolved tomato
    and the cherry tomatoes and bring to a simmer. Cover and simmer gently, stirring occasionally, for about
    15 minutes until the aubergine is tender. Season and discard the herbs.
3   Preheat the oven to 180°C/350°F/gas 4.
4   Cook the pasta according to the packet instructions but for 2 minutes less than usual. Drain and toss
    with the pesto, then with the aubergine sauce. Spread in a large, shallow baking dish.
5   Stir the eggs into the ricotta, then stir in the cream until smooth. Season and pour over the aubergine
    and mushroom mixture. Scatter the cheese over evenly and bake in the preheated oven for about
    35 minutes until the top is golden and just set.

347
vegetable & smoked mozzarella pasticcio

PREPARATION TIME 15 minutes* COOKING TIME 45 minutes SERVES 4

I AUBERGINE, CUT INTO 1cm (½IN) PIECES
I RED ONION, SLICED LENGTHWAYS
I HEAD OF CHICORY, CUT INTO 1cm (½IN) PIECES
I LARGE RED PEPPER, CUT INTO STRIPS
2 LARGE GARLIC CLOVES, CRUSHED
PINCH OF CHILLI FLAKES
VIRGIN OLIVE OIL

SALT AND FRESHLY GROUND BLACK PEPPER
375G (13oz) PENNE RIGATE
I QUANTITY GRILLED TOMATO SAUCE
  (SEE PAGE 18), WARMED
200G (7oz) SMOKED MOZZARELLA, GRATED
150G (5oz/SCANT ⅔ CUP) RICOTTA
6 TBSP FRESHLY GRATED PARMESAN

1   Preheat the oven to 220°C/425°F/gas 7.
2   Put the aubergine, onion, chicory, pepper, garlic and chilli into a roasting tin. Trickle over a little oil, add
    seasoning and stir the vegetables to coat evenly. Spread out and then bake in the preheated oven for
    25–30 minutes until soft and lightly charred. Leave the oven on.
3   Meanwhile, cook and drain the pasta according to the packet instructions. Mix with the vegetables
    and tomato sauce.
4   Spread half of the vegetable mixture in an oiled 20 x 20 x 5cm (8 x 8 x 2in) baking dish.
    Cover with three-quarters of the mozzarella, the ricotta and half of the Parmesan.
    Top with the remaining vegetable mixture followed by the remaining cheeses.
5   Bake for 15–20 minutes until bubbling and the top is browned.
    Leave to stand for 5 minutes before serving.

*   Assumes the sauce is already made.

348
mushroom & ricotta cannelloni

PREPARATION TIME 10 minutes* plus 15 minutes soaking and optional 2 hours standing
COOKING TIME 45 minutes* SERVES 4

15G (½oz) DRIED MUSHROOMS
300G (10oz) BROWN-CAP/CHESTNUT MUSHROOMS,
  FINELY CHOPPED
SMALL KNOB OF UNSALTED BUTTER
250G (9oz/1 CUP) RICOTTA
2–3 TSP THYME
ABOUT 1 TBSP LEMON ZEST

2–3 TSP RED PESTO (SEE PAGE 19)
SALT AND FRESHLY GROUND BLACK PEPPER
8 CANNELLONI TUBES
I QUANTITY FRESH TOMATO SAUCE (SEE PAGE 18)
  OR WINTER TOMATO SAUCE
  (SEE PAGE 19), WARMED
50G (2oz) PARMESAN, SHAVED

1   Pour 85ml (3fl oz/scant ⅓ cup) boiling water over the dried mushrooms and leave to soak for
    15 minutes. Drain and finely chop.
2   Fry the fresh and dried mushrooms in the butter in a large, preferably non-stick frying pan
    for 10–15 minutes until the liquid has evaporated and they are beginning to brown.
    Leave to cool on kitchen paper.
3   Combine the ricotta with the mushrooms. Stir thyme, lemon zest and red pesto to taste into
    the ricotta. Season. If possible, cover and leave for 2 hours or overnight.
4   Preheat the oven to 200°C/400°F/gas 6.
5   Cook the cannelloni tubes (see page 15), drain, rinse and drain again. Fill with the mushroom mixture.
    Place in an oiled large, shallow baking dish. Pour over the sauce, sprinkle with the Parmesan
    and bake in the preheated oven for about 30 minutes until bubbling and golden.

*   Assumes the tomato sauce is already made.

349
souffléed macaroni cheese

PREPARATION TIME 10 minutes COOKING TIME 30 minutes SERVES 4

350G (12oz) MACARONI

1 LEEK, FINELY CHOPPED

50G (2oz) UNSALTED BUTTER

50G (2oz) PLAIN FLOUR

570ML (1 PINT/SCANT 2½ CUPS) MILK

1 BAY LEAF, TORN ACROSS

175G (6oz/SCANT ¾ CUP) RICOTTA

115G (4oz) FONTINA, GRATED

115G (4oz) PARMESAN, FRESHLY GRATED

4 LARGE EGGS, SEPARATED

SALT AND FRESHLY GROUND BLACK PEPPER

1   Preheat the oven to 190°C/375°F/gas 5.
2   Cook the pasta for about 1 minute less then usual, then drain well.
3   Meanwhile, fry the leek in the butter until soft, then stir in the flour for 1 minute. Gradually add the milk
     and bay leaf, stirring constantly. Bring to the boil, stirring, then cook gently for 5 minutes. Discard the bay
     leaf. Off the heat, stir in the ricotta, fontina, half the Parmesan, and the egg yolks and pasta. Season.
4   Whisk the egg whites until soft peaks form. Stir a few spoonfuls into the sauce, then carefully fold in the
     remainder in 3 batches.
5   Transfer the mixture evenly into a large, shallow baking dish, scatter over the remaining Parmesan and
     bake in the preheated oven for about 15–20 minutes until puffed, golden and just set in the centre.

350
lentil & tomato cannelloni with spinach sauce

PREPARATION TIME 20 minutes COOKING TIME 1 hour SERVES 4

350G (12oz) GREEN LENTILS
1 ONION, FINELY CHOPPED
2 CELERY STICKS, FINELY CHOPPED
VIRGIN OLIVE OIL
3 GARLIC CLOVES, FINELY CHOPPED
3 LARGE WELL-FLAVOURED TOMATOES, SEEDED
 AND CHOPPED
1 TBSP CHOPPED OREGANO

150G (5oz) FRESH BROWN BREADCRUMBS
SALT AND FRESHLY GROUND BLACK PEPPER
8 SHEETS FRESH LASAGNE VERDE
175G (6oz) BABY SPINACH
2 TBSP PLAIN FLOUR
350ML (12FL oz/1½ CUPS) MILK
3 TBSP FRESHLY GRATED PARMESAN

1   Cook the lentils in plenty of boiling water for about 30 minutes until tender. Drain well.
2   About 5 minutes before the lentils are ready, fry the onion and celery in a little oil in a frying pan until softened, adding two-thirds of the garlic 2 minutes before the end. Stir in the drained lentils, the tomatoes and oregano. Simmer for about 10 minutes, stirring occasionally, until thickened. Stir in about three-quarters of the breadcrumbs. Season.
3   Meanwhile, cook the lasagne (see page 15) and spread on a tea towel to drain.
4   Preheat the oven to 200°C/400°F/gas 6.
5   Fry the remaining garlic in 1 tbsp oil in a small saucepan for 1 minute, then add the spinach and cook, stirring, until wilted. Stir in the flour. Off the heat, slowly pour in the milk, stirring. Return to the heat, bring to the boil, stirring, and simmer for 2 minutes. Season. Spread about one third in the bottom of a shallow baking dish.
6   Divide the lentil mixture among the lasagne sheets and roll them up. Place, seam side down, close together on the spinach sauce. Pour over the remaining sauce. Combine the remaining breadcrumbs with the Parmesan and sprinkle over the sauce.
7   Bake in the preheated oven for 20–25 minutes until the top is crisp and golden.

351
aubergine timballo

PREPARATION TIME 10 minutes* COOKING TIME 35 minutes* SERVES 4

300G (10oz) CAVATAPPI, FUSILLI OR CURVED
 MACARONI
3 AUBERGINES, TOTAL WEIGHT ABOUT 625G
 (1LB 6oz), CUT INTO 5MM (¼IN) THICK SLICES

VIRGIN OLIVE OIL
1 QUANTITY GRILLED TOMATO SAUCE (SEE PAGE 18)
225G (8oz) BUFFALO MOZZARELLA, SLICED
50G (2oz) PARMESAN, GRATED

1   Preheat the oven to 190°C/375°F/gas 5.
2   Cook and drain the pasta according to the packet instructions but giving it 2 minutes less than usual.
3   Meanwhile, brush the aubergine slices with oil and grill until tender and browned. Use most of the slices to line a 23cm (8½in) springform cake tin, allowing them to overhang the sides, taking care not to leave any gaps; reserve a few slices for the top.
4   Combine the pasta with the tomato sauce.
5   Pack half of the pasta mixture into the tin. Cover with a layer of mozzarella slices and a sprinkling of Parmesan. Add the remaining pasta, packing it down well. Cover with the overhanging and reserved aubergine slices. Bake in the preheated oven for about 20–25 minutes until heated through. Leave to stand for 5–10 minutes before carefully turning on to a warmed plate, if liked, and removing the tin.

*   Assumes the tomato sauce is already made.

352

elicoidali with aubergines, tomatoes & green olives al forno

PREPARATION TIME 15 minutes COOKING TIME 40 minutes SERVES 4

I LARGE ONION, HALVED AND THINLY SLICED

115G (4oz) SUN-DRIED TOMATOES PACKED IN OIL,
    DRAINED WITH I TBSP OIL RESERVED

2 GARLIC CLOVES, CRUSHED

I LARGE AUBERGINE, DICED

400G CAN CHOPPED PLUM TOMATOES

227G JAR PIMENTO-STUFFED GREEN OLIVES, DRAINED

SALT AND FRESHLY GROUND BLACK PEPPER

225G (8oz) ELICOIDALI*

115G (4oz) BUFFALO MOZZARELLA, DICED

150G (5oz) PARMESAN, FRESHLY GRATED

115G (4oz) BABY SPINACH

2 TBSP PINE NUTS, CHOPPED

WHITE SAUCE

25G (1oz/1½ TBSP) BUTTER

25G (1oz/2 TBSP) PLAIN FLOUR

570ML (1 PINT/2½ CUPS) MILK

1   Preheat the oven to 190°C/375°F/gas 5.
2   Fry the onion in the oil from the tomatoes until turning golden brown, adding the garlic for the last 2 minutes. Stir in the aubergine and sun-dried tomatoes for 1 minute, then add the chopped tomatoes.
3   Cover the pan and simmer gently for 10–15 minutes until the aubergines are tender. Stir in the olives, season and pour into a baking dish.
4   While the aubergine is cooking, cook the elicoidali according to the packet instructions but for 1 minute less than usual, and then drain well.
5   Meanwhile, make the white sauce (see page 17). Stir in the mozzarella and three-quarters of the Parmesan, followed by the spinach and pasta. Pile evenly over the aubergine mixture, scatter over the pine nuts and the remaining Parmesan.
6   Bake in the preheated oven for about 30 minutes until bubbling and golden.

*   Penne, rigatoni or sedani can also be used.

353

spaghettini, tomato & taleggio al forno

PREPARATION TIME 10 minutes COOKING TIME 35 minutes SERVES 4

225G (8oz) SPAGHETTINI

I ONION, FINELY CHOPPED

VIRGIN OLIVE OIL

3 GARLIC CLOVES, CHOPPED

SMALL HANDFUL OF FLAT-LEAF PARSLEY LEAVES,
    CHOPPED

1½ TSP DRIED OREGANO

SMALL HANDFUL OF BASIL LEAVES, SHREDDED

I EGG, BEATEN

115G (4oz/SCANT ½ CUP) RICOTTA

SALT AND FRESHLY GROUND BLACK PEPPER

450G (1LB) WELL-FLAVOURED PLUM TOMATOES,
    SLICED

85G (3oz) TALEGGIO, SLICED

2 TBSP FRESHLY GRATED PARMESAN

1   Preheat the oven to 190°C/375°F/gas 5. Oil a 20cm (8in) loose-bottomed cake tin.
2   Cook the spaghettini according to the packet instructions, giving it 2 minutes less than usual. Drain well.
3   Meanwhile, fry the onion in a little oil until soft. Add the garlic and fry for 1 minute. Combine with the spaghettini and herbs.
4   Blend the egg into the ricotta and then mix into the pasta. Season and put half into the prepared tin. Press down lightly and add half the tomato slices and Taleggio. Cover with the remaining pasta, press down lightly and arrange the remaining tomatoes and Taleggio on top. Sprinkle with the Parmesan.
5   Cover the top of the tin with foil and bake in the preheated oven for 20 minutes. Uncover and bake for a further 5 minutes or so until it is just set and the top is brown.

tomato-topped gorgonzola, spinach & leek rigatoni

PREPARATION TIME 10 minutes COOKING TIME 25 minutes SERVES 4–6

275G (9oz) RIGATONI*
675G (1½LB) LEEKS, THINLY SLICED
OLIVE OIL
450G (1LB) BABY SPINACH
PINCH OF FRESHLY GRATED NUTMEG
SALT AND FRESHLY GROUND BLACK PEPPER
115G/4oz GORGONZOLA, CRUMBLED
5 WELL-FLAVOURED TOMATOES, SLICED

1–2 TBSP CHOPPED FLAT-LEAF PARSLEY
2 TBSP FRESHLY GRATED PARMESAN

WHITE SAUCE
25G (1oz/1½ TBSP) BUTTER
25G (1oz/2 TBSP) PLAIN FLOUR
425ML (15FL oz/1⅞ CUPS) MILK
2 TBSP WHOLEGRAIN MUSTARD

1   Preheat the oven to 190°C/375°F/gas 5.
2   Cook the pasta according to the packet instructions but giving it 1 minute less than usual. Drain well.
3   Meanwhile, fry the leeks in a little oil for 3–4 minutes. Add the spinach and cook briskly, turning frequently, until wilted and the liquid has evaporated. Add the nutmeg and seasoning to taste. Combine with the pasta.
4   Make the sauce (see page 17) and stir in the mustard and seasoning.
5   Cover the bottom of an oiled baking dish with a layer of the pasta mixture. Sprinkle over half the Gorgonzola, then add another layer of the pasta mixture followed by half of the sauce. Repeat the layers, ending with a layer of sauce. Arrange the tomatoes slices on top. Scatter over the parsley and Parmesan, season.
6   Bake in the preheated oven for 20 minutes until the tomatoes are well cooked.

*   Penne, sedani, fusilli and eliche can also be used.

mushrooms, gorgonzola & tagliatelle al forno

PREPARATION TIME 10 minutes COOKING TIME 25–30 minutes SERVES 4

350G (12oz) TAGLIATELLE VERDE
2 SHALLOTS, FINELY CHOPPED
VIRGIN OLIVE OIL
1 GARLIC CLOVE, FINELY CHOPPED
350G (12oz) BROWN-CAP/CHESTNUT MUSHROOMS, THINLY SLICED
6 TBSP LOW-FAT CRÈME FRAÎCHE

85G (3oz) GORGONZOLA, CRUMBLED
2 WELL-FLAVOURED TOMATOES, PEELED, SEEDED AND CHOPPED
1 EGG, BEATEN
SALT AND FRESHLY GROUND BLACK PEPPER
115G (4oz) MOZZARELLA, GRATED

1   Preheat the oven to 180°C/350°F/gas 4.
2   Cook and drain the tagliatelle according to the packet instructions, giving it 1 minute less than usual.
3   Meanwhile, fry the shallots in a little oil until softened. Add the mushrooms and garlic and cook, stirring, until the mushrooms have just softened. Stir in the crème fraîche and Gorgonzola and warm through gently, stirring; do not allow to boil.
4   Add the tagliatelle and tomatoes, then remove from the heat and stir in the egg and seasoning, using plenty of black pepper. Pour into an oiled shallow baking dish, sprinkle over the mozzarella and cover with foil.
5   Bake in the preheated oven for 15–20 minutes until the mozzarella has melted and browned.

pasta & gorgonzola puff

PREPARATION TIME 10 minutes COOKING TIME 25–30 minutes SERVES 4–6

50G (2oz/scant ¼ cup) **UNSALTED BUTTER, MELTED**

2 TBSP **DRY BREADCRUMBS**

175G (6oz) **SPAGHETTI**

50G (2oz/scant ½ cup) **PLAIN FLOUR**

570ML (1 pint/2¼ cups) **MILK**

1 TBSP **DIJON MUSTARD**

175G (6oz) **GORGONZOLA, CRUMBLED**

6 EGGS, SEPARATED

FRESHLY GROUND BLACK PEPPER

1   Preheat the oven to 190°C/375°F/gas 5. Brush the inside of a 2.4 litre (4¼ pint/9½ cup) baking dish thoroughly with some of the butter. Sprinkle in the breadcrumbs so they adhere evenly.

2   Cook the spaghetti according to the packet instructions but for 1 minute less than usual and drain well.

3   Make a white sauce (see page 17) with the remaining butter, the flour and milk. Remove from the heat and stir in the mustard, cheese, egg yolks and cooked pasta. Season using plenty of black pepper.

4   Whisk the egg whites until stiff but not dry. Stir 2 tbsp into the pasta mixture, then fold in the remainder in 3 batches. Transfer to the baking dish and bake in the preheated oven for 20–25 minutes until puffed and golden and lightly set in the centre.

mushroom & squash al forno

PREPARATION TIME 10 minutes COOKING TIME 35 minutes SERVES 3—4

I BUTTERNUT SQUASH, PEELED, SEEDED AND CUT
   INTO ICM (½IN) CUBES
325G (11oz) CHESTNUT/BROWN-CAP MUSHROOMS,
   HALVED OR QUARTERED, DEPENDING ON SIZE
I SPRIG OF ROSEMARY
3 GARLIC CLOVES, LIGHTLY CRUSHED

VIRGIN OLIVE OIL
SALT AND FRESHLY GROUND BLACK PEPPER
250G (9oz) PENNE
250ML (9FL OZ/1 CUP) HALF-FAT CRÈME FRAÎCHE
70G (2½oz) PARMESAN, FINELY GRATED
70G (2½oz) FRESH BREADCRUMBS

1 Preheat the oven to 200°C/400°F/gas 6.
2 Put the squash, mushrooms, rosemary and garlic into a non-stick roasting tin, trickle over a little oil,
   season and stir the ingredients together. Spread in an even layer and bake in the preheated oven
   for about 30 minutes until soft and slightly charred, stirring a couple of times.
3 Meanwhile, cook and drain the pasta according to the packet instructions.
4 Toss the pasta with the cooked vegetables (discard the rosemary) and then gently stir in the crème
   fraîche and half the Parmesan. Season. Tip into a gratin dish, sprinkle over the breadcrumbs and
   remaining Parmesan and place under a preheated hot grill until crisp and golden.

rotolo

PREPARATION TIME 15 minutes* COOKING TIME 45 minutes* SERVES 4

2-EGG QUANTITY OF PASTA DOUGH (SEE PAGE 10)
750G (1LB 10oz) BABY SPINACH
UNSALTED BUTTER
175G (6oz) SOFT GOATS' CHEESE, RIND REMOVED,
   CRUMBLED
175G (6oz/¾ CUP) RICOTTA, CRUMBLED

85G (3oz) PARMESAN, FRESHLY GRATED
FRESHLY GROUND BLACK PEPPER
I WHOLE EGG AND I EGG YOLK, BEATEN
3 TBSP DOUBLE CREAM
RED PEPPER AND TOMATO SAUCE (SEE PAGE 123),
   TO SERVE

1 Cook the spinach in a large covered pan until wilted. Drain well and squeeze out as much water as
   possible. Chop finely.
2 Heat a little butter in a frying pan and stir in the spinach for 2—3 minutes, until all the moisture has
   evaporated. Cool slightly, then stir in the goats' cheese, ricotta and two-thirds of the Parmesan.
   Season with plenty of black pepper. Stir in the egg and egg yolk.
3 Roll out the pasta dough by hand to a rectangle about 30 x 40cm (12 x 16in).**
   Place on a large piece of muslin.
4 Using a spatula, spread over the filling to within 1cm (½in) of the edges. Roll up like a Swiss roll, dampen
   the ends and pinch them together. Wrap the roll tightly in the muslin and tie the ends with string.
5 Place in a fish kettle or large flameproof dish of boiling water, half cover with a lid and simmer for
   20—25 minutes, turning carefully twice. Lift out carefully and leave to cool before unwrapping.
6 Preheat the oven to 200°C/400°F/gas 6.
7 Using a large, sharp knife cut the roll into 1cm (½in) slices and arrange in a buttered gratin dish.
   Melt a small knob of butter in the cream, pour over the slices and sprinkle with the remaining
   Parmesan. Bake in the preheated oven for about 15 minutes until golden. Serve with the tomato sauce.

*   Times for making pasta dough or red pepper and tomato sauce not included.
** If using a pasta machine, roll 3 strips about 40cm (16in) long, lay them side by side,
   overlapping slightly. Moisten the overlap with water to stick the edges together.

VEGETABLE & VEGETARIAN DISHES

359
broccoli & pasta bake

PREPARATION TIME 10 minutes COOKING TIME 25 minutes SERVES 4

225G (8oz) PENNE RIGATE
1 LARGE HEAD OF BROCCOLI, DIVIDED INTO FLORETS
150G/5oz PARMESAN, FRESHLY GRATED
4 TBSP PINE NUTS, LIGHTLY TOASTED

SIMPLE WHITE SAUCE
25G (1oz/1½ TBSP) UNSALTED BUTTER
2 TBSP PLAIN FLOUR
570ML (1 PINT/2½ CUPS) MILK
1 TBSP WHOLEGRAIN MUSTARD

1 Preheat the oven to 200°C/400°F/gas 6.
2 Cook the pasta according to the packet instructions, adding the broccoli for the last 4 minutes.
   Drain the pasta and broccoli thoroughly. Tip in an even layer in a gratin dish.
3 Meanwhile, make a white sauce with the butter, flour and milk (see page 17).
   Remove from the heat and stir in the mustard and half the cheese.
   Pour over the broccoli and pasta. Scatter over the pine nuts and remaining cheese.
4 Bake in the preheated oven for about 15 minutes until golden.

210

VEGETABLE & VEGETARIAN DISHES

360
pappardelle with fresh artichokes

PREPARATION TIME 15 minutes COOKING TIME 15 minutes SERVES 4

6 ARTICHOKES
½ A LEMON
2 GARLIC CLOVES, FINELY CHOPPED
1 DRIED CHILLI, SEEDED AND FINELY CHOPPED

4 TBSP EXTRA-VIRGIN OLIVE OIL
2 TBSP BOILING WATER
500G (1LB 2oz) PAPPARDELLE
FRESHLY GRATED PARMESAN, TO SERVE (OPTIONAL)

1 Remove the outer leaves from the artichokes and cut off the tough tips from the remaining leaves.
   Cut the artichokes into quarters. Rub the cut surfaces with half a lemon. Remove the hairy 'choke'
   and thinly slice each segment.
2 Fry garlic and chilli in the oil for 2 minutes. Add the artichoke slices and cook gently, stirring,
   for about 3 minutes before adding the boiling water. Cover and simmer for 10 minutes.
3 Meanwhile, cook the pasta according to the packet instructions. Drain, reserving about ½ cup of
   the cooking water. Toss the pappardelle with the artichoke mixture. If the pasta seems too dry,
   add sufficient of the reserved pasta cooking water. Serve with freshly grated Parmesan, if liked.

361
spinach & cheese pasticcio

PREPARATION TIME 10 minutes COOKING TIME 1 hour 10 minutes SERVES 4

125G (4½oz) TAGLIATELLE

500G (1LB 2oz) SPINACH

300ML (10FL oz/scant 1¼ cups) MILK

300G (10oz) SOFT GOATS' CHEESE, CHOPPED*

85G (3oz/scant ⅓ cup) RICOTTA*

ABOUT 50G (2oz) PARMESAN,
    FRESHLY GRATED (OPTIONAL)**

3 EGGS, BEATEN

SALT AND FRESHLY GROUND BLACK PEPPER

RED PEPPER AND TOMATO SAUCE
    (SEE PAGE 123) OR ½ QUANTITY GRILLED TOMATO
    SAUCE (SEE PAGE 18), TO SERVE (OPTIONAL)

1 Preheat the oven to 180°C/350°F/gas 4.
2 Cook the tagliatelle for 2 minutes less then usual, then drain well.
3 Meanwhile, cook the spinach without any additional water in a large pan, stirring frequently,
   until wilted and softened. Drain, then squeeze out excess moisture. Combine with the milk, cheeses,
   eggs and seasoning. Mix with the drained pasta and pour into a oiled, large, shallow baking dish.
4 Bake in the preheated oven for about 1 hour until lightly browned and just set in the centre.
5 To turn out the pasticcio, invert on to a warm plate and give a slight shake. Serve with the sauce, if liked.

* The proportions can be varied, to taste.
** The addition of Parmesan will depend on the amount of goats' cheese used and the mildness of its flavour.

farfalle, artichoke,
mushroom & egg salad

PREPARATION TIME 10 minutes plus 2 hours standing COOKING TIME 10 minutes SERVES 4

400G (14oz) FARFALLE

225G (8oz) MIXED MUSHROOMS SUCH AS SHIITAKE,
    OYSTER, CHANTERELLE AND ENOKI

2 SHALLOTS, FINELY CHOPPED

2 GARLIC CLOVES, FINELY CHOPPED

285G JAR ROAST ARTICHOKES IN OIL, DRAINED
    (RESERVE THE OIL) AND HALVED

1 TBSP BALSAMIC VINEGAR

SALT AND FRESHLY GROUND BLACK PEPPER

2 EGGS, BOILED TO TASTE, PEELED AND CHOPPED

LEAVES FROM A BUNCH OF FLAT-LEAF PARSLEY,
    FINELY CHOPPED

1   Cook and drain the pasta according to the packet instructions.
2   Meanwhile, break the mushrooms into pieces if large. Fry the mushrooms and shallots in a little of the artichoke oil in a large frying pan over a brisk heat, until lightly browned, adding the garlic 2 minutes before the end.
3   Toss the mushrooms with the pasta, artichokes, balsamic vinegar and seasoning. Cover and leave in a cool place (preferably not the fridge) for at least 2 hours.
4   Just before serving, toss the egg with the parsley and seasoning. Scatter over the pasta salad to serve.

363

tagliatelle with courgette ribbons

PREPARATION TIME 15 minutes plus 30 minutes standing COOKING TIME 10 minutes SERVES 4

350G (12oz) SMALL COURGETTES

SALT AND FRESHLY GROUND BLACK PEPPER

225G (8oz) DRY WHITE BREADCRUMBS

50G (2oz) PARMESAN, FRESHLY GRATED

2 EGGS, BEATEN

400G (14oz) TAGLIATELLE

OIL, FOR DEEP FRYING

KNOB OF UNSALTED BUTTER, MELTED

SMALL HANDFUL OF BASIL LEAVES,
    SHREDDED

1   Cut the courgettes into fine ribbons lengthways using a mandoline, food processor or vegetable peeler with firm pressure. Layer with salt in a colander and leave for 30 minutes. Rinse well and dry thoroughly.
2   In a shallow bowl, combine the breadcrumbs with black pepper and half the cheese. Pour the eggs into another shallow bowl. Dip the courgette ribbons individually first into the egg, allowing the excess to drain off, then into the breadcrumb mixture to coat well and evenly.
3   Cook and drain the pasta according to the packet instructions.
4   Meanwhile, deep-fry the courgette ribbons in batches in hot oil for 1–2 minutes until crisp and golden. Drain on kitchen paper. Toss the pasta with the butter, basil and remaining cheese and transfer to a warm large, shallow serving dish. Pile the courgette strips on top.

cavatappi with courgettes, tomatoes & capers

PREPARATION TIME 10 minutes plus 30 minutes standing COOKING TIME 10 minutes SERVES 4

400G (14oz) COURGETTES, CUT INTO SHORT STRIPS
SALT
4 LARGE WELL-FLAVOURED PLUM
  TOMATOES, CHOPPED
2 GARLIC CLOVES, FINELY CHOPPED

3 TBSP CAPERS
2 TBSP CHOPPED OREGANO
2 TBSP WHITE WINE VINEGAR
EXTRA-VIRGIN OLIVE OIL
350G (12oz) CAVATAPPI*

1 Put the courgettes in a colander, sprinkle salt over and leave for 30 minutes. Rinse well, squeeze and pat dry with kitchen paper.
2 Meanwhile, combine the tomatoes, garlic, capers, half the oregano, the vinegar and 3 tbsp olive oil. Set aside for 15 minutes.
3 Cook and drain the pasta according to the packet instructions.
4 Meanwhile, quickly fry the courgettes in a little oil until lightly browned. Add the tomato mixture to the pan to warm through. Toss with the cavatappi and remaining oregano.

* Fusilli lunghi, fusilli or farfalle can also be used.

VEGETABLE & VEGETARIAN DISHES

213

tagliatelle with courgettes, ricotta & basil

PREPARATION TIME 10 minutes COOKING TIME 10 minutes SERVES 4

1 GARLIC CLOVE, THINLY SLICED
4 TBSP VIRGIN OLIVE OIL
325G (11oz) TAGLIATELLE
450G (1LB) SMALL, FIRM BABY COURGETTES,
  QUITE THINLY SLICED
JUICE AND GRATED ZEST OF 1 LARGE LEMON

25G (1oz) PARMESAN, FRESHLY GRATED,
  PLUS EXTRA TO SERVE
225G (8oz/SCANT 1 CUP) RICOTTA
SMALL HANDFUL OF BASIL LEAVES, SHREDDED
2 TBSP PINE NUTS, LIGHTLY TOASTED
SALT AND FRESHLY GROUND BLACK PEPPER

1 Warm the garlic in the oil for 5 minutes; do not allow to become too hot. Discard the garlic.
2 Meanwhile, cook and drain the pasta according to the packet instructions.
3 While the pasta is cooking, fry the courgettes in batches in the garlic oil until softened and flecked with brown. Return all the courgettes to the pan. Add the lemon juice to warm through.
4 Toss the courgettes with the pasta, Parmesan, ricotta, lemon zest, basil, pine nuts and seasoning. Serve with extra Parmesan.

Index

ANCHOVIES: black olive pasta with
broccoli, capers & anchovies 70
bucatini with melting onion
& anchovy sauce 75
farfalle with peppers, anchovies & capers 62
fusilli with sun-blush tomatoes,
anchovies & olives 38
linguine with anchovies, chilli & olives 31
orecchiette with cauliflower,
anchovies & tomatoes 66
penne with cauliflower,
anchovies & garlic 89
puffed spinach & anchovy bake 93
spaghetti alla puttanesca 64
spaghetti with anchovies, lemon, chillies
& thyme pangritata 39
spaghetti with capers, olives & anchovies 41
spaghetti with cherry tomatoes,
anchovies & basil 65
spaghetti with garlic,
anchovies & parsley 30
spaghetti with summer puttanesca sauce 40

ARTICHOKES: artichoke
& mushroom lasagne 194
cavatappi with artichokes,
mushrooms & peas 178
elicoidali with artichokes, peppers,
courgettes & prosciutto 135
farfalle, artichoke, mushroom
& egg salad 212
fusilli with artichokes, tomatoes & olives 32
lumache with pancetta & artichokes 137
pappardelle with fresh artichokes 210
penne with artichoke,
tomatoes & olives 167
tagliarini with artichokes & gremolata 29

ASPARAGUS: agnolotti with
asparagus & Parma ham 129
fettuccine with asparagus,
peas & lemon 160
fusilli with asparagus & Parma ham 141
riccioli with prawns & asparagus 80
tagliatelle, asparagus, broad bean
& courgette salad 168
tagliatelle with asparagus & Parmesan 173
tagliatelle with peas, asparagus
& saffron sauce 186

AUBERGINES: aubergine timballo 205
baked peppers & aubergine
with three cheeses 202
cavatappi with roast aubergines,
peppers & basil 188
elicoidali with aubergines, tomatoes
& green olives al forno 206
lumache with chicken, aubergine
& oregano 132
mushroom & aubergine pasticcio 202
penne with aubergines, olives & basil 180
penne rigate with aubergines & ricotta 193
sausage & aubergine lasagne 149
tortiglioni with aubergine & tomato 179

AVOCADO: cavatappi with tomatoes,
avocado & basil 52

BEANS: broad bean & basil cannelloni 200
conchiglie with broad beans,
nuts & lemon sauce 159
gnocchi with borlotti beans & pancetta 150
linguine with new potatoes,
beans & pesto 166
macaroni, beef & beans 134
penne with broad beans,
parsley & pecorino 181
tagliatelle with broad beans
& goats' cheese 177
tagliatelle with green beans & herbs 168
béchamel sauce 17, 79

BEEF: baked rigatoni alla Bolognese 146
cannelloni with roast beef,
shallots & garlic 145
lasagne 139, 143
macaroni, beef & beans 134
ragù 16
tagliatelle alla Bolognese 113, 120
Bolognese sauce 113, 120, 143

BRESAOLA: tagliatelle with
bresaola, peas & leeks 125

BROCCOLI: black olive pasta with
broccoli, capers & anchovies 70
broccoli & pasta bake 210
cannelloni with sausages & broccoli 143
casareccia with broccoli & Gorgonzola 174
conchiglie with broccoli,
walnuts & pancetta 129
eliche with broccoli, breadcrumbs,
sultanas & pine nuts 155
orecchiette with broccoli,
sun-dried tomatoes & thyme 159
pennette with broccoli,
pine nuts & chilli 182
riccioli with broccoli,
Parmesan & pine nuts 156
riccioli with broccoli,
Taleggio & almonds 179
trofie with broccoli sauce 155

CARBONARA sauce 40

CAULIFLOWER: orecchiette with
cauliflower, anchovies & tomatoes 66
orecchiette with cauliflower,
chorizo & black olives 116
penne with cauliflower,
anchovies & garlic 89
strozzapreti with cauliflower,
pancetta & parsley 139
strozzapreti with cauliflower,
saffron & tomatoes 170

CELERY: penne rigate with
cheeses, celery & almonds 163

CHEESE: black pepper tagliatelle
with three-cheese sauce 176
cheese & herb agnolotti 129, 183, 195
conchiglie with Gorgonzola & walnuts 57
linguine with Gorgonzola & watercress 32
panzarotti 190
pasta, basil & goats' cheese frittata 30
pasta & Gorgonzola puff 208
pasta with roast garlic, thyme
& crumbled goats' cheese 54
penne rigate with cheeses,
celery & almonds 163
souffléed macaroni cheese 204
spaghetti with goats' cheese,
rocket & walnuts 48
trofie with goats' cheese & lemon 160

CHICKEN: campanelli with chicken,
prosciutto & basil 130
chicken & prosciutto cannelloni
on spinach & mushrooms 144
chicken & spinach pasticcio 127
chicken & walnut cannelloni 127
chicken soup with tortellini 23
chicken-stuffed pasta shells 123
conchiglie with chicken,
cherry tomato & herb sauce 126
fusilli, chicken & fennel salad 44
fusilli lunghi chicken with avocado
& green pesto sauce 138
garganelle with chicken & watercress 124
gnocchi with chicken ragù 135
lasagne 122
lumache with chicken,
aubergine & oregano 132
Mediterranean chicken & pasta al forno 117

penne with chicken, leeks & Gorgonzola121
pennette with chicken livers & marsala 147
spiced chicken tortellini 23, 120
tagliatelle with chicken, courgettes
& red pepper 133
tagliatelle with chicken, lemon & basil 151
tagliatelle with chicken & sage 113

CHICKPEAS: quick pasta with
chickpeas & spinach 187

CLAMS: linguine with red clam sauce 86
linguine with white clam sauce 64
tonnarelli with prawns, clams & rocket 87

COD: cod, prawn & leek lasagne 78
smoked fish raviolini 76
spaghetti with cod & pangritata 72

COURGETTES: cavatappi with
courgettes, tomatoes & capers 213
courgette & ricotta cannelloni 196
fusilli with courgettes,
tomatoes & basil 182
linguine with mussels & courgettes 81
tagliatelle with courgette ribbons 212
tagliatelle with courgettes,
ricotta & basil 213
torchiette with courgettes,
lemon & pine nuts 154

CRAB: cavatappi with crab & basil 45
crab & dill cannelloni 74
crab & prawn ravioli 100
crab in conchiglie with red pesto sauce 95
riccioli with crab, avocado
& fresh tomatoes 90
tagliarini with crab & fennel 94
taglioni with crab sauce 102

EGG pasta 9–12

EGGS: farfalle, artichoke,
mushroom & egg salad 212

FENNEL: bucatini with sardines,
lemon & fennel 68
fusilli, chicken & fennel salad 44
macaroni, fennel, pine nut
& cheese al forno 199
pappardelle with roast fennel
& dolcelatte 192
tagliatelle with slow-cooked
fennel & garlic 198

FRITTATA 30, 35, 107

GNOCCHI 12, 43, 58, 59

HADDOCK: haddock, spinach
& pasta al forno 84
smoked fish & mushroom cannelloni 79
smoked fish pie 77
smoked fish raviolini 76

HAM: agnolotti with asparagus
& Parma ham 129
fusilli lunghi with asparagus
& Parma ham 141
tagliatelle with Parma ham,
peas & lemon 117
taglioni with Parma ham,
peas & parsley 125

HERB pasta 10, 195

LAMB: bigoli with lamb,
tomatoes & olives 121
braised lamb shanks with pasta 145
lamb ragù 107, 108
pappardelle with lamb & rosemary 131

LEEKS: fusilli with leeks,
garlic & Parmesan 186
lasagne 78, 122
pappardelle with mushrooms & leeks 172
pasta, leeks & cheese al forno 176

214

penne with chicken,
leeks & Gorgonzola 121
tagliatelle with bresaola, peas & leeks 125
tomato-topped Gorgonzola, spinach,
leek & rigatoni 207
LEMON sauce 56
LENTILS: chifferi with lentils
& pancetta 142
gnocchi with lentil sauce 188
lentil & tomato cannelloni
with spinach sauce 205
spinach & lentil lasagne 191
LETTUCE: cavatappi with
minted lettuce & peas 157
LOBSTER: fidelini with lobster,
basil & wilted tomatoes 82
green fettuccine & lobster
with vodka cream sauce 92

MEATBALLS 106, 119, 148
MINESTRONE 27
MUSHROOMS: cavatappi with
prawns, mushrooms & tomatoes 81
farfalle, artichoke, mushroom
& egg salad 212
farfalle with mushrooms, sun-dried
tomatoes & spinach 184
fettuccine with mushrooms,
pancetta & wine 110
lasagne 94, 195, 196
lasagnette with mixed mushrooms
& herbs 161
mushroom & ricotta cannelloni 203
mushroom & salami al forno 151
mushroom & squash al forno 209
mushrooms, Gorgonzola & tagliatelle
al forno 207
orecchiette with mushrooms & tomato 185
pappardelle with mushrooms & leeks 172
pappardelle with roast mushrooms 174
smoked fish & mushroom cannelloni 79
strozzapreti with peppers & mushrooms 180
MUSSELS: cavatelli with mussels,
tomatoes & chilli 103
linguine with mussels & courgettes 81
orecchiette with smoked mussels,
spinach & cashews 91
smoked mussel & pimento pasta salad 80
tagliatelle with mussels & pesto 82
taglioni with mussels, wilted greens
& lardons 71

NUTS: cavatappi with spinach,
raisins & pine nuts 53
chicken & walnut cannelloni 127
conchiglie with broad beans,
nuts & lemon sauce 159
conchiglie with broccoli,
walnuts & pancetta 129
conchiglie with Gorgonzola & walnuts 57
eliche with broccoli, breadcrumbs,
sultanas & pine nuts 155
farfalle with rocket, walnuts & dolcelatte 47
fettucine with scallops, buttered pine
nuts & shredded lettuce
fidelini with walnut sauce 33
green & white tagliatelle with
pine nuts & Parmesan 49
macaroni, fennel, pine nut
& cheese al forno 199
orecchiette with smoked mussels,
spinach & cashews 91
orecchiette with tomatoes,
rocket & pine nuts 47
penne rigate with cheeses,
celery & almonds 163
pennette with broccoli, pine nuts & chilli 182

pennette with tomato & almond sauce 54
riccioli with broccoli, Parmesan
& pine nuts 156
riccioli with broccoli,
Taleggio & almonds 179
spaghetti with goats' cheese,
rocket & walnuts 48
spaghetti with parsley & pine nuts 46
spaghetti with tomatoes,
olives & walnuts 51
tagliatelle with rocket,
pine nuts & thyme 55
torchiette with courgettes,
lemon & pine nuts 154
trenette with pine nuts & herbs 52
trenette with quick spinach
& walnut sauce 57

ONIONS: bucatini with melting
onion & anchovy sauce 75
gemelli with melting onion sauce 189

PANCETTA: bucatini with pancetta,
tomatoes, olives & herbs 136
bucatini with pancetta,
tomatoes & chilli 147
bucatini with sausage & pancetta 125
cavatappi with pancetta,
peppers & tomatoes 122
chifferi with lentils & pancetta 142
conchiglie with broccoli,
walnuts & pancetta 129
conchiglie with pancetta, peas & ricotta 136
fettuccine with mushrooms,
pancetta & wine 110
gnocchi with borlotti beans
& pancetta 150
lumache with pancetta & artichokes 137
orecchiette with peas, pancetta & sage 140
pancetta-stuffed tomatoes 37
spaghetti with tuna,
pancetta & tomatoes 66
strozzapreti with cauliflower,
pancetta & parsley 139
tagliatelle with pancetta,
rocket & Gorgonzola 147
taglioni with mussels,
wilted greens & lardons 71
taglioni with seared scallops,
pancetta & tomatoes 95
PANZAROTTI 190
PASTA: buying 7, 8
cooking 14–15
home-made 8–13
stuffed 11, 13, 15, 63, 76, 100, 120,
134, 183, 184, 190, 195, 209
PEAS: cavatappi with artichokes,
mushrooms & peas 178
cavatappi with minted lettuce & peas 157
chifferi with peas & Parmesan 157
farfalle with peas, mint & ricotta 175
fettuccine with asparagus, peas & lemon 160
fettuccine with peas, prosciutto & sage 131
orecchiette with peas, pancetta & sage 140
orecchiette with peas & feta 157
pasta e piselli (pasta & peas) 50
riccioli with peas & saffron 52
tagliatelle with bresaola, peas & leek 125
tagliatelle with Parma ham,
peas & lemon 117
tagliatelle with peas, prosciutto & basil 131
taglioni with Parma ham, peas & parsley 125
PEPPERS: ditali with tomatoes, garlic
& grilled peppers 181
farfalle with hot-smoked salmon
& red peppers 64
fidelini-stuffed peppers 42

fusilli lunghi with fresh tuna
& roast peppers 67
potato gnocchi with red pepper
& red pesto sauce 43
red pepper & tomato sauce 123, 209
riccioli with peppers & cherry tomatoes 187
spaghetti with grilled peppers & garlic 48
spaghetti with simple
red pepper sauce 41
strozzapreti with peppers
& mushrooms 180
tagliatelle & tiger prawns
with red pepper sauce 98
tagliatelle with red peppers
& mozzarella 171
warm pasta with mixed
peppers & tomatoes 50
ziti with red peppers & basil 194
PESTO 10, 18, 19, 33, 38, 47
PORK: cavatappi with pork ragù 114
pasta with pork, spinach & lemon 126
pork & spinach cannelloni 144
tonnarelli with pork & mushrooms 112
POTATOES: linguine with new potatoes,
beans & pesto 166
potato gnocchi with red pepper
& pesto sauce 43
spinach & potato gnocchi with fontina 59
PRAWNS: bucatini with squid, prawns,
lemon, parsley & garlic 102
cavatappi with prawns,
mushrooms & tomatoes 81
conchiglie with prawn sauce 100
crab & prawn ravioli 100
fettuccine with tiger prawns,
tomatoes & basil 96
fusilli lunghi with prawns,
fennel & tomatoes 94
lasagne 78, 79
pasta, prawns & pesto 41
prawn & pasta al forno 91
quick tagliatelle with
prawns & red pesto 87
riccioli with prawns & asparagus 80
spaghetti with prawns,
tomatoes & capers 69
tagliatelle & tiger prawns
with red pepper sauce 98
taglioni with prawns & spinach 82
tonnarelli with prawns, clams & rocket 87
PROSCIUTTO: bucatini with prosciutto,
radicchio, capers & lemon 111
cannelloni with spinach
& prosciutto filling 148
eliche with prosciutto,
peppers & peas 140
elicoidali with artichokes, peppers,
courgettes & prosciutto 135
fettuccine with peas, prosciutto & sage 131
lumache with prosciutto,
rocket & capers 128
penne with mushrooms
& frazzled prosciutto 138
penne rigate with spinach, prosciutto
& crumbled goats' cheese 140
tagliatelle with peas, prosciutto & basil 131
tonnarelli with radicchio,
rosemary & prosciutto 137
tortellini with spinach,
ricotta & prosciutto 150
PUTTANESCA sauce 40, 64

RADICCHIO: bucatini with prosciutto,
radicchio, capers & lemon 111
tonnarelli with radicchio,
rosemary & prosciutto 137
tonnarelli with radicchio & Taleggio 193

RAGÙ: beef ragù 16, 111, 113
  chicken ragù 135
  lamb ragù 107, 108
  pork ragù 114
  Sardinian ragù 107
RED MULLET: linguine with roast
  red mullet & cherry tomatoes 71
ROCKET: cavatappi with rocket,
  tomatoes & olives 31
farfalle with rocket, walnuts & dolcelatte 47
fusilli, rocket & tomato frittata 35
gnocchi, rocket, tomato
  & black olive salad 46
orecchiette with tomatoes,
  rocket & pine nuts 47
spaghetti with goats' cheese,
  rocket & walnuts 48
tagliatelle with rocket pesto 47
tagliatelle with rocket, pine nuts & thyme 55
ROTOLO 209

SAFFRON pasta 10
SALADS: farfalle, artichoke,
  mushroom & egg salad 212
fusilli, chicken & fennel salad 44
gnocchi, rocket, tomato & black
  olive salad 46
Mediterranean seafood & pasta salad 84
Mediterranean vegetable & pasta salad 43
olive & triple tomato salad 59
roast vegetable, seafood & pasta salad 92
smoked mussel & pimento pasta salad 80
tagliatelle, asparagus, broad bean
  & courgette salad 168
warm fresh tuna salad niçoise 72
warm fusilli & seafood salad 69
warm pasta, mushroom
  & grilled vegetable salad 169
SALMON: farfalle with hot-smoked
  salmon & red peppers 64
fettuccine with smoked salmon,
  dill & ricotta 89
green & white tagliatelle with
  smoked salmon, spinach & lemon 73
salmon ravioli 63
salmon shells with pesto
  & tomato sauce 75
spaghetti with salmon eggs & chives 57
SARDINES: bucatini with sardines,
  lemon & fennel 68
spaghetti with flaked sardines & tomatoes 70
SAUSAGES: bucatini with sausage &
  pancetta 125
cannelloni with sausages & broccoli 143
elicoidali, sausages & peppers al forno 115
mushroom & salami al forno 151
orecchiette with cauliflower,
  chorizo & black olives 116
penne with chorizo, rocket & tomatoes 112
penne with sausages & mushrooms 114
penne rigate with sausages al forno 119
sausage & aubergine lasagne 149
sedani with tomatoes, sausages
  & mushrooms 108
strapiozi with sausages, mixed
  peppers & tomatoes 128
strozzapreti with sausages,
  onions & peppers 115
vermicelli, chorizo & mozzarella torta 118
SCALLOPS: black spaghettini with
  scallops, white wine & parsley 83
fettucine with scallops, buttered pine
  nuts & shredded lettuce
scallop & prawn lasagne 79
tagliatelle with scallops, peppers & basil 97
taglioni with seared scallops,
  pancetta & tomatoes 95

SEAFOOD: conchiglie
  with seafood sauce 97
linguine with seafood, saffron & tomatoes 98
Mediterranean seafood & pasta salad 84
quick linguine with seafood 65
roast vegetable, seafood & pasta salad 92
seafood cannelloni 76
seafood linguine en papillote 88
seafood spaghetti with saffron 93
seafood tossed with spaghetti,
  lemon & rocket 86
shellfish spaghetti with
  sun-blush tomatoes 99
warm fusilli & seafood salad 69
SOUPS 22–28
SPINACH: cannelloni with
  spinach & prosciutto filling 148
cavatappi with spinach,
  raisins & pine nuts 53
chicken & prosciutto cannelloni
  on spinach & mushrooms 144
chicken & spinach pasticcio 127
fusilli with spinach, sun-dried
  tomatoes & olives 36
fusilli lunghi with spinach
  & Gorgonzola 167
lentil & tomato cannelloni
  with spinach sauce 205
lasagne 191, 195
pasta with pork, spinach & lemon 126
penne rigate with spinach, prosciutto
  & crumbled goats' cheese 140
pork & spinach cannelloni 144
puffed spinach & anchovy bake 93
quick pasta with chickpeas & spinach 187
rotolo 209
spinach & cheese pasticcio 211
spinach & potato gnocchi with fontina 59
spinach & ricotta gnocchi 51
spinach & ricotta ravioli 184
tagliatelle with spinach,
  lemon & Parmesan 186
tagliatelle with spinach & ricotta 187
tomato-topped Gorgonzola,
  spinach & leek rigatoni 207
tortellini with spinach,
  ricotta & prosciutto 150
trenette with quick spinach
  & walnut sauce 57
warm pasta salad with
  spinach, tomatoes & olives 34
SQUASH: mushroom & squash al forno 209
pappardelle with roast squash
  & grilled goats' cheese 158
ravioli with squash & prosciutto 134
ricotta, Parmesan & squash ravioli 192
squash & mushroom lasagne 196
SQUID: bucatini with squid, prawns,
  lemon, parsley & garlic 102
linguine with squid, basil & chilli 101
spaghetti with squid, tomatoes & herbs 100
STEAK: pappardelle with steak
  & mushrooms 109
tagliatelle with steak & onions 110
SWORDFISH: spaghetti with swordfish,
  lemon, capers & rocket 101

TAPENADE 33
TOMATOES: bucatini with roast tomatoes 164
cavatappi with rocket, tomatoes & olives 31
cavatelli with fresh tomatoes,
  herbs & mozzarella 39
eliche with tomatoes, olives & basil 48
fettuccine with fresh tomatoes & basil 45
fusilli, rocket & tomato frittata 35
gnocchi, rocket, tomato & black
  olive salad 46

green & white tagliatelle with
  ricotta, tomatoes & basil 180
linguine, tomatoes, peppers
  & black olives en papillote 178
olive & triple tomato salad 59
orecchiette with tomatoes, rocket
  & pine nuts 47
pancetta-stuffed tomatoes 37
pappardelle with roast cherry
  tomatoes, basil & ricotta 177
penne with creamy tomato
  & basil sauce 172
penne with spicy tomato sauce 181
sauces 14, 15, 18, 19
tagliatelle with Sicilian tomato pesto 38
tagliatelle with tomatoes,
  mozzarella & herbs 173
tonnarelli with tomato
  & red pesto sauce 42
trenette with wilted tomatoes 35
warm pasta salad with spinach,
  tomatoes & olives 34
warm pasta with mixed
  peppers & tomatoes 50
TORTA 118
TUNA: fusilli lunghi with
  fresh tuna & roast peppers 67
fusilli with tuna, olives & garlic 62
penne with tuna in
  tomato & olive sauce 69
pipe with tuna, lemon & basil 74
rotelle with tuna & rocket 89
spaghetti with tuna,
  pancetta & tomatoes 66
strozzapreti with fresh tuna,
  chilli, tomatoes & olives 65
tuna & broccoli bake 103
warm fresh tuna salad niçoise 72
TURKEY: fusilli with turkey,
  mortadella & mozzarella 132
tagliatelle with turkey,
  marsala & mushrooms 142
turkey meatballs al forno 148

VEGETABLES: agnolotti with
  grilled vegetable dressing 183
cavatappi with spring vegetables
  & herbs 164
elicoidali with roast vegetables & pesto 201
fusilli lunghi with grilled
  Mediterranean vegetables 162
lasagne 197, 198
marille with roast vegetables & fontina 185
marille with spinach, aubergines
  & peppers al forno 201
Mediterranean vegetable & pasta salad 43
pasta provençal 171
penne with Mediterranean vegetables 162
sedani with roast vegetables
  & olives al forno 199
tagliatelle, asparagus, broad bean
  & courgette salad 168
tagliatelle alla primavera 165
taglioni with summer vegetables
  & fresh herb sauce 163
tonnarelli with roast peppers,
  aubergines, fennel & olives 169
vegetable & smoked
  mozzarella pasticcio 203
warm pasta, mushroom
  & grilled vegetable salad 169

WATERCRESS: garganelle with
  chicken & watercress sauce 124
linguine with Gorgonzola & watercress 32
linguine with watercress & capers 45
WHITE SAUCE 17

216

INDEX